Democracy with Dharma

The Successful Indian Experiment

Salvatore Babones

Vitasta

Published by
Renu Kaul Verma
Vitasta Publishing Pvt Ltd
4348/4C, Ansari Road, Daryaganj
New Delhi-110 002
info@vitastapublishing.com

ISBN: 978-93-47098-46-8

First Edition 2025
MRP ₹795

Typeset by Shubhpreet Kaur
Cover Design by Smriti Maheshwari
Printed by Vikas Computer and Printers, New Delhi

Contents

List of Abbreviations *v*

Preface *vii*

An Electoral Autocracy? 1

The Minister Monk 39

The Legacies of Partition 74

An Extraordinary Democracy 110

Muslims in a Hindu Nation 147

Not Only Toleration 183

The New Establishment 219

References *255*

Index *303*

List of Abbreviations

BJP : Bharatiya Janata Party (Indian People's Party)
CAA : Citizenship Amendment Act
CPJ : Committee to Protect Journalists
EIU : Economist Intelligence Unit
GRI : Pew Research Center's Government Restrictions Index
HYV : Hindu Yuva Vahini (Hindu Youth Brigade)
IAMC : Indian American Muslim Council
INC : Indian National Congress
JUH : Jamiat Ulama-i-Hind (Council of Muslim Theologians of India)
JNU : Jawaharlal Nehru University
NES : National Election Studies
RSF : Reporters sans frontières (Reporters Without Borders)
RSS : Rashtriya Swayamsevak Sangh (National Volunteer Organization)
SHI : Pew Research Center's Social Hostilities Index
SP : Samajwadi Party (Socialist Party)
UP : Uttar Pradesh (Northern Province)
USCIRF : United States Commission on International Religious Freedom
V-Dem : Varieties of Democracy Institute

***(Please note:** Some of the abbreviations originate from Hindi/Urdu/French. The English versions are literal translations to aid understanding.)*

Preface

Dharma is the basis of democracy which Asia must recognise, for in this lies the distinction between the soul of Asia and the soul of Europe.

–Sri Aurobindo Ghose[1]

Indian democracy is the politics of superlatives. Everyone knows that India, with nearly a billion registered voters, is the world's largest democracy. Few realise that, with an annual income per capita of less than Rs 2.62 lakh (US $ 3,000) in 2024, it is also the world's poorest. Or at least: it is by far the world's poorest country to be able to boast of more than a few decades of competitive elections under the rule of law with routine transfer of power between competing parties. India has been a democracy of some kind ever since it became an independent country in 1947, and it has been unambiguously a liberal democracy since the end of the 21-month 'Emergency' of 1975-1977. The only other non-Western country that comes close to matching India's record of free and fair elections is Japan, where democracy was imposed by American forces after 1945. By contrast, India's democracy is entirely home-grown.

That said, much of the Western political science profession now believes that India is not a democracy. The leading democracy-rating organisation, Sweden's Varieties of Democracy Institute, categorises India as an 'electoral autocracy.'[2] Princeton University's Ashoka Mody believes that Indian democracy began 'unraveling' under its first Prime Minister, Jawaharlal Nehru, went into a 'death spiral' in the 1970s under his daughter Indira Gandhi (no relation to the Mahatma), and 'veered into dangerous territory' in the 1980s and 1990s before the current Prime Minister, Narendra Modi, 'mounted a merciless assault on democracy' after taking office in 2014.[3] Christophe Jaffrelot of Sciences Po in Paris characterises 'Modi's India' as an 'authoritarian vigilante state.'[4] The University of Sydney's Debasish Roy Chowdhury and John Keane call India an 'elective despotism,' writing that 'with power-sharing democracy on its knees, blindfolded, elections prove useful to its killers.'[5] Oxford University's Maya Tudor asks 'has India really departed the shores of democracy?' and answers with the one word: 'yes.'[6]

For most of India's on-the-ground political commentators, things are not so dire. The Berkeley-educated Indian policy analyst Rahul Verma objects to the prevailing international consensus, arguing that 'claims of Indian democracy's death are highly exaggerated' and labelling accusations like those cited above as 'an injustice to India's journey as a democracy.'[7] India's most prominent liberal political journalist, Shekhar Gupta, asked that 'all those who said India's democracy was dead and buried, over, that we were no-hopers under fascist rule, please sit down and drink Kool-Aid.'[8] He apparently misinterpreted the American idiom. India's most prominent journalistic critic of Narendra Modi, Rajdeep Sardesai, believes that 'the 2024 elections must be seen as arguably the most unfair election in the history of Indian politics,' but that nonetheless, 'the humble voter could hold powerful politicians to account.'[9] And India's most prominent opposition politician, Rahul Gandhi, quite sensibly said after the 2024 elections that:

> The fight for democracy in India is an Indian fight. With all due respect, it has nothing to do with anybody else. It's our problem. And we'll take care of it. We will make sure that democracy is secure.[10]

The Gandhi family scion is correct: India's democracy has always been India's fight. The widespread myth that India inherited its democracy from England is belied by the fact that India is the only one of the United Kingdom's major colonial possessions that became and remained a democracy. It is true that India's representative institutions were modelled on the British parliamentary system. But so, too, were the constitutions of Pakistan, Sri Lanka, and Myanmar, all of which emerged out of the British Empire in South Asia. Pakistan inherited a British constitutional legacy that was nearly identical to that of India, along with the Indian Civil Service and the British Indian Army, both of which were split in two to form the modern state institutions of India and Pakistan. Yet within two years of independence, Pakistan became officially an Islamic republic. It experienced its first military coup in 1958. Pakistan didn't hold proper elections until 1970, and when it did, the country erupted into civil war.

If things have turned out differently in India, the credit must go to the leaders who shaped the country's understanding of itself as a unified political community. Highly literate political activists like Jawaharlal Nehru, Rajendra Prasad, B R Ambedkar, V D Savarkar, Subhas Chandra Bose, V K Krishna Menon, and the 'father of the nation' M K 'Mahatma' Gandhi gave India a democracy literature that was even more impressive than that left by the American founding fathers 150 years earlier. Most Western countries, including the United Kingdom, primarily derived their democratic principles from the United States. Not India. The revolutionary intellectuals of India's national liberation movement charted the way to a distinctively Indian political philosophy that, although informed by American and European precedents, drew much more extensively on India's own experiences. Call it '*dharma* democracy.'

Dharma is one of those words that linguists often say is untranslatable, but in reality there is a very close English equivalent to the word that captures nearly all of its meanings: duty. The philosopher and second President of India, Sarvepalli Radhakrishnan, famously defined *dharma* simply as 'right action.' Thus *sanatana* (eternal) *dharma* encompasses the sacred responsibilities all people owe to God; *yuga* (era) *dharma* mandates adherence to the customs of the society in which one lives; *sva* (own) *dharma* dictates the expectations of a person's specific position in society. Each is a form of propriety, describing forms of behaviour appropriate to a specific context. For example, a king's *raja dharma* as a ruler may clash with his *pitri dharma* as a father if he believes that his son is not strong enough to succeed him. His regal duty as a king demands that he ensure the future security of his people, while his parental duty demands that he advance the career of his son. *Dharma* is an infinitely flexible term because it can be applied to an infinite number of situations, but ultimately it all comes down to duty. As Radhakrishnan explained, 'every form of life, every group of men has its *dharma*, which is the law of its being.'[11]

Independent India emerged as a democracy in 1947 because India's independence leaders shared an overwhelming sense of *rashtra dharma*: duty to the nation. This is not quite the same thing as *rajya dharma* (duty to the state). It is a commitment to the people of a country, as a people—what the Italian revolutionary Giuseppe Mazzini called a 'community of duty.' Mazzini characterised the nation as 'a common faith, a tradition distinct from that of other nations, and constituting the past, present, and future generations of our people an historical unity.'[12] This romantic ideal had a great influence on the leaders of India's national liberation movement, including Mahatma Gandhi. In fact, Gandhi included a chapter on 'Italy and India' in his foundational work, *Hind Swaraj, or Indian Home Rule*, originally published in 1909 and promptly banned by the British. It is precisely the chapter in which he first formulated the idea of non-violent resistance. Directly citing the example of Mazzini, Gandhi said that in order to achieve freedom, 'what we need to do is to sacrifice ourselves.'[13]

The literary works of India's independence leaders are suffused with the idea of duty to the nation, although it was not always clear just what 'nation' people owed their duty to. Many thought that democracy meant duty to the whole world. The Indian nationalist Sri Aurobindo (again citing Mazzini) wrote in 1908 that 'the weakness of European democracy and the source of its failure' was that 'it took as its motive the rights of man and not the *dharma* of humanity.'[14] Others were more clear that they held a duty specifically to the Indian nation. When Bal Gangadhar Tilak departed for London in 1918 to press for Indian home rule, he described it as 'a mission of *dharma*' on behalf of 'the fortunes of the whole of India.'[15] Of course, the leaders of national liberation movements throughout the Third World professed duties toward the nations they aspired to lead. Mao Zedong even had 'serve the people' inscribed over the entrance to the Communist Party compound in Tiananmen Square.

But India's independence leaders were of a different mould, and a different mind. With the possible exception of Nehru, they were more concerned to ensure the success of the independence struggle than that of their own careers. Gandhi may be the only "father" of a non-Western nation who clearly had no ambition to lead it. His *dharma* was to inspire, not to govern, and he seems to have been aware of it. He and the other founders of India wrote extensively about their aspirations for the Indian nation, and fully expected to be held accountable by history for living up to their ideals. We don't have to tease implicit political philosophies out of their speeches and letters. They left behind a veritable library full of books spelling out their vision for the future of their nation, and ruminating on the meaning of nationhood itself.

India's independence literature is the world's most voluminous, and arguably its most introspective. It is too little read even by Indians today. It deserves to be read by the world.

In contrast to America's founding fathers, India's independence leaders went far beyond debating the simple mechanics of government. These minutiae do appear in their writings, and much ink—and some blood—over issues like reserved parliamentary seats for specific community groups, the degree to which the law should support social reform, and even the extent of the franchise. These were all important questions that needed to be answered in the runup to India's independence, but the major literary works of India's founding fathers focused on what it meant to be a nation, who was and wasn't Indian, the meaning of nationhood for India, and the duties of citizens toward the new Indian nation. India's constitution-making body, the Constituent Assembly that sat from late 1946 to early 1950, debated such matters as the national flag, the national emblem, the national anthem, the national song (not the same thing), the national language, and even what the country should be named. Everyone agreed that India was an old nation, even if no one agreed just what nation it was.

This question of colonial India's future national identity had been unsettled by the demand made by many Muslim intellectuals that a separate Muslim-majority country be carved out of British India. The prospective (and later the actual) partition of British India into the successor states of India and Pakistan loomed large in the writing of India's independence leaders, as did the prospective relations among adherents of different religions in a democratic, Hindu-majority India. All recognised that independent India would have many Muslim citizens, even if Muslim separatists succeeded in their campaign to create an independent Pakistan.

It is an inescapable fact that all of India's most prominent, most literary independence leaders were Hindu. Some Muslim intellectuals remained in India after Partition, but they did not enjoy anything close to the stature of those who left to form Pakistan. Thus, while British India's Muslim intellectuals were busy developing the theory of Islamic nationhood, the challenge of theorising a pluralistic Indian nationhood fell almost entirely to Hindus.

The nature of nationhood is something most people take for granted today, but it was hotly debated in the first half of the twentieth century. World War One marked the end of the era of empire, while World War Two brought the end of colonialism and the rise of the nation-state. After the Western allies made 'national self-determination' one of the major peace aims of World War One, would-be national leaders from Ho Chi Minh to Lawrence of Arabia converged on the Paris Peace Conference to argue for recognition of their would-be nations.

India was represented by Edwin Montagu, the British Secretary of State for India. None of India's native independence leaders were present, but they were all very well aware that empires were being broken up—that the Russian, Ottoman, and Austro-Hungarian empires were divided into more than a dozen new nations, and that many of them were being recognised as independent states. And although a century later there may be a rough consensus as to which communities constitute "nations" and which do not, there was no such consensus back in 1919.

Much like the empires that had been broken up after World War One, British India was also a patchwork of had-been and would-be nations. It included, at various times, a collection of territories that have since become the distinct modern nations of India, Pakistan, Bangladesh, Burma, Sri Lanka, the Maldives, and Singapore, as well as parts of Malaysia and Yemen. Nepal and Bhutan were British client states that ultimately remained independent; Sikkim was a British client state that did not. Hundreds of 'princely states' within what is now modern India were nominally sovereign under British rule, and Hyderabad made a serious bid for independence in 1947, going so far as to appeal to the United Nations Security Council for help. There were also non-British colonial enclaves in Goa under the Portuguese and Pondicherry under the French. All of the entities of this now-disparate region could have become part of modern India. The fact that some did and some didn't is an accident of history, not a product of fate.

Thus it is not surprising that Indian nationalism had to wrestle with the definition of the term 'nation' in a way that Pakistani (or indeed Nepali, Burmese, or Sri Lankan) nationalism never did. Nationalism as an ideology gets short shrift these days, especially among Western intellectuals, but at the time of India's independence struggle, it was all the rage, especially among Western intellectuals. Even today, the Western political class that disparages nationalism as a primitive survival from an earlier era is nonetheless keen to promote 'nation-building' in faraway countries that suffer from chronic violence and civil war, or to defend the distinct nationhood of smaller countries against the irredentist claims of their larger neighbours.

India's independence leaders were very aware that they had to define and build a nation before they could liberate it. The nation that nearly all of them sought to build was a multireligious India encompassing today's India, Pakistan, and Bangladesh. Their *rashtra dharma* was to ensure the emergence of a peaceful, democratic, but most of all united India.

In this endeavour, they failed. India was partitioned at independence, and violently so. It is impossible to understand the political fault lines of today's India without realising that a few months before the declaration of Indian independence on 15 August 1947, it still wasn't clear that British India would be divided into separate Hindu- and Muslim-majority countries. It wasn't only that the borders were undetermined; the actual decision to partition the country was not announced until 3 June 1947. But prescient people could see it coming. The prospect of an upcoming partition on the basis of religion encouraged radicals to expel or murder their neighbours of different faiths in order to ensure a local majority for their own communities. It was thus that the ethnic cleansing of India had begun a full year earlier, in August 1946. It continued through the proclamation of the new countries of India and Pakistan, and well beyond that. At a low level, it continues today.

The Indian *rashtra*, or nation, that we know today is

the product of Partition. It is not the nation that India's independence leaders fought for, or expected to achieve. All analyses of Indian nationhood, and thus ultimately of Indian democracy, must account for this discrepancy. The nation of India's pre-1947 national liberation movement is not the nation of the modern Indian nation-state. Nor is the theorisation of Pakistani nationhood much clearer. Pakistan was supposedly carved out of British India in 1947 as a homeland for the country's Muslims, but approximately one-third of the Muslims of British India remained in independent India. India has thus remained a multi-religious country, in contrast to Pakistan and Bangladesh, which have become more and more uniformly Muslim. India's continuing commitment to religious pluralism thus raises an obvious question: if India was always destined to be an inclusive secular democracy, why was Pakistan created at all?

That question lies at the heart of India's democratic *dharma*. The Bharatiya Janata Party (BJP) that has led India's central government since 2014 promotes a vision of India as a single, unified, undifferentiated nation—more a recision than a healing of the scars of Partition. Though often portrayed as a reactionary movement, the BJP is in fact a modernising force in Indian politics, fighting elections on a nationwide basis and seeking supporters across all castes, classes, and even creeds. It is an unabashedly nationalist party dedicated to what it sees as the rejuvenation of the Indian nation. It is also in practice an unabashedly Hindu party, though it resists the label 'Hindu nationalist' that is almost universally applied to it by the international press. In a country that is 80 per cent Hindu, the BJP is widely (and, it must be said, often credibly) accused of treating India as a Hindu *rashtra*: that is to say, a specifically Hindu nation. The BJP's party theorists characterise their nationalist ideology as inclusive. Many opponents, of course, disagree.

Westerners who are neither political scientists nor overly familiar with Indian politics might be nonplussed by the assertion that a major Indian political party might think of India as a Hindu nation. After all, the one thing that most Westerners know about India is that India is a Hindu country, just as the United States is routinely referred to as a Christian country. And this despite the fact that neither of these countries has an official state religion.

The United States wears its Christian founding lightly, notwithstanding occasional disputes over the separation of 'church' and state. The very word 'church' itself reflects the fact that Christianity is the default religion. But then, the United States did not fight a civil war on the basis of religion. Sensitivities regarding religion in India cannot be overstated. Americans might celebrate the spectacle of a newly elected politician taking an oath of office on the *Bhagavad Gita*, but an Indian politician who tried to do the same would be vilified for attempting to undermine India's secular state.

There is a fine line between a democratic system that enshrines respect for religious minorities and one that mandates a purely secular state. It is the line between religious toleration and religious pluralism; it is the line that separates liberalism from multiculturalism. The BJP claims to be a liberal political party that preaches religious toleration against a secular intellectual establishment that argues for religious pluralism. Implicit in the BJP's worldview is the idea that every Indian citizen, regardless of religion, owes the same *rashtra dharma* to the nation—which, in India's case, happens to be a nation that is overwhelmingly Hindu. The BJP does not maintain that people must be Hindu to be truly Indian, but it does insist that Indians respect the Hindu character of the Indian nation. It uses Hindu-centric rhetoric the way an American conservative might speak of America's Christian heritage or appeal to the country's Judeo-Christian values. But although this kind of language might be considered only mildly exclusionary in the United States, many BJP critics consider it deeply offensive in India.

The BJP's main political opponent, the Indian National Congress (INC), was once a typical Third World national liberation movement. Historically, it attempted to unite all pro-independence forces in the country under a single political umbrella. In most other postcolonial countries, these united front movements evolved into dictatorial family dynasties. That was almost the fate of the INC. Upon independence, the INC leader Jawaharlal Nehru became India's first Prime Minister. He remained in office for nearly seventeen years, dying in harness in 1964. After an interlude of only twenty months, he was succeeded in 1966 by his daughter, Indira Gandhi. After a decade in power, she engineered a state of emergency, suspended elections, imprisoned her opponents, and ruled by decree for twenty-one months beginning in June 1975. But Indian democracy held firm, and the INC was swept from power when elections were eventually held in 1977. Yet today a diminished INC is still India's second party, still the major national opposition to the BJP, and still run by the Nehru-Gandhi family.

All told, the Nehru-Gandhi family—father, daughter, and grandson—governed India for thirty-seven of its first forty-two years as an independent country. India's politics have, however, been highly competitive at least since the 1990s, and today's INC is thoroughly committed to genuine multiparty democracy. Under its fourth generation of family leadership, it has evolved into a postmodern political party that in many ways seems more at home on social media than in stadium rallies. It retains the socialist predilection for a managed economy that characterised its early years, but has evolved away from their Third World communitarianism toward a more individualistic, more Western-style understanding of social justice. The INC still presumes to speak for India's political class, but it is no longer politically dominant. It is committed to a pluralistic view of the nation, but it faces the dilemma that its staunch secularism sits awkwardly with the extreme religious conservatism of some of the Muslim communities it purports to defend—and aspires to represent.

If the BJP and the INC represent respectively the modern and postmodern currents of Indian politics, a plethora of regional and caste-based parties represent its premodern back-channels. Although it is wrong to paint them with too broad a brush, many of them are typical of the clientelist 'big man' politics that dominate most of the postcolonial world. The characteristically Indian form of politics-as-patronage is the caste-based party, though these overlap with other forms of organisation, and caste loyalty should not be overstated.

Besides caste-based parties, India also has several minority ethnolinguistic parties, a panoply of local family-run parties, and a residual communist party that remains active only in a few scattered states. These regional parties, like the caste-based ones, tend to lack truly national policy programmes. Most of the successful non-BJP, non-INC political parties in India centre on the larger-than-life personality of one prominent politician. As a result, most of these parties are unstable and unable to compete on the national stage, except in coalitions.

The pluralistic politics of social justice and personal fulfilment pursued by today's INC would be familiar to Western readers as the politics of the Democratic Party in the United States, Labour in the United Kingdom, or the Social Democrats in Germany. Other Western countries have similar parties. The INC is an avowedly nationalistic party, and might not want to be likened to these international peers, but the comparison is clear enough. Today's INC is the party of academics, intellectuals, civil servants, and minorities; it supports quiet diplomacy and human rights; its leaders get invited to speak at international book festivals. Foreign commentators (and Indian intellectuals abroad) treat it as the natural party of government. The INC may not be entirely familiar to people in other countries, but it requires no special explanation. And India's dozens of particularistic regional parties, though each difficult for outsiders to penetrate, are not difficult to understand in the aggregate. Every country has single-issue parties, but in India, there are many of them.

The BJP, by contrast, is a purely Indian phenomenon. As an unabashedly nationalist party, it is widely misunderstood and often unthinkingly condemned by foreigners. Its distinctively Indian understanding of nationhood translates poorly into English terminology. Eager to score political points, the BJP's opponents within India actively encourage international misperceptions of the party and its policies. The BJP is routinely characterised as authoritarian, dangerous, extremist, fascist, hateful, majoritarian, racist, and undemocratic, with comparisons routinely being drawn between BJP India and Nazi Germany. All of this is pure nonsense. There are supporters of the BJP who jingoistically call for the recognition of India as a Hindu nation in which people of other faiths should merely be tolerated, not accepted or embraced. There are also equally jingoistic critics of the BJP who claim that the party wants to turn India into a

'Hindu Pakistan.' Neither view accurately reflects the party, its history, its ideology, or its behaviour in government.

Whether or not the BJP's own brand of *dharma* democracy offers the best adaptation of liberal democratic values to India's particular circumstances is for Indians to judge. With 180 million members, the BJP is the world's largest political party, and its leader Narendra Modi is arguably the world's most popular politician. Although Modi is often portrayed in the international media as a ruthless oppressor of farmers, of Muslims, of 'lower' caste Hindus, and of the poor, that image is contradicted by hard data from opinion surveys and falls completely flat at the polls. It may be that Modi is popular because Indians don't actually want a liberal democracy, but there are no serious signs of that. The counterintuitive conclusion of this book is that Indians' sense of *rashtra dharma* has made the country more supportive of its liberal institutions and consequently more tolerant of all of its citizens. Duty-based democracy is a model that works for India. It might be a model worth trying elsewhere, too.

The BJP certainly did not set out to make India a more liberal nation, but it has succeeded in doing so. That conclusion might shock old India hands, but it should come as no surprise to students of history. After all, the single most powerful law of historical development is the law of unintended consequences.

***

The purpose—one might say, the *dharma*—of this book is to offer Western readers a dispassionate account of the operation of Indian democracy. It analyses Indian democracy from both a comparative perspective (benchmarking India against other, well-established democracies) and an historical perspective (benchmarking today's BJP-run India against prior INC governments). Personally, I am a non-religious American sociologist living and working in Sydney, Australia. I have no personal connection to India, the Hindu faith, or the BJP, and I have no axes to grind. Others may seek to use my words for their own purposes, but my purpose in writing them is simple: I believe that Indian democracy is an extraordinary success story, and I want to tell it. If I were Indian, I would be very proud of my country's democracy. Not being Indian, I am content to lay out the facts, offer my analysis, and hope that my readers find themselves better-informed at the end of the book than they were at the beginning.

The study of modern India is extraordinarily politicised. I am a comparative social scientist with deep expertise in the quantitative analysis of country indicators, but I am not an expert on India as such. In researching this book, I quickly discovered that most of the established experts on India are, frankly, unreliable. With only a few exceptions, most books on Indian democracy, whether written by Indians or foreigners, are written with the obvious intention of boosting one side in Indian politics while demonising the other. The scholarly literature is rife with hagiography, selective amnesia, and outright misrepresentations of historical facts. Thus instead of relying on historians for the main facts to support my analyses, as a social scientist usually would, I generally had to read the primary sources for myself. This was immensely time-consuming, but also immensely rewarding. I learned an enormous amount from all this detailed intellectual spadework, and I loved learning it.

As an outsider to Indian studies who has taken a strictly empirical approach to the study of Indian democracy, I have been greatly aided by the fact that nearly all of the relevant sources are in English. Anyone who wants to obtain a deep understanding of Indian culture must master many languages: Hindi as a lingua franca, Sanskrit as the language of classical learning, Urdu as the language of independence-era Muslim intellectuals, and a dozen or more regional tongues. But the language of academic discourse, political journalism, and the social sciences in India is English. The dominance of English is highly controversial in India, but for me it was obviously very convenient. Nonetheless, as a comparative social scientist I have published on China (extensively), eastern Europe, and Latin America without colleagues ever raising the objection that I did not speak the relevant languages. Western scholars of India, however, have objected so vehemently to my trespassing on their turf as to put my name on online watchlists and write to my university demanding that I be fired. That may sound crazy, but it is true.

Thus I would like to acknowledge at the beginning that although five years of continuous research have given me some expertise on Indian democracy, I am not an expert on Indian culture or religion. This book presents the facts on Indian democracy as seen from the perspective of a sceptical quantitative and comparative sociologist who came to the subject with an interest in democracy, not (initially at least) with any particular interest in India itself. After five years of study, I have formed strong opinions about the history and trajectory of Indian democracy, but I started with no opinions at all. I set out on this project only with curiosity. Why did Indian democracy survive when so many other postcolonial democracies failed? And if that riddle can be solved, can the solution be exported? The answers to these two questions may determine whether the world can hope to become a community of friendly democracies, or is destined to remain a battleground between freedom and despotism. It may be that a world of opposing camps is the best we can hope for. But if a democratic future for the world is at all within reach, it's worth a little academic trespassing to help us get there.

This book is dedicated to A.V.C.

Salvatore Babones
Sydney, Australia

An Electoral Autocracy?

On 22 March 1977, the front page of *The Times of India* carried a cartoon showing the recently unseated Prime Minister Indira Gandhi (1917-1984) pushing a baby stroller out of the capital, followed by the faceless men of her inner cabinet.[16] In the stroller were a crown, bags of loot, a toy tractor, and a caricature of her son Sanjay Gandhi (1946-1980) holding a 'horror' comic book. Mrs. Gandhi, universally known by that title, had ruled the country for nearly two years under emergency powers that had made her a near-dictator; Sanjay had been her heir apparent, and was associated with many of the worst transgressions of her reign.[17] The human rights abuses of Indira Gandhi's 1975-1977 period of 'Emergency' rule included mass home demolitions in the name of slum clearance, and in the cartoon, Sanjay is shown asking to be taken to one of his newly sanitised 'townships.' Having suffered an historic election defeat, the political dynasty that had ruled India for three decades seemed to be finished forever. Indira Gandhi and her favourite son had not only been rejected by the voters; they were suddenly also being ridiculed in the press.

Yet, Indira Gandhi returned as Prime Minister at the very next election, winning a super-majority of 353 seats in the 531-seat Lok Sabha in January 1980. Her supposedly hated son Sanjay also won election to the Lok Sabha representing the Uttar Pradesh constituency of Amethi, which would (like his mother's constituency of Raebareli) come to be known as a 'family seat.' The thirty-three-year-old Sanjay died just six months later in a recreational plane crash while performing aerobatic stunts. He was replaced in his parliamentary seat—and in his mother's succession plans—by his staid older brother Rajiv Gandhi (1944-1991).

Notwithstanding the excesses of the Emergency, the Gandhi family was back in charge of Indian politics, chastened, but not discouraged. When Indira Gandhi was assassinated in 1984, her son Rajiv succeeded her. Riding a wave of sympathy into the 1984 elections, Rajiv won his own, even larger electoral mandate of 414 parliamentary seats.

In the 1980s, Indians may have rejected Indira Gandhi's dictatorship, but they had not rejected Indira Gandhi, or the political family she headed. India's opposition parties may have come together to prevent a decline into despotism, but they had not yet developed sufficiently large and loyal voter bases to maintain themselves in power. The most important opposition party, the Jana Sangh, had never won more than 10 per cent of the vote before 1977. After the Emergency, the Jana Sangh was reconstituted as today's Bharatiya Janata Party (literally translated, it means 'Indian People's Party' or the BJP), which did not break the 10 per cent threshold until 1991.

Throughout the 1980s, the main national opposition to the Gandhi family came from the scattered remnants of rump Congress diehards—politicians who had been ejected from the party by Indira Gandhi in a series of splits and purges. The only other nationally organised group, the communists, generally supported the Gandhi family's line of the Indian National Congress (INC).

In short, after the Emergency of 1977-1979, India returned to being what political scientists call a 'dominant party system' or 'one-party dominant system.'[18] Historically, experts have disagreed on whether or not a country can meaningfully be classified as a democracy when one party or one person so dominates the political system that no other party has a realistic chance of defeating it.[19] On the one hand, if a dominant party or individual that upsets the electorate can be ousted by an opposition coalition just as Indira Gandhi was in 1977, it might be argued that the system is democratic. On the other hand, if voters are not consistently offered a coherent alternative political vision, but in effect have only a periodic up-or-down vote on continued rule by a dominant party, then the dominant party system comes dangerously close to the model of endorsement-by-plebiscite favoured by dictators since the time of Napoleon.[20]

Quantitative measures of democracy are generally kind to the early years of Indian democracy, before the interlude of the Emergency. The oldest quantitative democracy rating system, the 'Polity' dataset developed by the American political scientist Ted Gurr, rated India a middling democracy under its founding Prime Minister, Jawaharlal Nehru (1889-1964).[21] Post-independence India received 5 points on a scale ranging from -10 (full autocracy) to +10 (full democracy), losing points mainly due to a lack of any serious electoral competition.[22] India's Polity score jumped to 8 points as competition picked up after Nehru's death, faltering down to 6 points during Indira Gandhi's Emergency. Polity has rated India at a near-perfect score of 9 points since 1998, although the data series currently ends in 2018. That placed India just below the top tier of thirty-two mostly European countries that earned perfect scores, and slightly above the United States and United Kingdom (both with only 8 points).

It might sound strange to rate Indian democracy above Anglo-American democracy, but the Polity methodology offers broad evaluations, not fine distinctions. It captures, via expert evaluations, such basic criteria as the competitiveness and openness of elections, the presence of institutional constraints on government decision making, and the degree of winner-take-all partisan factionalism. The United States and United Kingdom lose points for being highly partisan in the evaluation of Polity's experts. Whether or not partisanship really makes countries less democratic is in the eye of the beholder; this is a choice made by the designers of the Polity database, not an absolute truth about democracy. The overall take-away from the Polity analysis is that independent India has always been a democracy, but that it lacked meaningful political competition under Nehru and during the 1975-1977 Emergency.

Not all political scientists agree with Polity's broad-brush approach to democracy measurement, nor with its relatively benign evaluation of India. In the 2010s, a new democracy evaluation initiative took shape: the Varieties of Democracy Institute (V-Dem). Based at Sweden's University of Gothenburg and funded by the European Commission (the executive arm of the European Union), the European Research Council, all three Scandinavian national research agencies, and several European foundations, V-Dem immediately established itself as the most authoritative source of information on the quality of the world's democracies. In contrast to the more sedate Polity project,

V-Dem published media-friendly, professionally edited reports targeted at a general audience. It also used statistical methods that were light years ahead of Polity's. Such a well-funded, well-promoted, and well-researched data source was bound to be taken seriously.

In 2017, V-Dem opened its inaugural democracy report with the rhetorical question: 'Is there evidence of a global democratic backslide?' The answer, inevitably, was 'yes.'[23] India was ranked number 73 out of 174 countries on V-Dem's flagship Electoral Democracy Index.

Since then, things have only gotten worse. In its 2021 annual report, V-Dem controversially characterised India as an 'electoral autocracy' where democracy had 'broken down.'[24] In 2024 V-Dem went even further, calling India an 'increasingly oppressive electoral autocracy' with democratic credentials worse than at the depths of the Emergency in 1976.[25] Despite being rated one of the world's best democracies by the Polity project and roughly on a par with the European Union's newer members by the Economist Intelligence Unit (EIU), for five years running India has been labeled a non-democracy by the world's most authoritative democracy rating organisation. The label has stuck.[26]

The case against India

According to the historical data compiled by V-Dem, India's democracy reached its apogee in 1998, when it was ranked number forty-five in the world. The late 1990s and early 2000s in India were times of political instability and weak coalition governments. India's ranking slowly declined under a succession of more stable BJP and Congress-led governments until Narendra Modi came to power in 2014. By that point, India had declined to number seventy-one, receiving its lowest democracy score since the Emergency. Then things went steadily downhill. By the end of Modi's first term in office, India's international ranking had fallen to 107. In 2023, India was ranked number 110 in the world, just one step above Iraq (ranked 111). It was ranked well below such seriously troubled democracies as South Africa at fifty-three, the Solomon Islands at sixty-seven, and Sri Lanka at seventy-five.

The Maldives, a small island country just off the coast of India, was ranked number seventy in the world by V-Dem (forty places above India), despite a constitution that denies citizenship to all non-Muslims. Under the country's strict Sharia law, apostasy is punishable by death. In the 2023 presidential election, the leading candidate was disqualified because he was in prison. In that election, campaign finance laws were 'not effectively enforced,' state media 'blurred the boundaries between governmental functions and campaign activities,' and the incumbent 'received preferential treatment from state media,' according to the European Union observer mission.[27] That should have come as no surprise, since Maldives law requires that all published material be approved by a state censorship board.[28] In the ensuing 2024 Maldives parliamentary elections, the new president's party won sixty-six of the ninety-three seats in the country's parliament, a swing of sixty-three seats in its favour.

It is relevant to consider the cross-national and historical context for India's recent democracy rankings because these scores have been statistically calibrated by V-Dem to be 'consistent' across space and time.[29] The extraordinary statistical sophistication of the V-Dem approach is precisely why the dataset has been called 'the de facto gold standard in empirical democracy research.'[30] Thus it should be taken seriously that according to V-Dem, Indian democracy is in worse shape today than it was during Emergency, a time when elections and civil rights were suspended, most opposition members of parliament were imprisoned, and the Prime Minister arbitrarily rewrote the Constitution with no meaningful checks on her power. It should also be taken seriously that V-Dem currently ranks India far below South Africa (a racially divided state under one-party rule), the Solomon Islands (where Australian troops must be called in to maintain order during polling), Sri Lanka (which recently experienced a constitutional crisis), and the Maldives (with all the problems detailed above).

The founder and director of the Varieties of Democracy Institute, the political scientist Staffan Lindberg, has publicly defended V-Dem's current India rankings on multiple occasions.[31] V-Dem's 2024 democracy report pulls no punches. It backs up its negative evaluation of Indian democracy by claiming that:

> India's autocratization process has been well documented, including gradual but substantial deterioration of freedom of expression, compromising independence of the media, crackdowns on social media, harassments of journalists critical of the government, as well as attacks on civil society and intimidation of the opposition. The ruling anti-pluralist, Hindu-nationalist Bharatiya Janata Party (BJP) with Prime Minister Modi at the helm has for example used laws on sedition, defamation, and counterterrorism to silence critics. The BJP government undermined the constitution's commitment to secularism ... [and] continues to suppress the freedom of religion rights. Intimidation of political opponents and people protesting government policies, as well as silencing of dissent in academia are now prevalent.[32]

Nor is V-Dem alone in making such allegations. The quasi-official American think tank Freedom House (which receives most of its funding from the US State Department) considers India to be only 'partly free.'[33] The World Justice Project (an offshoot of the American Bar Association) ranks India at seventy-nine out of 142 countries for the rule of law.[34] The journalism campaigning organisation Reporters Without Borders (known by its French acronym RSF) ranked India number 161 out of 180 countries for press freedom in 2023.[35] According to RSF, the year 2022 'signalled the end of pluralism in the mainstream media.' Things are allegedly even worse for religious freedom. The Washington-based Pew Research Center ranked India as the second-worst country in the world for 'social hostilities involving religion' in 2021 (the most recent year for which data are available) and number thirty-eight out of 198 countries for 'government restrictions on religion.'[36]

The highly respected United States Holocaust Memorial Museum ranks India the fifth most likely country in the world to experience 'mass killings'—the main ingredient of genocide.[37] Most of the predictor variables used in its models are taken from the V-Dem database. This is also the case for many of the other human rights rankings that have proliferated in recent years. For example, Human Freedom Index compiled by America's Cato Institute and Canada's Fraser Institute ranks India at 109 out of 165 countries for 'human freedom,' but most of its indicators are drawn from V-Dem, with additional data from Freedom House, the World Justice Project, and a few other sources.[38] The Academic Freedom Index, on which India is ranked number 130 out of 179 countries (just below the Hamas-administered Gaza Strip) is based entirely on V-Dem data.[39] The University of Würzburg Democracy Matrix, which ranks India at eighty-five out of 176 countries, similarly consists of a reanalysis of V-Dem data.[40]

There now exists a widespread public consensus, reflected in dozens of articles in prominent newspapers and magazines as well as in academic books, that Indian democracy has failed catastrophically since Narendra Modi became Prime Minister in 2014. That consensus appraisal may or may not be correct. But it ultimately derives from a single (though admittedly highly reputed) data source, the V-Dem database. This poses an epistemological challenge. Had the V-Dem project not been funded in 2014 and published its first rankings in 2017, the world might never have known about the supposed dramatic deterioration in the quality of Indian democracy. Other rating systems have shown either no decline in Indian democracy (Polity), a slight decline beginning in 2017 (EIU), or a more serious decline beginning in 2019 (Freedom House). In the absence of V-Dem, there would likely be no serious talk of an 'electoral autocracy' emerging in India.

It is quite likely that India's downward slide in the EIU and Freedom House rankings have themselves been influenced by V-Dem. Both organisations base their rankings on evaluations made by international experts, who must be aware of V-Dem's widely publicised downgrading of Indian democracy. As Freedom House explains, its analysts 'use a broad range of sources, including news articles, academic analyses, reports from nongovernmental organizations, individual professional contacts, and on-the-ground research' to make their evaluations.[41] With dozens of fine-tuned judgements to make about each of 210 distinct countries and territories, one suspects they must also have consulted Wikipedia. To take just example of the challenges faced by Freedom House's analysts, consider the question: 'Do laws, policies, or persistent socioeconomic conditions effectively impose rigid barriers to social mobility?' This must be answered for such obscure countries as Grenada, Kiribati, Lesotho, and Turkmenistan about which they may have little knowledge and less experience. The potential for a country's highly publicized ratings on one index to influence its scores on another is unavoidable.

Conceptualising 'democracy'

Philosophical exercises notwithstanding, the V-Dem project did get funded in 2014, the V-Dem rankings do exist, and academic experts generally consider V-Dem to be world's premier democracy rating system.[42] The V-Dem rating system is solidly grounded in the most widely-accepted theoretical framework for conceptualising democracy, and its measurement approach utilises the most sophisticated statistical tools available. The data collection exercise underlying V-Dem's ratings is the most extensive ever conducted for creating a governance index. The V-Dem project team codes 228 distinct democracy indicators for 202 distinct countries or territories (some no longer extant), with historical coverage going back as far as 1789. These are complemented by expert survey data for an additional 256 indicators.

Nearly all of V-Dem's survey indicators are evaluated by five or more 'country experts' who code democracy indicators for a particular country. For India, which is especially well-covered, many indicators are coded by a dozen or more experts. Most of V-Dem's country experts reside in the country being studied, and V-Dem reports that across the entire project, 'three-fourths of the Country Experts have PhDs and roughly 70 per cent are employed by a university.'[43] Regional managers and country coordinators play key roles in the recruitment and oversight of country experts, but V-Dem does not name a regional manager for South Asia or identify any of its country coordinators on its website.[44] These supervisory roles may be points at which biases could enter the V-Dem coding process, but given the political sensitivity of its India rankings, it is likely that V-Dem's upper management pays close attention to its India team.

The headline-grabbing Electoral Democracy Index that forms the core of the V-Dem is calculated from 23 major indicators that are mostly coded by country experts, which are combined with general evaluations about countries' constitutions that are made by the project team. These many sources feed into five main component indices that cover:

1 suffrage (who can vote)
2 leaders (are they elected)
3 the quality of elections
4 freedom of association
5 freedom of expression

A complicated but mathematically straightforward formula aggregates these five component indices into each country's overall score on the Electoral Democracy Index. This main index is designed to run from zero to one, with the lowest score ever recorded for an independent country being for Oman in the late 1960s (with a score of 0.007) and the highest score being for Denmark in the early 2010s (0.922). There is no formal cutoff for status as a democracy, but the V-Dem 'Regimes of the World' spinoff project uses the index score 0.500 to differentiate between 'democracies' and 'autocracies.'[45] It is on this basis and not on any direct analysis of leadership behaviour that V-Dem characterises India as an 'electoral autocracy.'

The Electoral Democracy Index is designed to measure a concept that political theorists call 'polyarchy.'[46] This term was introduced in 1953 by the American political theorist Robert Dahl, who defined it as 'a process, sometimes called democracy, in which nonleaders control leaders.'[47] He further clarified that 'democracy is a goal, not an achievement,' and that polyarchy is 'the main sociopolitical process for approximating (although not achieving) democracy.'[48] In other words, democracy is the ideal state in which everyone has an equal say in government, and polyarchy is a means for achieving that end. Dahl's early formulations of polyarchy were strictly procedural; for example, he gave a detailed eight-part definition in 1956 that closely resembled the American primary system of first selecting candidates and then voting on them.[49]

By 1971, Dahl's views had evolved. Instead of simply demanding that people have the opportunity to express their preferences at the polls, Dahl had come to believe that democracy must be embedded within a wider framework of supporting institutions. His updated list of eight 'institutional guarantees' that are required for democracy was:

(1) Freedom to form and join organisations
(2) Freedom of expression
(3) Right to vote
(4) Eligibility for public office
(5) Right of political leaders to compete for (a) support and (b) votes
(6) Alternative sources of information
(7) Free and fair elections
(8) Institutions for making government policies depend on votes and other expressions of preference[50]

Dahl's later formulations of polyarchy were generally expansions or restatements of this list, which has become widely accepted by political theorists.[51] Of course, there are many competing definitions of democracy. Some of them (like Dahl's early conceptualisation) focus narrowly on the process of voting. Others expand the concept so much as to claim that no country can be a democracy without a minimum basic income to universal access to healthcare. While some might consider Dahl's institutional guarantees too broad, others (in particular the EIU) consider them too narrow.[52] But few Western liberals would disagree entirely with Dahl's list—or seriously object to any of its eight specific criteria.

The V-Dem project is a pragmatic attempt to transform Dahl's eight polyarchy principles into a practical measurement tool. First, it collapses Dahl's eight institutional principles of polyarchy into five component indices. Dahl's 'alternative sources of information' is subsumed under V-Dem's freedom of expression component; information about 'eligibility for public office' is collected by V-Dem, but does not seem to enter into the main Electoral Democracy Index; and Dahl's final principle calling for institutional accountability is left implicit by V-Dem. These seem to be reasonable compromises, and in any case Dahl published many different versions of his criteria for polyarchy. Taken together, V-Dem's five component indices unquestionably represent a reasonable attempt to encapsulate what it calls 'Dahl's sub-components' of polyarchy.[53]

The five component indices that underlie V-Dem's Electoral Democracy Index are constructed using a mixture of objective and subjective, direct and indirect methods. The first two components covering the extent of suffrage and methods for selecting leaders are based on relatively objective criteria that are directly coded by the V-Dem team. There is very little 'wiggle room' in the determination of each country's score on these components. The third component, which deals with the quality of elections, is generated indirectly by using advanced statistical methods to combine multiple country experts' evaluations of eight different aspects of a country's elections. These range from the mostly objective, such as the accuracy and completeness of the voter registry, to the completely subjective, such as the freeness and fairness of elections. Questions like these leave much space for differences in interpretation.

The final two components, covering freedom of association and expression, are also generated indirectly through a statistical analysis of evaluations made by country experts. For freedom of association, country experts answer six different questions, some of them relatively objective, such as questions asking if any parties banned, while others are much more subjective, such as questions asking if the government suppresses civil society organisations. For freedom of expression, they answer nine different questions, focusing mainly on the media but also including individual expression (evaluated separately for women and men) and academic freedom. These are all highly subjective. Freedom of expression is the most controversial component of the Electoral Democracy Index, and the most vulnerable to bias. It is also the component on which India has fallen fastest in the Modi era, and on which it currently scores the worst.

From conceptualisation to measurement

Measurement in the social sciences is not as simple as pulling out a scale. It is challenging enough to arrive at an agreed conceptualisation of such an amorphous and contested idea as democracy. It is even more difficult to measure it properly. The process of moving from conceptualisation to measurement is what social scientists call 'operationalisation.' Operationalisation involves breaking down concepts into things that can actually be measured, whether directly or indirectly, objectively or subjectively. Obviously, social scientists would prefer direct, objective measures, but these are not always available. Very sophisticated statistical techniques have been developed for converting indirect and even subjective evaluations into well-validated quantitative measures, and the techniques used by V-Dem really are state-of-the-art.

That said, 'garbage in, garbage out' is a universal principle of statistical modelling, and the V-Dem data incorporate some very serious, but strangely overlooked flaws.

Operationalisation of suffrage

The first and most serious is in its operationalisation of suffrage: the proportion of the citizens of a country who are allowed to vote. In its ratings for 2023, V-Dem gave a perfect score (1.000) on suffrage to 175 of the 179 countries evaluated. Thailand received an almost-perfect score of only 0.994, presumably because its constitution denies the vote to ordained priests and monks. That leaves only four countries without universal suffrage: the United Arab Emirates (0.360), Qatar (0.350), Somalia (0.002), and Saudi Arabia (0.000). Leaving aside the vexed question of exactly how these problematic cases are evaluated, the net result is that suffrage is virtually irrelevant when it comes to determining a country's ranking on V-Dem's final Electoral Democracy Index. Since nearly every country in the world gets the same perfect score, an index that didn't include suffrage would return almost exactly the same result as the existing V-Dem index.

The countries receiving perfect scores for universal suffrage include China, North Korea, Vietnam, and Eritrea, and many other countries that don't actually have elections, or at least not real elections. As the V-Dem documentation explains, the suffrage measure 'covers legal *de jure* restrictions, not restrictions that may be operative in practice *de facto*.'[54] It answers the question 'what share of adult citizens as defined by statute has the legal right to vote in national elections?'—even if there are no elections. This reflects, at best, a literalist reading of Dahl's theory of polyarchy; indeed, support for this approach can be found in Dahl's writings.[55] Nonetheless, it probably offends most people's democratic sensibilities. Perhaps more importantly, it also complicates the operationalisation of democracy, since it transforms what most analysts would consider the single-most important aspect of democracy (the right to vote) into the least important component of a country's relative rankings.

Election of leaders

The second component index, covering the election of leaders, suffers from similar problems. Here 126 countries receive perfect scores (1.000), indicating that the chief executive and members of the legislature are elected. India receives a near-perfect score (0.996) because, until 2023, the Lok Sabha included two appointed members. Again, there are major anomalies in the scores for this component. Among the countries receiving perfect scores for the election of leaders are Russia and Belarus (but not China and North Korea), because 'a popular election is minimally defined and also includes sham elections with limited suffrage and no competition.'[56] Once again, although this operationalisation decision can be defended with reference to Dahl's theories, it is obnoxious to most intuitive thinking about democracy. And once again, this operationalisation decision makes the election component largely irrelevant to countries' overall democracy scores.

In fact, among countries that (by more conventional measures) really are democracies, these first two components of the V-Dem Electoral Democracy Index do not differentiate at all regarding the quality of their democracies. In other words, all countries that have leaders or legislatures who are elected via universal suffrage get the same perfect score. Yet these are the only two components of the Electoral Democracy Index that are measured directly and objectively. The mathematical consequence of this is that literally all of the differentiation across democratic countries in their V-Dem rankings comes from the indirect, more generally subjective component indices. The universal suffrage and elected leaders components do help differentiate China and North Korea from the rest of the world, and they do result in Saudi Arabia being ranked last in the rankings, but these are not useful results. They tell us nothing that we didn't know already.

Quality of elections

Thus with two component indices down, there are only three remaining components that determine nearly all of the variability of interest in V-Dem's Electoral Democracy Index. The third component index, the quality of elections, uses a statistical model to convert the answers of multiple experts on eight different questions into a single index score. The eight questions cover the completeness of the voter registry, the electoral commission's autonomy and administrative capacity, the prevalence of vote buying, violence at the polls, and other voting irregularities, and an overall judgement of the extent to which elections are 'free and fair.' India scores 0.510 on a scale from 0 to 1, on par with the United Arab Emirates (where political parties are banned) and just below Vietnam (where only the Communist Party is allowed to run).

A naive analyst might expect meaningful party competition to be at the heart of measuring the quality of elections, but (incredibly) the actual competitiveness of elections does not at any point enter into the calculation of V-Dem's Electoral Democracy Index. Instead of operationalising the quality of elections in terms of substantive criteria like competitiveness, V-Dem focuses mainly on procedural criteria. Thus when compared to Vietnam, India scores much higher on electoral commission autonomy and experts' overall impression that elections are free and fair, but much worse on vote buying and violence at the polls. Of course, no one buys votes in Vietnam because there is no choice who to vote for. In any case, a comprehensive empirical study of allegations of vote buying in India conducted by political scientists, Pradeep K Chhibber and Rahul Verma found that 'the well-known myths about vote buying in India are just that—myths.'[57]

India's score on the component index for quality of elections has declined steeply since 2014, when Narendra Modi first took office. Nearly all of the decline has come from a fall in the perceived autonomy of the Election Commission of India (ECI), which has been compounded by perceptions of increased voting 'irregularities' and an increasing perception that India's elections are no longer 'free and fair.' Both of these additional factors are sufficiently vague that they may represent spillover effects from the first: that is, country experts may feel that the ECI is permitting irregularities, thus tilting the playing field and making the elections less fair. India's rating on election commission autonomy has fallen from a level slightly better than Canada's to a level somewhat worse than Gaza under Hamas. Such a shift, if true, would represent a catastrophic threat to Indian democracy. But is it true?

Subjectivity and bias

The Election Commission of India is highly respected, but it is not without its critics. Freedom House gives the ECI perfect marks for impartiality, but notes that 'in recent years ... its impartiality and competence have been called into question.'[58] Academic research reinforces this perception, with the most comprehensive recent study of the ECI concluding that although party officials from across the political spectrum 'generally regarded the ECI in a positive light,' the absolute majority gained by Narendra Modi in 2014 has allowed him to employ 'the tactic of limiting the ECI's authority from within, by appointing pliant election commissioners.'[59] An Indian non-governmental organisation called the Constitutional Conduct Group has organised repeated open letters questioning the independence of the ECI, including one that called the 2019 elections 'one of the least free and fair elections that the country has had in the past three decades.'[60] All of this points to a perception of increasing partiality.

But the V-Dem rates the ECI's autonomy today as being lower than it was during the Emergency, and dramatically lower than at any other time in India's history. This may be nothing more than a case of historical amnesia. Political scientist Alistair McMillan describes the ECI during the post-independence period of INC dominance as having "become absorbed into the Congress system of government and lost sight of its broader remit to maintain the democratic structure of the Indian political system."[61] He details how prior INC governments made serious attempts to stack the ECI in 1989 and 1993; in 2009 the chief commissioner himself asked that a fellow commissioner be removed from office due to pro-INC partiality, a request that was denied by the INC-appointed President.[62] Historical inconsistencies like these illustrate the possibility that subjective evaluations might be conditioned on the political preferences of the country experts making the evaluations.

It is no secret that the BJP in general and Narendra Modi in particular are widely reviled among social scientists, both within India and in the West. A little over a year after Modi took office, a group of 139 prominent academics at American universities signed an open letter claiming that:

> Modi's first year in office as the Prime Minister of India includes well publicized episodes of censorship and harassment of those critical of his policies, bans and restrictions on NGOs leading to a constriction of the space of civic engagement, ongoing violations of religious freedom, and a steady impingement on the independence of the judiciary.[63]

Many of the signatories would have been prime candidates to serve on V-Dem's panel of country experts for India. In 2019, a group of thirty-seven international development scholars published a letter condemning Modi's 'human rights record and divisive politics,' claiming that 'activists and critics have been jailed, killed and accused of being anti-national.'[64] In 2023, a group of 522 scholars from India and around the world signed an open letter condemning the Indian government for censoring a documentary that was critical of Modi.[65] Many more examples could be cited.

It must be noted that the antipathy of scholars for Narendra

Modi is very much reciprocated by his government. The BJP is widely (and credibly) perceived to be mounting a national campaign to change the character of the academy.[66] The BJP has sought to influence the direction of India's most politically symbolic university, the Jawaharlal Nehru University (JNU), through the appointment of sympathetic university leaders.[67] It has also been suggested that organisations affiliated with the BJP have influenced the selection of leaders at Delhi University.[68] It is an article of faith among BJP supporters that India's schools and universities have long been bastions of INC partisanship (or worse: outright communist control), and they are probably correct. After all, the INC controlled India's education ministry throughout the second half of the twentieth century, and today's academic establishment is the heir to yesterday's politicised hiring practices.

In light of the ongoing intellectual war being fought between the BJP and the Indian intellectual establishment (and the alignment of Western intellectuals with their Indian counterparts) it would be a miracle if V-Dem's subjective indicators did not reflect an anti-BJP, anti-Modi bias. One obvious interpretation of V-Dem's determination that the ECI was much less autonomous in the 2020s than at any other time in India's history is that although there have been multiple occasions on which the ECI has been politicised, this is the first occasion on which it has been politicised by the BJP. In other words, the deterioration in the autonomy of the ECI is real, but it is not unprecedented, and it is probably less severe than reported. This view would be consistent with the limited body of academic research that focuses on the ECI. The implication of this would be that the quality of Indian elections is not as bad as V-Dem says it is, but was never as good as V-Dem says it was.

A similar analysis holds for V-Dem's fourth component index, which covers freedom of association. This component is based on six indicators, once again using a statistical model to convert the answers of multiple experts into a single index score. Four of the six indicators are relatively straightforward questions that ask for objective information about opposition parties: are they banned, do they face barriers, are they truly autonomous, and are they allowed to meaningfully contest elections. Since Modi came to office in 2014, India has faced modest downgrades on barriers to opposition and opposition autonomy, and in both cases the downgrades are justified. It is certainly true that the BJP has selectively prosecuted wrongdoing by opposition leaders, and it is equally true that the BJP has selectively recruited opposition leaders into its ranks. It has sometimes done both at the same time.[69] Such hardball political tactics do not make a country undemocratic, but they do make a country less democratic.

These minor downgrades have had little effect on India's overall democracy score. Much more important are the final two, almost entirely subjective indicators that feed into the freedom of association component. These measure government control over and repression of civil society organisations. The latter is so subjective that V-Dem offers its expert coders several historical benchmarks to guide their evaluations. Based on these benchmarks, India's average expert evaluation exactly splits the difference between 'Mugabe's Zimbabwe, Poland under Martial Law, Serbia under Milosevic' and 'post-Martial Law Poland, Brazil in the early 1980s, and the late Franco period in Spain.'[70] According to V-Dem's country experts, government repression of civil society in India today is more severe than in Saudi Arabia or Gaza, and much, much more severe than in Pakistan or the

West Bank. This is plainly preposterous. But it is not the worst example of bias in India's democracy evaluations.

As bad as it gets: Freedom of expression

The V-Dem methodology is not kind to India. According to its flagship Electoral Democracy Index, Indian democracy reached its zenith in the late 1990s and early 2000s, a period of political instability and weak coalition governments. At its highest point, in 1998, Indian democracy was ranked only forty-fifth in the world. By the time Narendra Modi took office in 2014, India had fallen twenty-five places to number seventy-one. Over the next nine years, India fell another thirty-nine places to number 110. Over the full quarter-century of decline, India's scores on V-Dem's two objective component indices (universal suffrage and elected leaders) remained exactly the same. India fell fifty-two places on the quality of its elections and forty-five places on freedom of association, both serious drops. But the catastrophic decline that put India over the edge from 'democracy' to 'autocracy' was a ninety-seven-place fall in its global ranking for freedom of expression.

The conclusion (repeatedly emphasised by V-Dem over multiple reports) that India and China merely represent different varieties of autocracy—one, an 'electoral autocracy' and the other, a 'closed autocracy'—can mainly be attributed to this one component of democracy.[71] At number 138 in the world, India's freedom of expression is ranked sixteen places below Pakistan's and exactly halfway between Palestine's West Bank and Gaza. It is ranked far below Brazil (number thirty-six), where freedom of online speech has come under serious threat and mainstream publishers have faced arbitrary enforcement and potentially gratuitous prosecutions.[72] Similar accusations have been levelled at India, but India's online publishing takedown orders have been more narrowly focused, and its prosecutions of journalists have mainly targeted non-traditional news outlets.[73] Another big difference is that Brazil's restrictions have come overwhelmingly from the political left, while India's have come from the right.

At issue is not whether or not it is proper for democracies to censor—clearly, more censorship means less freedom of speech, and by implication, less democracy—but the degree of additional censorship that is required to justify a difference in the rankings of 102 places. The censorship allegations made against India and Brazil seem to be broadly similar, and a close observer of both countries might be puzzled by the huge gap in their freedom of expression scores. Whether both countries belong in the thirties or the 130s or somewhere in between, it seems like their scores should fall into the same range. Similarly, it is reasonable to compare evaluations of freedom of expression in India over multiple decades. India's 2023 V-Dem score for freedom of expression is only marginally higher than during Indira Gandhi's Emergency (1975-1977), and much lower than the scores given for the Nehru years (1950-1964). This seems indefensible.

The Emergency speaks for itself. But the Nehru years are much less known. One of Nehru's first act as Prime Minister was to amend the Constitution to restrict freedom of speech. He did this in 1951, before independent India had even held its first elections, ensuring that he went into those elections with the new restrictions already in place. The First Amendment to the Indian Constitution (1951) included a 'statement of objects and reasons' in which Nehru frankly admitted that:

During the last fifteen months of the working of the

> Constitution, certain difficulties have been brought to light by judicial decisions and pronouncements specially in regard to the chapter on fundamental rights. The citizen's right to freedom of speech and expression guaranteed by article 19(1)(a) [the personal freedoms clause] has been held by some courts to be so comprehensive as not to render a person culpable even if he advocates murder and other crimes of violence. In other countries with written constitutions, freedom of speech and of the press is not regarded as debarring the State from punishing or preventing abuse of this freedom.[74]

Nehru's First Amendment permitted the government to impose 'reasonable restrictions' on personal freedoms (including freedom of speech and expression) 'in the interests of the security of the State.' It was fiercely resisted by the press at the time, with journalists staging nationwide protests.[75] *The Times of India* editorialised that 'Mr Nehru, once the spirited advocate of civil liberties in India, is now presiding over their obsequies.'[76] The *Washington Post* editorialised that the First Amendment would usher in 'dictatorship in the strictest, most literal, sense of the word.'[77] The *New York Times* called the ensuing Press (Objectionable Matters) Act of 1951 'a repressive code as stringent as any that ever existed under the British.'[78] Under the Act, journalists were treated like a 'criminal tribe' who 'lived in a state of 'perpetual terror,' according to period accounts.[79]

Yet Nehru's India under the 1951 Press Act, like Brazil today, gets top marks from V-Dem's expert coders for freedom of expression. This final V-Dem component index is based on nine indicators, all of them highly subjective. It includes questions like:

- Is press censorship 'limited' or 'routine'?

- Is media self-censorship 'common' or does it occur only 'on a few highly sensitive political issues'?
- Does the media 'cover all newsworthy parties' equally at election time?
- Is it possible to code the extent to which people 'are able to openly discuss political issues in private homes'?[80]

The evaluations made by V-Dem's country experts are aggregated via a statistical model to create its freedom of expression component index. This is, perhaps, a challenge that must be faced, but it is not a process on which a high degree of confidence can be placed. Wherever possible, objective indicators should be used to validate these subjective expert evaluations.

Freedom of expression is, by its very nature, a subjective quality: not only is the evaluation of freedom inherently subjective, but the very experience of freedom is subjective, too. But six out of V-Dem's nine freedom of expression indicators involve media coverage, which can (to some extent) be exposed to external validation. Interestingly, the V-Dem media indicator for which no validation is possible is the one on which India performs the worst: media self-censorship. The media self-censors everywhere in the world, and although it seems incongruous that V-Dem rates self-censorship as 'common' in India while being restricted to 'a few highly sensitive political issues' in Pakistan, only those journalists who are self-censoring can know for sure.[81] Social scientific research based on interviews with top mainstream journalists in Pakistan suggests that the situation there is much more dire than reflected by V-Dem.[82] And although there is a large academic literature on media self-censorship in Pakistan, there is no equivalent literature about India.

Like self-censorship, government censorship effort is

difficult to quantify, and although there are many popular press articles on media censorship in India, there are hardly any academic studies of the subject. On the topic of media bias, V-Dem's experts rate India at the middle of the scale, giving India a score that corresponds to the description 'print and broadcast media cover some opposition parties or candidates more or less impartially, but they give only negative or no coverage to at least one newsworthy party or candidate.'[83] Here, India's multiparty democracy may weigh against it. In a two-party system like that found in the United States, there are only two clearly 'newsworthy' parties, and thus there is little scope for bias to affect the way that experts answer a question like this. But in India, experts who support fringe parties can always (reasonably) believe that their 'newsworthy' parties are being excluded from coverage, even if the two major parties (the BJP and the INC) receive equal time.

Similarly, on the range of media coverage, V-Dem's experts believe that in India 'major media represent a variety of political perspectives but they systematically ignore at least one political perspective that is important.'[84] Which perspective do they ignore? The experts aren't asked. But for passing over marginal perspectives, the Indian media are relegated to number 130 in the world. To anyone familiar with Indian newspapers and television, it would seem hard to believe that the Indian media are the second worst in South Asia (just pipping Bangladesh at number 132) for the breadth of their political coverage, but once again this proposition is difficult to refute objectively. Only a large-scale empirical study could definitively resolve the debate. It would also require a major study to determine the number of 'major print and broadcast outlets' that 'routinely criticise the government.'[85] Whatever the objective truth of India's ranking of number 138 in the world, it seems inconceivable that India, with the only free media in the region, is the worst country in South Asia for government-critical reporting.

Unfortunately, these reality checks are only meaningful to people who are already familiar with the region and its media landscape. Luckily, there is one V-Dem media indicator that can be objectively validated: the harassment of journalists. On this indicator, India is rated at the second-lowest rung on a five-point scale, with the descriptor 'some journalists occasionally offend powerful actors but they are almost always harassed or worse and eventually are forced to stop.'[86] This places India at number 138 in the world. Yet it is quite easy to identify many prominent journalists in India who have publicly opposed Prime Minister Narendra Modi for a decade or more without being 'forced to stop.' Included among them are Rajdeep Sardesai (the lead political reporter for *India Today*), Suhasini Haidar (foreign affairs editor of *The Hindu*), Tavleen Singh (lead political columnist for the *Indian Express*), and many others. These journalists may be little known outside the country, but they are household names in India.

The V-Dem harassment of journalists indicator specifically asks if journalists have been 'threatened with libel, arrested, imprisoned, beaten, or killed' by the government. The claim that India is unsafe for journalists has been made so many times in so many different venues that it has become a trope. It is such a trope that the article on India in the multi-authored handbook *Press Freedom in Contemporary Asia* was published under the double entendre title *Killing Press Freedom in India*.[87] Beyond V-Dem and perhaps influencing the V-Dem expert panel, the RSF World Press Freedom Index highlights 'violence against journalists' as one of the main reasons for India's low ranking.[88]

According to RSF, India 'is one of the world's most dangerous countries for the media.' That is a provocative claim. Luckily, it is a claim that can be tested against hard statistical data.

The claim that India is a dangerous country for journalists originates in statistics compiled by the Committee to Protect Journalists (CPJ). According to CPJ data, forty-three journalists were killed in India from 2001 to 2023. That gives an annual rate of 1.3 per billion people per year, which compares very favourably to the 9.5 per billion rate in the rest of the world excluding China (which is not covered by CPJ data).[89] India is safer than the United States, where the rate of journalist killings is 1.6 per billion per year. Comparing the nine full years of INC rule before Modi came to power (2005-2013) to the nine full years of Modi's BJP government (2015-2023), fifteen journalists were killed under the INC versus twenty-one under the BJP. That is an uptick, but one that still leaves India roughly half as dangerous as the United States over the same period. Although many cases of individual tragedies can be cited, there is no factuality to the claim that India is a particularly dangerous country for journalists.

Academic freedom

Another freedom of expression indicator that can be objectively verified is academic freedom. According to V-Dem, there has been a serious decline in academic freedom in India since Modi took office, with the country falling from number 109 in the world in 2013 to number 144 in 2023. As with many other indicators, the situation today is rated as being worse than during the Emergency, with nine country experts agreeing that 'academic freedom and freedom of cultural expression are practiced occasionally, but direct criticism of the government is mostly met with repression'.[90] Like the coding for harassment of journalists, this is only a descriptor attached to a five-point scale measuring academic and cultural freedom with regard to political issues, not a qualitative evaluation made by the country experts themselves. Still, it might seem extreme to anyone familiar with Indian academia to place it on the second-lowest out of five rungs, ranking academic freedom in India below that in Hamas-administered Gaza, Chinese-administered Hong Kong, military-ruled Thailand, and communist-ruled Cambodia—to say nothing of neighbouring Pakistan.

As with all subjective evaluations, exactly where India belongs on the academic freedom scale is difficult to judge, but academia is a querulous profession, and academic freedom is a hot topic in both the general and the trade press. Academics are so rarely fired for their controversial views that when one is, it generally makes the headlines. Thus the number of politically motivated firings of academics in India might be compared to the number in a Western comparison country, not to arrive at an exact score for academic freedom in India, but to provide a rough reality check on India's recent downgrade. In the United States and Canada, it is near impossible to fire tenured professors, meaning that dismissals mainly affect non-tenured professors without permanent positions, making them difficult to track. India's university system, however, resembles that used in the United Kingdom, Australia, and New Zealand, where academics with 'permanent' positions can be fired, though with difficulty.

The United Kingdom, Australia, and New Zealand thus offer a reasonable benchmark for how many academics might be fired for their political views even in well-regarded Western democracies. In these three countries, at least six academics have been dismissed from paid (i.e., not merely honorary) positions specifically for expressing politically unpalatable opinions during 2019-2023. These cases include incidents at the University of Bristol (2021), Cambridge University (2019), the Open University (2021 and 2023), Solent University (2020), and the University of Sydney (2019).[91] This list excludes academics who resigned under pressure, whose claims of political persecution are still being litigated, or who were technically dismissed for administrative violations despite widespread acknowledgment that the underlying motivation was political. Nor does it include academics who were stood down from leadership positions, censured by learned societies, or deplatformed from speaking engagements. These are hard, unambiguous firings.

Six cases might not sound like a lot, until contrasted with India. It is difficult to identify even a single case of an academic being dismissed from a paid position in India for political reasons over the same period. The most widely reported case of compromised academic freedom occurred in 2023 at Ashoka University, where a junior economics professor came under severe public criticism for publishing a research paper that suggested possible vote-rigging in the 2019 elections. He resigned despite a public outpouring of support from colleagues and the university's administration.[92] Later, he took up a more senior (but non-permanent) position at another institution.[93] Less prominently, one academic was allegedly forced to resign in 2019 and another was summarily dismissed in 2022 over hate speech incidents at the relatively obscure Lovely Professional University.[94] The founder and chancellor of this private university is a senior opposition politician. Another academic was dismissed from the Madras School of Social Work in 2021, but it is not clear whether he was fired for his politics or (as he himself claims) for gossiping with colleagues about his managers.[95]

The Madras incident was the only case of an academic firing identified by the political scientist Niraja Gopal Jayal in a major review of academic freedom in India published in 2023 and covering incidents through mid-2021. Jayal taught at JNU for thirty-five years before moving to London, where she holds professorial chairs at Kings College and at the London School of Economics. An outspoken critic of Narendra Modi and the BJP, she concluded in her review that:

> The range and comprehensiveness of the recent assault on academic freedom [since 2014] is wide: From the politicization of appointments of heads of universities and even faculty appointments at every level, to constraints on the freedom to teach, research, and disseminate knowledge both in professional circles and in the public domain, to threats to campus integrity by vigilante intimidation and violence directed at students and teachers.[96]

These are all serious allegations, but they are the kinds of allegations that academics make in every Western democracy. Other reviews of academic freedom in India report similarly commonplace complaints. A 2022 article in the trade journal *Times Higher Education* reported 'intimidation and harassment' of scholars who are critical of the government, with academics being 'called into meetings with university officials'[97] Calling an academic in for a meeting is a typical senior administrator response to controversial research and teaching everywhere. Another comprehensive and thoroughly hostile review of the state of academic freedom in India published in 2023 by *Al Jazeera* claimed that 'academics faced the axe for being critical of the BJP and its Hindu nationalist affiliates,' but did not name a single academic who had been dismissed.[98] Instead, it reported claims from professors that they had been denied privileges like sabbaticals and travel funding—all complaints that are part and parcel of academic life.

When it comes to serious transgressions of academic freedom, the absence of evidence is not evidence of absence, but the absence of evidence with regard to India is nonetheless striking. A recent report on academic freedom in tiny New Zealand documented dozens of cases of interference in teaching and research that are similar to claims made about India.[99] As for outright dismissals, India has more than fourteen times the population of the United Kingdom, Australia, and New Zealand combined, and a similarly structured university system. If academics really do face serious oppression in India, there should be dozens of clear-cut cases of academic dismissals on political grounds. It seems unlikely that such cases exist, but are not being reported. The fact that many less severe cases of perceived infringement have been widely reported in both the Indian and the international press demonstrates that there is no shortage of journalistic hype around such cases, should they arise. Outright firings of academics may be only the visible tip of a much larger academic oppression iceberg, but in the absence of that tip, the existence of the iceberg must at least be called into question.

The 'India rankings'

None of this is meant to imply that academics do not face political pressure in India, or that anti-government reporters are never harassed by the Indian government. It is meant to illustrate the reality that evaluations of freedom of expression and association are highly subjective, and prone to political bias. The V-Dem case against Indian democracy rests almost entirely on such subjective evaluations made by country experts who cannot possibly have direct evidence for most of the indicators they are asked to score and who may themselves be politically interested in the rankings outcomes. The same is true of V-Dem's evaluations of other countries, but there are few other countries where the V-Dem rankings have become such a focus of the national political conversation. Between 2020 and 2024 (both years inclusive), the V-Dem rankings were mentioned in 853 articles indexed in the Proquest International Newsstream database (a standard industry source). India was mentioned in 401 of those articles. The V-Dem rankings are, in effect, the India rankings.

The publication of salacious claims about the decline of Indian democracy has become something of a cottage industry among political scientists. For example, in early 2024 the highly respected Pew Research Center teased its latest global democracy report with the headline 'Who likes authoritarianism?'[100] Top of the list was India, with 85 per cent of the population saying that 'rule by a strong leader or the military would be a *good* way of governing their country' [emphasis in the original]. Scroll 102 pages into the full report, past the appendices to the raw data tables, and the full picture is revealed for those who have the skill to read it. In India, 82 per cent of people say that governance by experts would be good, 80 per cent direct democracy by the people, 79 per cent representative democracy by elected officials, 72 per cent military rule, and 67 per cent strongman rule.[101] In other words, Indians seemed to opt for every form of government.

This phenomenon is so common in survey research that it has a name: 'acquiescence bias.' Pew actually warns about this on its own methodology page, advising against the use of 'agree-disagree' questions (especially among less-educated respondents and when a survey is conducted in person) and recommending that 'a better practice is to offer respondents a choice between alternative statements.'[102] But instead of informing readers that in India—a relatively low-education country where the survey was conducted in person—the high number of people agreeing to military and strongman rule likely reflected nothing more than acquiescence bias, Pew combined the two categories into a new indicator it called "support for authoritarianism."[103] It did not bother to report that its own data showed that these were the two least favoured types of government among the five offered.

Pew's technically precise but substantively mendacious approach to reporting Indian 'authoritarianism' is mirrored in V-Dem's approach to reporting Indian 'autocracy.' By creating an arbitrary Electoral Democracy Index cut-off below which a country would be classified as an autocracy, V-Dem was able to classify India as an autocracy starting with its 2021 report (backdating India's slide into autocracy to its 2019 elections).[104] Why would that matter to V-Dem? Because by classifying India as an autocracy, V-Dem was able to publish the alarming statistic that 'autocracies are home to 68% of the world's population'.[105] If that meant putting democratic India on par with totalitarian China, so be it. The numbers don't lie, and they help V-Dem justify its continued funding by seeming to substantiate its ever-shriller warnings about democracy in decline.

The only problem with this approach is that the numbers do lie. Examined from a statistical standpoint, V-Dem hardly measures democracy at all. In fact, V-Dem doesn't even mention the single most serious objective shortcoming of Indian democracy: the fact that the state-wise apportionment of parliamentary seats was frozen by Indira Gandhi at 1971 levels to promote her population strategy on the argument that states that were 'successful' in reducing population growth should not be 'penalized' with the loss of Lok Sabha seats. India's relatively wealthier southern states have always had lower fertility than its northern ones, and in deference to their sensibilities parliamentary representation has remained frozen ever since. Due to differential population growth over the ensuing five decades, voters in the south Indian states of Kerala and Tamil Nadu now have more than 50 per cent greater parliamentary representation (on a per capita basis) than voters in poor north Indian states like Bihar and Uttar Pradesh.[106] One can only wonder if it is not discussed because the discrepancy strongly disfavours the BJP.

Instead of focusing on objective shortcomings like unequal representation, V-Dem's democracy ratings are driven almost entirely by the subjective degree of personal freedom felt by each country's expert class. This harsh verdict is substantiated by a 2024 study conducted by political scientists, Andrew T Little and Anne Meng. They studied the discrepancy between recent trends in objective and subjective indicators of democracy, concluding that:

> Most existing studies of global backsliding are based largely if not entirely on subjective indicators that rely on expert coder judgment. Our study surveys objective indicators of democracy ... and finds little evidence of global democratic decline during the past decade. [...] Although we cannot rule out the possibility that the world is becoming less democratic exclusively in ways that require subjective judgment to detect, this claim is not justified by existing evidence.[107]

The situation with V-Dem is even worse, since even its objective indicators are highly suspect. The two objective component indices calculated by V-Dem, covering universal suffrage and elected leaders, are coded in purely pro forma terms. Nor does V-Dem's quality of elections component index serve to properly differentiate among countries that are nominally democratic. That leaves the highly subjective freedom of association and freedom of expression component indices to bear almost the entire weight of ranking countries on V-Dem's Electoral Democracy Index. The result is that countries where a single party wins 82 per cent of the seats in parliament (Mongolia in 2020), where an incumbent president wins with 95 per cent of the vote (Ivory Coast in 2020), or where elections have been suspended entirely (Tunisia in 2023) can substantially outperform a competitive multiparty democracy like India. Such perversions do not result from an inherent flaw in Dahl's 'polyarchy' model of democracy. They result from preventable errors in operationalising Dahl's criteria into practical indicators that can be measured using empirical data.

The operationalisation choices made by V-Dem may have sounded good in theory, but they have failed when confronted with real-world data. India is not, like Russia, an 'electoral autocracy' where people have as little meaningful opportunity for self-government as in 'closed autocracies' like China and North Korea. India is a real democracy, but one that since 2014 has elected leaders whom many of its own intellectuals (and most intellectuals abroad) find distasteful. India faces many challenges, and the quality of Indian democracy may or may not be on a par with that of the leading Western countries. It is, however, certainly much higher than indicated by V-Dem. There is no definitive way to measure democracy, but by any measure that counts, India's democracy is in better shape than that of just about any other developing country. In many measurable ways, it outperforms the established democracies of the Western world, too.

The Minister Monk

Democracy is a slippery concept. Reduce it to the mere holding of elections, and all sorts of unsavoury regimes creep in. Restrict it with qualifiers like 'real' or 'true', and every country can be said to fall short. But there is one form of democracy that most people in the developed countries of North America, Western Europe, and East Asia accept as a practical working model, and that is liberal democracy. Liberal democracy is just as routinely denounced by the leaders of countries like China, Iran, and Russia. These patterns reflect real differences in political institutions between liberal and illiberal countries.

If liberal democracy is to be an ideal, or even a working principle, it must have a definition. All attempts at definition are politically suspect, so it's best simply to turn to the dictionary. That mother of all dictionaries, the *Oxford English Dictionary*, defines liberal democracy as 'a democratic system of representative government in which individual rights and civil liberties are officially recognised and protected, and the exercise of political power is limited by the rule of law.'[108] By that standard, and subject to all sorts of critical objections about majoritarian threats, slippery slopes, and uncertain futures, there is no doubt that twenty-first century India is a liberal democracy. But India is not a typical liberal democracy. Most of the world's liberal democracies are rich, secular, and Western. India is none of those things. Its income per capita is a tiny fraction of that of the United States or the European Union, and India is a deeply religious country where 75 per cent of the population claims to pray every day.[109]

India is arguably the only poor, religious, non-Western liberal democracy in the world. There are no truly comparable success stories against which the country can be benchmarked. Its uniqueness makes it difficult for rich, secular Westerners (and, for that matter, rich, secular, Western-educated Indians) to recognise a liberal democracy when they see it operating in such an unfamiliar context. India's democratic institutions may resemble those in the rich, secular West, but India's electorate is strikingly different. As a result, the outcomes of elections are different, even if the processes are the same. Obviously, the people of Uttar Pradesh and Bihar want very different things from the people of New York or London. The electorates are so different that the comparison is almost laughable. But to understand how a genuine, Western-style liberal democracy would operate in the Indian context requires the imagination to make just such comparisons.

Bookstores, academic journals, and the mass media are full of shrill attacks on Indian democracy, warning of India's supposed descent into dictatorship and nascent fascism. An equally shrill response might be to label these attacks neocolonial, elitist, and of course racist. And there the conversation would end.

A more productive way to confront scepticism about the quality of Indian democracy is to respond by asking what a successful liberal democracy would look like in a country that is poor, religious, and non-Western? For example, it is unrealistic to expect a uniformly high standard of law enforcement in a country where illiteracy is still so common that political parties use registered campaign symbols to help voters identify them on ballot papers. Village constables have to be able to read the law before they can responsibly enforce it. Even in Western countries, failures of police procedure are routine. In a country like India, the best that can be expected is that local lapses are corrected at higher levels, and that an independent minded Supreme Court ultimately rights the wrongs of illegal arrests, censures prosecutorial overreach, and overturns flawed lower court decisions. It is inevitable that a local constable somewhere in a country of 1.4 billion people will deprive someone of the due process of law. The important thing is that such transgressions be identified and redressed.

Similarly, it is also unrealistic to demand that political parties steer clear of religion in a country where religious identity is so central to daily life that the very laws that govern marriage, divorce, and inheritance differ according to people's religions. It is arguably inappropriate for politicians to seek votes by appealing to voters' religious values. But would India be a fully functioning democracy if politicians ignored the wishes of their constituents in order to avoid upsetting minority religious communities—or urbane liberal critics? Muslim-baiting in India, like race-baiting in the United States or indeed Muslim-baiting in Western Europe, is morally wrong. Nevertheless, such unsavoury practices occur in all liberal democracies, not because they are illiberal, but because they are democratic. In a genuine liberal democracy like the United States, Australia, Sweden, or indeed India, some politicians will appeal to the electorate's worst impulses. Liberal principles like freedom of speech and freedom of assembly make this possible.

Even accounting for differences in wealth and religion between India and the West, there is still the challenge of imagining what a genuine non-Western liberal democracy should look like. The standard story we tell ourselves about the growth of democracy—that a rising urban middle class challenged the authority of aristocratic hereditary rulers and demanded a greater say in the political life of the country—is just that: a story we tell ourselves, about ourselves. It is not so much a theory of democracy as a history of democracy in Western Europe and North America. Most of these Western nations developed their governing institutions over a period of several centuries, arriving at full liberal democracy relatively late in their national lives. In contrast, most non-Western nations emerged between 1945 and 1975 with shallow-seeded democracies that generally failed to take root. India alone among major post-colonial countries has been continuously governed by the same democratic constitution it wrote for itself upon achieving independence.

A distinctively Indian democracy

In the developed West, modern liberal democracy germinated, sprouted, and matured organically as part of the same process that led to the development of modern nation-states. The state preceded democracy by millennia, but the nation grew up along with it. Thus in failed states today, democracy-building is still inseparable from nation-building. In India, nation-building efforts began in the late nineteenth century, built up steam in the interwar years, and culminated in a three-year constitutional convention that sat from late 1946 to early 1950. The

Constitution of India ran to 234 pages in the official illustrated calligraphy edition; it is reputed to be the longest constitution in the world. But as history demonstrates, a detailed constitution is not enough to secure the survival of a democracy. The participants in India's constitutional debates were aware that their real task was not the writing of a democratic constitution, but the founding of a democratic nation.

Much like the United States Constitution, the Constitution of India was the product of compromise, and just like the American founding fathers had set aside some difficult issues to be dealt with later, so too did India's independence leaders. Among these were the choice of a national language, the issue of reserved parliamentary seats for members of the lowest caste groups, and even equal protection under the law for people of different religions. Again and again, India has 'punted' on constitutional reform, leaving open questions that are too controversial to answer definitively. As a result, nation-building remains an ongoing process for India, and even today, India faces multiple calls for regional autonomy and continuing separatist terrorism. Rather than define the meaning of Indian nationhood once and for all, Indians have repeatedly chosen compromise and ambiguity, all in the interest of everyone just getting along.

Many of these questions are now coming to a head. In recent years, the Indian government has been criticised both at home and abroad for seeking to establish a religiously exclusionary vision of India as a specifically Hindu nation. That India's current leaders as well as their major domestic rivals are committed nationalists is clear enough. Both the governing Bharatiya Janata Party (BJP) and the opposition Indian National Congress (INC) claim nationalism as a guiding value.

The advocacy of a specifically 'Hindu' nationalism for India is, however, much more controversial. After the formation of independent India in 1947, the INC governed the country for most of the remainder of the twentieth century, advocating a 'socialist, secular' vision of Indian nationhood. When the BJP later became the dominant force in Indian politics following the 2014 elections, its critics routinely (and derisively) labeled it a 'Hindu nationalist' party. This may or may not be a fair assessment, but it must be acknowledged that if the BJP has one core identifying trait, it is its unabashed 'Hinduness'.

The BJP accepts India's secular constitution, but its leaders openly embrace Hindu religious language, values, and symbolism. The party's unofficial colour is saffron, the Hindu sacred colour of fire, and its official symbol is the lotus, the Hindu sacred flower of creation. The BJP, however, does admit non-Hindu members and does run non-Hindu candidates—though in relatively low numbers, The BJP even collaborates with non-Hindu parties when it considers it strategically convenient to do so. In short, the BJP does everything it can to succeed in a religiously plural society, but when all is said and done, the party is inextricably linked with the idea that India is a fundamentally (but not necessarily fundamentalist) Hindu nation.

Critics maintain that the BJP's implicit—and sometimes, when the mask falls, explicit—understanding of India as a Hindu nation is incompatible with the core principles of liberal democracy. But is that really so? After all, the United States is a democracy, and it is in many ways a Christian nation. The United States Congress opens its sessions with a prayer, and presidents routinely close their speeches by asking God to bless America. No one seriously believes that the 'God' referred to is any other but the God of the Bible. American

Christians overtly campaign on the basis of religion, and exert a strong influence over government policies despite the strict constitutional separation of church and state. Everyday government practices like the taking of oaths on the Christian Bible (though allowing for alternatives to be used on request) reflect the deep embeddedness of a presumption of Christianity in the United States. Americans are free to pursue whatever religion they choose, or none at all, but the American nation as such is Christian in origin, practice, and outlook.

Other Western democracies come even closer to embracing state religions. Many European countries have established churches that receive direct government subsidies and play central roles in state ceremonies. In the United Kingdom, the sovereign is still the titular head of the Church of England, and must, by law, be Anglican.

In Belgium, Germany, and the Netherlands, major political parties include the word 'Christian' in their names. In Ireland, the Catholic Church runs most of the country's publicly funded elementary schools, and until recently even state schools institutionalised Catholicism in the form of clerical oversight and graduation masses.[110] In Japan, a Shinto ceremony is embedded in the country's secular national institutions, and indigenous quasi-religious ceremonies are increasingly common at state occasions in Australia and New Zealand.

The key difference between India and these developed liberal democracies isn't the behaviour of the Indian government, but the character of Indian society. Western governments, despite their nominal retention of religious imagery and institutions, are embedded in relatively agnostic societies. Irish children may still attend Catholic schools, but Irish adults voted to permit same-sex marriage in 2015. Three years later, they voted by an even wider margin to legalise abortion. Both referendums were resisted by the Catholic church, though to no avail.

By contrast, Indian society, like most other non-Western societies, is deeply religious. As the political scientist Pradeep K Chhibber writes:

> India is a very religious society and religious practice is important to most Indians. This practice is frequent, multiple, and diverse. No politician can ignore this fact.

He goes on to point out that India is not the West, where in the not-so-distant past, the religious elite was opposed to democracy because the religious elite feared a loss of power. This fear was borne out of a legitimate concern that the modern nation-state would limit their authority.[111]

Anticlericalism holds no such sway in India. While these days any Western government that overtly embraced religious causes would likely find itself turned out of office at the next election, no Indian government can afford to ignore the fiercely held religious convictions of its electorate. In most of India, that means some form of Hindu convictions, but in some areas it can mean Muslim, Christian, or Sikh ones. Indian politicians who want to get elected must represent their constituents. The country wouldn't be much of a democracy if they didn't.

The colour of government

Uttar Pradesh (UP) is the kind of place most Westerners imagine when they think about India. It is home to the Taj Mahal, built by the Muslim emperor Shah Jahan (1592-1666) as a memorial to his favourite wife. It is also the home of holy sites like Varanasi, Ayodhya, Mathura, and Sarnath. It is the beating heart of the 'Hindi Heartland,' a densely populated region of small farms and sacred cows that straddles the middle reaches of the Ganges River. Its capital, Lucknow, was the centre of the 1857 Indian Mutiny against British rule—or the First War of Indian Independence, depending on your point of view.

Home to more than 235 million people, UP is by far India's largest state, accounting for more than one-sixth of the country's total population.[112] If UP were an independent country, it would be the fifth largest in the world. It would also be among the poorest in the world. With a state domestic product of roughly Rs 88,800 or $1,000 per capita, it would not be out of place in sub-Saharan Africa.[113] In fact, it is relatively poor even by African standards, with income levels more akin to Ethiopia and Rwanda than to economic powerhouses like Nigeria and South Africa. The population of UP is 19 per cent Muslim (as against 15 per cent for India as a whole) and 21 per cent Hindus from Scheduled Castes (as against 17 per cent for India as a whole).[114] Compared to other Indian states, UP has high levels of fertility, high levels of child mortality, and low levels of education.[115] It reflects all of India's modernisation challenges.

Most of all, however, Uttar Pradesh is big. The state's enormous voter base, central position, and symbolic significance have made it the most important political battleground in the country. The behemoth and the bellwether of Indian politics, UP accounts for eighty of the 543 seats in the Lok Sabha, the Indian parliament's decisive lower house. The electoral preponderance of UP will increase further if and when the Indian government reapportions the nation's parliamentary representation to account for population shifts since the allocation of seats was frozen in 1971. India's general elections are an overwhelming spectacle of democracy in action, but in this populous and prominent state, even local elections are fought on the scale of national elections in other countries.

The BJP was carried to national power in India's 2014 elections on the back of an outsized performance in UP, where it leapt from a total of just ten seats all the way up to seventy-one, sweeping almost the entire state. The BJP's seats in UP accounted for roughly one-quarter of all the seats it won nationwide. As a result, UP became a must-hold state for the BJP. Trading on its success, the BJP went all out to win the 2017 legislative assembly elections in the state, seeking to capitalise on Prime Minister Narendra Modi's personal popularity in a state where it had historically been a third-place finisher.

Prior to 2017, UP's state elections had been fought mainly on caste lines, but the BJP successfully shifted the debate over to cross-caste issues like corruption, the economy, and personal safety.[116] The result was a landslide victory for the BJP, giving it the opportunity to appoint the state's new chief minister. It chose one of the country's most outspoken, controversial, and divisive politicians, Yogi Adityanath.

The chief minister of Uttar Pradesh bears the title 'Yogi' because, quite literally, he is a yogi. In addition to being India's second most popular politician, he leads one of northern India's most prominent Hindu religious orders. Born Ajay Mohan Bisht, Adityanath is a colourful figure—if by 'colour' you mean 'saffron.' It's the only colour he wears. Hailing from a modest family (his father was a forest ranger), he took his current name on being initiated into the Gorakhnath Math religious order in 1994.[117] He got his start in politics around the same time, joining the campaign for the building of a temple in Ayodhya dedicated to Lord Ram (the 'Ram Mandir'). It was to be built on the site of a mosque that had been destroyed by a Hindu mob in 1992. Three decades later, as chief minister of UP, he had the opportunity to see this project through to completion.

In his intermingled roles of pastor and politician, Adityanath took an active role in local Hindu civil society in his religious order's bastion in eastern UP. In 2002 he organised a militantly—many would say violently—anti-Muslim youth organisation called the Hindu Yuva Vahini (HYV), or Hindu Youth Brigade.[118] In addition to protesting Muslim cow slaughter for beef consumption, the HYV took up a broad range of Hindu nationalist causes, including the Ram Mandir campaign. Controversially, the HYV has come to be seen as a 'private army' of militant young volunteers loyal only to the Yogi.[119] The HYV also played a role in revitalising the Hindu Mahasabha party, a fringe competitor to the BJP for the votes of extreme Hindu nationalists.[120]

Adityanath was first elected to the Lok Sabha in 1998, winning—or inheriting—the seat of his mentor and spiritual predecessor, the Gorakhnath Math's then-leader, Mahant Avaidyanath. He represented the Math's home city of Gorakhpur as India's youngest member of parliament, winning four reelections from the same constituency before resigning to take up the UP chief minister's role in the capital city of Lucknow. During his years in the Lok Sabha, Adityanath built an enthusiastic following as a young Hindu firebrand politician. In 2014, his mentor Mahant Avaidyanath passed away, and Adityanath succeeded him as *mahant* (chief priest) of the Gorakhnath Mandir, the central temple of the Gorakhnath Math. This temple is a major religious and civic establishment in the relatively poor area of eastern UP, hosting schools, cow rescue facilities, and even a hospital. It has also long been deeply engaged in local politics.[121]

It is not clear whether Adityanath sees himself as primarily a religious leader or a public servant; most likely, he recognises no distinction between the two roles. He was anointed as the intended future leader of the Gorakhnath Math at the age of twenty-one; his entire adult life has been spent within the strict religious discipline of monastic life. His many admirers see him as incorruptible. As *mahant* of the Gorakhnath Mandir, he acted as a modern-day Solomon. He reportedly held court every day in Gorakhpur to issue judgements on disputes referred to him by local people, a practice he is said to have continued after moving to Lucknow in 2017.[122] Supporters and opponents alike see him as the monk who became chief minister. As a duly elected (and genuinely popular) democratic politician, 'the Yogi' is a uniquely Indian phenomenon. In his person, religion and politics are inextricably intertwined.

Bad press and good politics

Yogi Adityanath's hardline Hindu reputation has been both a resource and a curse for the BJP. Nationally, the BJP has long sought to build bridges with Muslim voters.[123] Its national leader, Prime Minister Narendra Modi, gets positive ratings from at least a quarter of India's Muslims.[124] A small but rising proportion of India's Muslims vote for BJP candidates, with the BJP's Muslim supporters being richer, more educated, younger, and more female than the Muslim population as a whole.[125] Nonetheless, the BJP has in recent years focused its Muslim outreach on a group of poorer, 'lower' caste Muslims, better known as the Pasmanda ('left behind') community.[126] Muslims make up roughly 20 per cent of the population in UP, enough to tip the balance in closely-run state elections. Farther afield, bad press in UP can hurt the party's chances with Muslims all over the country, drive away potential coalition partners, and even threaten international relations with Gulf Arab countries.[127]

But bad press can be good politics, and Adityanath has had more than his share of it. Throughout the 2017 UP state election campaign, Adityanath warned of the threat posed by young Muslim 'Romeos' lurking on street corners and just outside college gates to seduce innocent Hindu 'Eves.'[128] Leaving aside the strangely mixed Western metaphor, this was highly incendiary rhetoric, and it was widely condemned by human rights campaigners and the mainstream press. Immediately on taking office as chief minister, he escalated this rhetoric into a very public campaign to protect the honour of UP's young women. Sexual harassment and sexual violence are serious problems throughout India, and Adityanath had rightly promised to make it safe for women to go out in public. But when, as chief minister, Adityanath ordered the formation of special police 'anti-Romeo' squads, no one was surprised when all hell broke loose.[129]

The anti-Romeo campaign was an invitation, almost a directive, to law enforcement that they should arrest suspicious-looking (by implication, Muslim) young men and crack down on young couples loitering in public. Inevitably, reports quickly emerged of police harassment and the summary punishment of suspected offenders.[130] In reality, however, allegations of extralegal actions taken by police were relatively muted. In one incident, a man was publicly humiliated by being forced to assume an embarrassing stress position, a mild form of corporal punishment formerly used in some Indian schools. In several other cases, police called the couple's parents to alert them of their children's behaviour. Stories emerged that HYV gangs were involved in anti-Romeo violence, but the extent to which such incidents were directly tied to official policy is open to question.[131] For example, a report that a man had his head shaved by the anti-Romeo police went viral, but it turned out that the punishment was inflicted by a civilian vigilante while police looked on. The three police officers present at the scene were promptly suspended pending investigation.[132]

In 2018, a whole year after the rushed initial roll-out, the UP police finally issued formal guidelines for the operation of anti-Romeo squads, mandating the use of body cameras, instituting the maintenance of proper records, and placing an emphasis on informal counselling.[133] In 2019, when police became lax in their anti-Romeo patrolling, Adityanath ordered a new push, adding domestic violence to the agenda and ordering extra foot patrols in rural areas.[134] Complaints about inappropriate moral policing died down, and Adityanath claimed to have succeeded in imposing law and order.[135] In the end, the anti-Romeo narrative generated a lot of alarmist press coverage, but it does not seem to have sparked the kinds of arbitrary enforcement or violent backlash anticipated by liberal intellectuals. For the most part, the HYV seems to have stayed in the background and let the police enforce the law.

Perhaps prompted by the BJP national leadership, or perhaps simply reflecting personal growth in the job, Adityanath toned down his anti-Muslim rhetoric after the 2019 national elections. However crude his methods, Adityanath was at least making a visible effort to deter violence against women. One might even believe that his concern for UP's women was sincere, if somewhat unsophisticated. Then on 14 September 2020, a 19-year-old woman was violently abducted, severely beaten, and gang-raped by a group of four men in a village near the small city of Hathras in western UP.[136] Initially hospitalised nearby, the victim was later transferred to a major hospital in Delhi, where she died of her injuries two weeks later. Police from UP somehow obtained possession of the victim's body before the family had a chance to pay their last respects. They transported it back to Hathras, where they cremated it in a remote field in the middle of the night, against the family's wishes and without the family present.[137]

The Hathras incident, though tragic, could have been a golden political opportunity for Adityanath to demonstrate his genuine commitment to women's safety by aggressively prosecuting the culprits without fear or favour. Instead, he remained silent as two junior members of his administration downplayed the severity of the incident, questioning whether a rape had technically occurred at all, as if the brutal assault were not a serious crime in itself.[138] Police did belatedly arrest the four accused men, but the government seemed more focused on quashing demonstrations than delivering justice.[139] These misplaced priorities seemed to be confirmed when Adityanath launched a major state-wide investigation into those who 'want to incite caste and communal riots'—by which he meant not the Hathras rapists and murderers, but people protesting his government's inaction.[140]

To be fair, Adityanath quickly suspended the police officers involved in the irregular cremation and ordered a state-level investigation into the affair.[141] Perhaps bowing to pressure from the national government, he referred the case to the Central Bureau of Investigation.[142] The four suspects were ultimately charged with gang rape, murder, and caste-based atrocities.[143] One was ultimately convicted and sentenced to life imprisonment, while the other three walked free, pending appeal.[144] One might say that although a horrific crime had been committed—and horrific crimes are committed everywhere—

the justice system had worked. Nonetheless, the perpetrators of the Hathras incident were not the Muslim Romeos that Adityanath had so often warned of. They were all Hindus, members of the Thakur caste. Adityanath is also a Thakur.

The politicisation of patriarchy

The Thakurs, known in the colonial era as Rajputs, are considered to have 'upper' caste status in UP, alongside the better-known Brahmins. Historically a village landlord caste, they account for less than 10 per cent of UP's population, but own more than 50 per cent of the state's land.[145] While not necessarily members of the business and managerial elite of modern high-tech India, they are a powerful local group and key BJP electoral constituency.[146] The idea that young Thakur men might engage in gang violence in rural India with impunity is an ingrained cultural prejudice, whether or not it is true.

The murdered woman, by contrast, was a member of a Scheduled Caste community. These caste groups are often referred to by the Sanskrit word *dalit* ('scattered'), originally an activist term but now widely used for the castes formerly known in English as 'untouchable.' Dalit castes are ranked at the bottom of India's historical caste system. Their members have full civil rights under Indian law but still face serious discrimination and disadvantage. In a state where caste politics are important—and where 17 Lok Sabha seats are actually reserved for Scheduled Caste candidates, including the Hathras seat—the BJP has in recent years worked hard to win over Dalit voters.[147] Adityanath's lackadaisical response to the Hathras incident suggested to many that the chief minister's ostentatious concern for the honour of UP's women did not extend to Dalits.[148] Or at least: not when they were assaulted by 'higher' caste Hindus.

Yet Adityanath could not let go of the myth of marauding Muslim Romeos. Before the Hathras charges were even handed down, Adityanath set out on a new campaign against an imagined Muslim threat to the honour of young Hindu women. Perhaps wary of bringing up the issue of rape, he focused instead on another intercommunal bugbear: religious conversion through illicit seduction and forced marriage. Thus on 24 November 2020, in the midst of the coronavirus pandemic, Adityanath's cabinet approved the Prohibition of Unlawful Conversion Ordinance 2020. The new law introduced serious penalties for forced conversions, forced conversions of members of vulnerable populations, and mass forced conversions. Even more controversially, it also introduced a requirement that interfaith couples inform government magistrates of their intention to marry at least two months in advance.[149]

The ordinance was immediately pronounced (and denounced as) the 'Love Jihad' law by the Indian and international press.[150] The Love Jihad trope has a long history in India, with Hindu groups mobilising against the 'kidnapping' and 'abducting and seducing' of Hindu women by Muslim men at least since the 1920s.[151] In a country where interfaith marriage is rare (and often highly stigmatised), sexual politics have always been highly charged. The last time Love Jihad mania broke out in a serious way, it wasn't even over Hindu girls in poverty-stricken UP. The focus was Catholic girls in the relatively prosperous south Indian state of Kerala.[152]

The first arrest under UP's new forced conversion law was a young Muslim man whose Hindu girlfriend's father had filed a complaint.[153] The suspect was actually accused of very serious crimes, including a threat to kill the woman and her parents. He spent fourteen days in jail before being released, though it seems this was not due to the forced conversion complaint, but to his efforts to evade arrest.[154] In the first three years of operation of the law, a total of 855 people were arrested in 433 distinct cases.[155] It appears that at least half of these cases involved either bona fide forced conversions or illegal marriages of minors. As of mid-2023, only four cases had gone to trial. The main effect of the law seems to have been to spur police to intervene to prevent the exploitation of young women by catching potentially forced marriages before they are solemnised and consummated. Under the law, only the couples involved and their immediate family can file complaints.[156]

It is not known how popular Adityanath's unlawful conversion law is with the people of UP, whether Hindu or Muslim. A major 2019-2020 survey on religion in India conducted by the Pew Research Centre found that 82 per cent Indians opposed women marrying outside of their religion, with the percentage being highest among Muslims, at 89 per cent. Ninety-nine per cent of all Indians reported being married to someone of the same religion.[157] Interfaith romances often stoke genuine fear and anger among parents and families, and can lead to intercommunal violence. Interfaith couples can marry under civil law (though this rarely occurs), and even civil marriages require a 30-day waiting and public notification period, to give parents and others the opportunity to objections, if they have any.[158] There is no national law in India covering conversion by marriage, but some Indian states have had laws on the books since the 1960s.[159] Studies show very little evidence of religious conversions through forced marriages, but in a country as large as India there is always scope for individual cases.[160]

India is a profoundly conservative country where the laws covering marriage, divorce, child custody, and inheritance differ by religion. As a result, an interfaith marriage generally requires one of the parties to convert to the other's religion; there are few mixed marriages in India. Seen from a Western liberal perspective, the obvious way to address the whole issue would be to get rid of religion-specific laws altogether. As it happens, the application of such a uniform civil code to all of India's people regardless of religion has long been one of the 'core issues' of the BJP and its predecessor party, the Jana Sangh.[161] In India's counterintuitive ideological landscape, support for special Sharia-based Muslim family laws is usually found among political liberals. It is the supposed Hindu nationalist who wants to impose uniform marriage laws on all citizens. Until Indian society is ready to move toward a religion-blind family law regime, anti-conversion laws may be the best political compromise that a poor state like UP can manage.

The defeat of caste politics

The controversy that perpetually swirls around Yogi Adityanath has little to do with the substance of his record as chief minister of Uttar Pradesh. He seems to have been a competent administrator by Indian standards, and a breath of fresh air by the standards of most Third World countries. Nor does the Yogi's saffron-infused sartorial style offend political sensibilities in India, where overt expressions of religious identity are an accepted feature of public life. The fact that he serves in government while simultaneously retaining his position as a major religious figure may seem strange, but in India, it is more of a personal quirk than a public transgression. Even Adityanath's overtly Islamophobic rhetoric, although certainly not acceptable from a liberal standpoint, is not particularly out of line with the rough-and-tumble of populist state-level politics in India. It is routinely criticised in India's elite English-language press, but it is only exceptional because Adityanath is seen to be a potential future Prime Minister, not merely a firebrand local politician.

The routine use of Islamophobic language by Adityanath is well-documented.[162] He has long been characterised in the media as anti-Muslim, and with good reason. Academic evaluations of Adityanath's words and actions have confirmed a consistent anti-Muslim sentiment.[163] The best defense offered by his most ardent boosters is that as head of the Gorakhnath Mandir, he has employed Muslims in executive positions in the organisation's schools, shops, and hospital, and as chief minister, he has worked with and promoted Muslims.[164] Against that, his many transparently Islamophobic statements and speeches weigh heavily in the scales.

Why would a national political party like the BJP make such a polarising figure as Yogi Adityanath the chief minister of India's largest state—especially a state that is the key to its electoral strategy for the entire country? The simplest and most obvious explanation is that he is popular. Adityanath was already a rising star when he was made a chief minister in 2017, and since then he has only become more popular. As of 2024, national surveys from the magazine *India Today* rated him the country's most popular state chief minister for each of the eight years he had been in office—and the competition was not even close. In 2024, more than 46 per cent of Indians nationwide named him as the best out of a field of thirty contenders, with the remaining twenty-nine chief ministers splitting the remaining 54 per cent of the vote.[165] It's hard to argue with that kind of popularity.

An alternative explanation is that the BJP wants to guard its hardline Hindu flank. In the 2017 UP state elections that ultimately led to his appointment as chief minister, Adityanath's HYV had actually fielded a slate of alternative candidates, reportedly to put pressure on the BJP.[166] While 'keep your friends close and your enemies closer' logic cannot be dismissed, journalists who have interviewed senior BJP sources suggest something much more straightforward: Prime Minister Modi and the then BJP president, Amit Shah simply thought that Adityanath could win elections. In a closely held decision that surprised both the BJP rank-and-file and the country's political commentariat, they reportedly chose Adityanath for his power to appeal to Hindus across caste lines—and potentially to conservative Muslims, as well.[167] In any case, they must have thought carefully about the appointment: they waited for a whole week after the election to put Adityanath forward as chief minister.

The BJP had won the 2017 UP elections with a landslide victory, taking more than three-quarters of the seats in the state's legislative assembly, but they actually received only a plurality of the votes. Looking forward to the 2019 national elections, the BJP leadership was anxious to use their newfound control of the UP administration to consolidate their position in the state. Their greatest challenge was the entrenched practice of caste politics in UP. Although Modi himself hails from a 'lower' caste background, the BJP is widely perceived to be an 'upper' caste party. Its chief competitor in UP, the Samajwadi Party (SP), is a family-run party dominated by members of the Yadav caste. Mulayam Singh Yadav (1939-2022), who founded the party, and his son Akhilesh Yadav have both served as UP chief minister. The SP often works with the Bahujan Samaj Party, an overwhelmingly Dalit party whose charismatic leader, Mayawati, is both figuratively and literally a Dalit icon, famous as the poor Dalit woman who rose to become chief minister of UP four times. She is also infamous for the enormous number of statues that she has raised to Dalit leaders, including herself.

As a Thakur, Adityanath himself hails from an 'upper' caste background, but as the *mahant* of the Gorakhnath Mandir, he spiritually stands outside the caste system.[168] Like most Hindu orders today, the Gorakhnath Math does not recognise caste distinctions.[169] Adityanath's cross-caste appeal seems to have been crucial to the BJP's success in the 2019 national elections. With Adityanath headlining the party's campaign, the BJP's vote in UP came in at just a sliver short of 50 per cent, well above its previous results in the state. In India's fractured party system, half the vote can represent a big win, and it did that year for Adityanath and the BJP. When the BJP decided to campaign in 2024 without Yogi Adityanath as its leading face, its Lok Sabha seat haul from UP fell from sixty-two to just thirty-three. Political journalist Rajdeep Sardesai reported that 'the Yogi was deeply unhappy with the BJP's choice of Lok Sabha candidates' for 2024, since 'hardly any of his suggestions were accepted.'[170] In the upcoming 2027 UP legislative assembly elections, it seems likely that Adityanath will be firmly back in charge.

Cooptation or capture?

Breaking the power of caste in UP politics in the 2017 election was no mean feat. In UP and throughout the country, Indian democracy has long been characterised by caste and family fiefdoms. The BJP portrays itself as a modernising party that fights against both. While it inevitably engages in the politics of caste and personality in making electoral alliances across India's thirty-six states and union territories, within its own ranks it stresses teamwork and meritocracy. In that regard, the BJP's best calling card is the Prime Minister himself. Narendra Modi is the son of a small-town railway station *chaiwala* (teaseller). He earned his bachelor's and master's degrees by mail, via correspondence school. He has no children. It was only in 2014 that the public learned that he even had a wife., and none of his siblings is involved in politics or big business.[171] He is squeaky clean, which is probably why the BJP tolerates his emerging personality cult.

Yet Adityanath, for all his faults, makes Modi look like a libertine. He doesn't just live like a monk; he is a monk. After a quarter century in politics, his declared net worth is less than $200,000.[172] He owns no land or vehicles. He is reputed to rise long before dawn to pray, practice yoga, and spend time with cows. As the chief priest of the Gorakhnath Mandir, he has disowned his biological family and vowed to live a life of chastity and discipline. His biological siblings live even more modestly than Modi's.[173] Unlike Modi, however, Adityanath has an organised base of support outside the BJP. As *mahant* of the Gorakhnath Mandir, he leads the Gorakhnath Math religious order. This is not a political organisation, and is unlikely ever to become one. But it is no coincidence that in a 2024 election in which the BJP suffered serious losses throughout UP, it held onto all five of the Lok Sabha seats in and surrounding Gorakhpur.

The Yogi is now a major figure in the BJP, but he is one of the few party leaders who could walk away if he wanted to and take several seats with him. It seems likely that, as a condition for appointing Adityanath as chief minister of UP, the BJP's Modi and Shah insisted that he wind down the HYV and sever his connections with the Hindu Mahasabha.[174] Whatever happened behind the scenes, the HYV was for the most part disbanded soon after Adityanath took office—despite a reported surge in applications to join.[175] The Hindu Mahasabha openly split with Adityanath, accusing him of 'dividing Hindus' and asking the Election Commission of India to bar him from future electioneering.[176] The HYV seems to have then been reconstituted in advance of the 2022 UP elections, before being nominally suspended again after Adityanath comfortably cruised to victory.[177] It remains both a source of contention and something of a mystery.

For academic critics of the BJP who view it as a right-wing, Hindu-nationalist party that has undermined India's 'secular, pluralist and constitutional liberal democracy' with its anti-intellectual majoritarian populism, the party's cooptation of Adityanath presents a conundrum.[178] The fact that the BJP has elevated a firebrand Hindu nationalist to the leadership of India's largest state seems to confirm their worst fears about Indian democracy. But the fact that in doing so, the BJP has reined in Adityanath's more egregious provocations and redirected his energies toward the delivery of secular, caste-blind government services suggest something else. It is possible, after all, that Modi and the BJP took a chance on Adityanath because they thought he could break the influence that caste and cronyism continue to exert on UP politics and deliver clean, effective government in its place.[179] By all accounts, Adityanath threw himself into the day-to-day work of government administration at a pace previously unheard of in UP.

In all the breathless reporting on Adityanath's idiosyncratic law and order initiatives, it was rarely noted that the chief minister inherited a police force that was riddled with corruption in recruitment and promotion.[180]

One of his first tasks was to implement a statewide crackdown on cheating that led to a decline of a million people choosing to sit for the qualifying exams. Denied the opportunity to cheat, candidates didn't bother to take the tests.[181] He also pushed hard to clean up a civil service that was plagued by low standards and chronic absenteeism, setting a personal example of long hours and dedication to duty.[182] When the coronavirus hit and the national government ordered a three-week lockdown, he organised a combined state and volunteer service to deliver food to people trapped in their homes.[183] The proportion of people who received the promised aid is unknown, but politically, that hardly matters in a state where historical failures have entrenched a culture of low expectations. Unlike his predecessors of the previous fifteen years, Adityanath actually forced civil servants to show up in their offices.[184]

Road building, metro construction, electricity provision, public health measures, the rapid construction of the Ram Mandir and associated infrastructure—whether or not Adityanath has actually succeeded in getting things done for the people of Uttar Pradesh, he has certainly made a point of doing them. Adityanath raised expectations with outsized promises of government efficiency, then worked very visibly to fulfil them. In a state that is as poor as most of sub-Saharan Africa, and potentially just as corrupt, he showed a level of dedication to duty that is hard to find anywhere in politics today. He might disrupt and offend, but no one could accuse the Yogi of lacking a strong sense of *dharma*. Precisely to whom he feels he owes his dharmic duty is, however, open to question.

The *dharma* of modernity

Dharma means duty. The word is sacred to several religions, and it can mean many things depending on the context, but people's duties (to humanity, to their societies, to their families, to themselves) are ultimately at the core of the concept. Its ancient meaning was 'that which binds fast all beings, each to each with bonds of rights and duties; binding these also together, in the unfailing law of Action and Reaction, from whence Reward arises for good and Punishment for ill and thus preserves mankind.'[185] In the *Bhagavad Gita* ('Sacred Song'), Krishna instructs his disciple Arjuna that:

> …as you discern your own *dharma*, you should not waiver. For the warrior, there can be found nothing greater than battle for the sake of *dharma*.[186]

There is no doubt that Adityanath is a warrior for *dharma*; the only question is: which *dharma* is he fighting for—the *rashtra* (national) *dharma* of his duty to India, or the *sanatana* (eternal) *dharma* of his duty to religion? As a monk who has renounced worldly affairs and devoted his life to spiritual service, he may believe that these two are one and the same thing.

Adityanath has demonstrated a lifelong commitment to Hindu nationalism, which can be understood as the 'belief that politics should be organised in accordance with the precepts of the Hindu scriptures and way of life.'[187] Although he represents the mainstream BJP as chief minister of UP, he and his monastic order have long been associated with the Hindu Mahasabha ('Hindu Great Assembly'), which is today a fringe party but was once a major political movement.[188] Just how Hindu is the minister monk? It seems safe to assume that he is as Hindu as he knows how to be. Yet despite many opportunities for mischief, the worst fears of Adityanath's many critics have not come to pass. Ironically, liberal critics seem to have forgotten that many of those fears actually did come to pass under Adityanath's predecessor as chief minister of UP, the young, modern-sounding, Australian-educated environmental engineer Akhilesh Yadav.

It was under the nominally secular Yadav administration that UP suffered its worst intercommunal violence of the post-independence period, the 2013 Muzaffarnagar riots. A prominent Indian academic and human rights activist who is a staunch critic of Adityanath and the BJP describes it thus:

> Between 27 August and 17 September ... massified violence targeted the Muslim community in Muzaffarnagar. At the onset, two Hindus accused and killed a Muslim youth for allegedly sexually harassing a Hindu woman and relative. In the violence that ensued, sixty-two people died, ninety-three suffered injuries, women were gang-raped, and approximately 40-50,000 people were displaced. Three months after the violence, relief centres were shut down.[189]

There is some debate over exactly what prompted the initial dispute (it seems to have actually been a traffic accident), but it should be noted that those killed and displaced were overwhelmingly Muslim.[190] Whoever was responsible for stoking the violence, it is clear who was responsible for providing relief in the aftermath of the riots: the UP government, then led by chief minister Yadav. Yet notwithstanding Yadav's technocratic reputation, the living conditions in the camps established by his UP government were characterised as 'appalling' by India's National Human Rights Commission.[191] Seemingly credible allegations were made that funds appropriated for support never made it to families in need.[192] Three years later, in 2016, at least 30,000 displaced Muzaffarnagar refugees still had not been rehoused.[193] None of these criticisms are drawn from BJP-linked sources.

If Yadav and the SP exhibited any sense of *dharma* in the aftermath of the Muzaffarnagar riots, it was the *sva* (own) *dharma* of clientelist politics and institutionalised corruption. It's no wonder that UP voters were ready for a change in 2017. They didn't elect Adityanath to be their chief minister as he was chosen by the BJP to lead the state only after the elections, but the voters certainly did opt for a new kind of *dharma* in their state leadership. Previously, they had consistently voted along caste and religious lines. In 2017, an increasing number of UP voters, though still not the majority, defected to the BJP, In the 2022 state elections, they confirmed that decision. With Adityanath as their standard bearer, the BJP took a plurality of 41.3 per cent of the vote. In 2023, Adityanath became UP's longest continuously serving chief minister, and he remains popular today. His approval rating in UP in 2024 exceeded 50 per cent.[194]

No one can know for sure whether Adityanath and the BJP won in UP because of their reputation for Hindu nationalism, or because of their success in delivering electricity, toilets, cooking gas, mini-buses, and stricter law enforcement. What is known is that the BJP proudly wears its *rashtra dharma* on its saffron sleeves. It is a national party that campaigns mainly on national issues and actively seeks the votes of all Indians. That includes Muslims, although they have so far had only moderate success in winning Muslim votes.[195] The party espouses a specifically Hindu vision of the Indian nation, but it is open to debate whether it does so primarily to exclude Muslims (the conventional view of South Asia experts and Western political theorists) or to unify Hindus (the BJP's own understanding of itself). The difference may be only one of emphasis, but it is far from pedantic.

India's first modern political party

When the Modi-Shah team at the top of the BJP elevated a relatively obscure monk from the parliamentary backbenches to be the public face of their party in India's make-or-break electoral heartland, they were in effect instrumentalising religion in the service of politics. That said, Adityanath has also been an effective tool for achieving the BJP's larger goal of forging a strong, modern, united India. The BJP is a modernising force in Indian politics that is first and foremost determined to forge a unified Indian nation, and only incidentally (but nonetheless indispensably) a nation that is distinctively Hindu in identity. Having emerged in a society where around four-fifths of the population consists of highly observant Hindus, the BJP has evolved a reflexively Hindu perspective on society. But its core programme is not the creation of a Hindu state. Its core program is national modernisation—in a predominantly Hindu country.

If, as its critics assert, the BJP has historically been Hindu and 'upper' caste, it is because any major political movement emerging in twentieth century India was likely to be Hindu and 'upper' caste. During the independence struggle, the INC was predominantly Hindu and 'upper' caste, and the modern INC is still led by an 'upper' caste family. Many prominent intellectual critics of Narendra Modi and the BJP are, inevitably, Hindus from 'upper' caste backgrounds as well.[196] The BJP has, however, consistently sought to neutralise or at least reduce the role of caste in Indian politics. It is an overwhelmingly Hindu party, often jingoistically so, and sometimes Islamophobically so. But caricatures that portray the BJP as a hive of hardline Hindu nationalists yearning for an irretrievable Hindu past miss the point. The BJP does not want to turn the clock back on social reform. Its vision for India is that of a strong country, proud of its Hindu heritage, but moving confidently into a nationalist future.

The party's promotion of Yogi Adityanath as its standard bearer in UP is consistent with that vision. Adityanath physically embodies the BJP's connection to organic Hindu society while at the same time symbolising its construction of a new Indian nation. In a strange but telling confluence of goals, the BJP isn't just modernising India or UP; it has modernised the Yogi, too. It has forced him to expand his priorities from temple construction and cow protection to include electricity distribution and sewage treatment, and taught him to exchange the clientelist *durbars* (courts) of the Gorakhnath Mandir for the bureaucratic managerialism of the chief minister's office. At the same time, the BJP has leveraged Adityanath's Hindu nationalist appeal into Hindu nationalist votes, not only in UP but around the country. The issues on which the BJP's candidates are campaigning may not always be particularly Hindu, but the society in which they are campaigning is, and that makes Adityanath a valuable electoral asset.

The BJP is not making India more Western, but it is making India more modern, and in doing so it is inevitably making it more liberal. It seems safe to surmise that Adityanath himself harbours no liberal ideals for UP or for India. Yet his tenure as chief minister has brought some degree of civil service reform, honesty in examinations, a law against forced conversion enforced by secular authorities, improved rule of law, and (relative) intercommunal harmony to a state as poor as Ethiopia. That may not have turned Uttar Pradesh into the European Union, but it represents movement in the right direction.

It is possible through selective quotation and the cherry-picking of evidence to portray the BJP as a reactionary force undermining an idealised Indian democracy. A more balanced appraisal is that the BJP is successfully building a modern political nation in a relatively poor, deeply religious, non-Western society. Politicians like Modi and Adityanath may not 'look' modern to Western eyes, but the BJP they lead is the most cutting-edge modern political party in India today—and through its election victories, it is increasingly forcing its opponents to modernise as well. The BJP does exploit the traditionalism of Indian society to win elections, but the modernisation of Indian society is at the heart of its electoral programme. The BJP's new India may lack some of the postcolonial grace of the old India it is displacing, but it is unambiguously the India of the future. Those who see it as a regressive throw-back to an imagined pre-modern past fail to recognise that, for good and for bad, the new India is firmly in the vanguard of contemporary global trends.

The race between power and ability

New India's shopping malls, mobile phones, consumer capitalism, online marketing, and microtargeted politics may not please everyone, but they are the inevitable byproducts of modernisation and development. Modernity itself has always been a slippery concept. In its ordinary English usage, 'modern' simply means 'present-day': modern ideas are today's ideas; modern methods are those currently in use; a modern person is up-to-date on the latest developments in technology and fashion. Modern is what we are now, as opposed to people (and practices) from the past. But how far past? Who and what, exactly, counts as pre-modern? In historical sociology, there is a firm answer to that seemingly vague question. Modernity is a done deal: the modern era was the period from the late fifteenth century to the middle of the twentieth century, and we now live in a post-modern world. As individuals, we may all want to be as modern as possible, but modernity itself is historically passé.

At least, that's the story for the Europeanised West. In other parts of the world, modernity may have arrived at different times—or sometimes not at all. In the social sciences, modernity is usually seen as a step-change, a one-time transformation from the 'traditional' world of the distant past to the 'modern' world of the ever-advancing present. It is not so much as a frame of time as a state of mind. The founding generation of sociologists contrasted what they saw as the rational organisation of modern lives dominated by formal, contractual relationships with the irrationality (or non-rationality) of traditional societies, where most social relations were based on family or kinship ties. For these pioneering social scientists, modernity didn't arrive everywhere all at once; modernisation was a process that every society went through at its own pace, and which some may still be experiencing.

Classical sociology associated the transition to modernity with changes in the character of social relationships from a focus on personal characteristics (shared kinship, religion, or caste) to impersonal membership in broad collectives, foremost among them, citizenship in the modern nation-state. Nations demanded states and states forged nations, leading to the two concepts becoming so intertwined as to be hyphenated. There were (as there still are) people who considered themselves to be members of stateless nations, but lacking access to the machinery of state institutions, most of these nations have faded from history, and those that remain are chronically beleaguered. There were also (as there still are) states that governed people who did not share a common sense of nationhood; many of these states have since disintegrated, and those that remain tend to be highly unstable. The hyphenated nation in its own state is the one stable form of modern social organisation.

Today, most of the world's leading democracies are nation-states, meaning that their populations broadly embrace a shared sense of nationhood (American, Australian, French, Japanese, etc.) under a unified system of administration (the state). Modern democracies where shared nationhood is contentious, like Belgium, Spain, and the United Kingdom, are the exceptions that prove the rule. In these countries, the ordinary operation of democracy has fractured, with regional separatist parties fighting elections on identitarian (as opposed to policy) platforms. The dominance of Flemish separatist parties in Belgian Flanders, of Catalan separatist parties in Spanish Catalonia, and of the Scottish National Party in the British region of Scotland demonstrates the breakdown of democratic politics in countries where a shared sense of national identity is lacking.

For many Third World countries, the problem of forging a unified nation has proved even more challenging than the struggle to achieve independent statehood. Many postcolonial independent states, especially in Africa and in parts of Asia, remain divided along tribal, sectarian, or other proto-national lines. Former colonial powers may bear the historical fault for these divisions, but the present-day responsibility for inculcating a shared sense of nationhood among the citizens of a state must be met by the formerly colonised. Having achieved independence, they have no choice but to rise to the challenge. In India, that challenge began on 15 August 1947, when the Indian nation took control of the Indian state. That the Hindus of British India were at the core of the new Indian nation was, at the time, taken for granted: after all, the parallel state of Pakistan had been created specifically for and at the behest of the Muslims of British India. But the Hindu character of the new Indian nation was not taken for granted.

Late on the eve of India's independence, the country's founding Prime Minister, Jawaharlal Nehru famously recalled that 'long years ago we made a tryst with destiny.' Proclaiming independence as the moment when 'the soul of a nation, long suppressed, finds utterance,' he traced India's quest for nationhood all the way back to 'the dawn of history.' Echoing the rhetoric of nationalists everywhere, he claimed that the Indian nation was not new, but was merely being reborn: 'We end today a period of ill fortune and India discovers herself again.' He exulted that 'at the stroke of the midnight hour, when the world sleeps, India will awake to life and freedom.'[197] The crowd, naturally enough, roared in approbation. But the strange fact is that, at that very moment, the borders of the newly independent country had not yet been announced. This meant that millions of people listening to Nehru on the radio did not know which new nation they were citizens of—India or Pakistan.

Hours after Nehru's well-remembered speech, the 'Father of Pakistan' Muhammad Ali Jinnah (1876-1948) took to the radio to proclaim with somewhat less fanfare that the 'Muslims of India have shown to the world that they are a united nation.'[198] It is easy for scholars, in retrospect, to condemn the illiberal exclusion of Muslims from the construction of modern Indian nationhood. But at that moment in 1947, the role that Muslims would play in independent India was far from clear. This ambiguous circumstance led another speaker on India's independence eve, the Hindu philosopher Sarvepalli Radhakrishnan (1888-1975), to lament that 'while India is attaining freedom, she is attaining it in a manner which does not produce joy in the hearts of people or a radiant smile on their faces.' In a premonition worthy of a true scholar-statesman, Radhakrishnan warned that 'our opportunities are great but ... when power outstrips ability, we will fall on evil days.'[199] In India (as in so many postcolonial states), power did rapidly outstrip ability, and those evil days came all too soon.

The Legacies of Partition

From the moment of its birth as an independent country, India has been defined by religion—and by its relationship to religion. In 1947, India was to many of its citizens (and to many outsiders) simply the Hindu-majority counterpart to Muslim-majority Pakistan. To others, India was destined to be a multifaith country governed by a staunchly secular state. The tension between these two views of Indian nationhood has never been resolved. In a traditional society where four-fifths of the population identifies as Hindu, the dominance of Hindu customs, symbols, and discourses is unavoidable. Nonetheless, for a country where a literal yogi can become a major politician, India retains a surprisingly strong separation between 'church' and state. Hindu identity is routinely leveraged to win votes, as are Muslim identity, Christian identity, and multiple linguistic, regional, and caste identities. But the Indian state itself is, in many ways, surprisingly secular.

For example, there are only three mandatory national public holidays—Republic Day, Independence Day, and the birthday of the 'father of the country' Mahatma Gandhi (1869-

1948). In addition, the central government declares a panoply of religious holidays including Good Friday and Christmas in addition to multiple Muslim, Buddhist, Sikh, Jain, and, of course, Hindu holy days. Individual states and union territories within India also declare lists of local religious holidays. This contrasts favourably with most Western countries, few of which celebrate non-Christian official public holidays. Defenders of India's reputation for secularism never tire of reminding Western critics that many of their democracies retain vestiges of state religions, like religious tests for hereditary monarchs or national cathedrals where state ceremonies are celebrated. Such symbols are anathema in India.

Or were. On 22 January 2024, India's Prime Minister Narendra Modi served as the *mukhya yajman*—or 'chief patron'—at a ceremony to consecrate the *Shri Ram Janmabhoomi Mandir* ('Temple of the Birthplace of Lord Ram'), or Ram Mandir. The troubled history of the site is history: a Hindu temple on the site was destroyed by the Mughal emperor Babur (1483-1530), who built a mosque on its ruins; a Hindu mob destroyed the eponymous Babri Masjid ('Babur Mosque') in 1992; India's trenchantly secular Supreme Court awarded the site to a Hindu trust in 2019, providing an alternative location nearby for a new mosque. The building of a Ram Mandir at Ayodhya had been a core policy of the BJP from its very founding as a political party, and the opening of the temple (even if not completely finished) in time for the 2024 elections was a big win for Narendra Modi and his UP chief minister, Yogi Adityanath.

There was never any doubt that Modi would play a prominent role in the opening of the Ram Mandir. But Modi was more than just an honoured guest at the temple consecration, as any serving politician might be at the opening of a major construction project. As the *mukhya yajman*, he ceremonially 'breathed life' into the idol of Lord Ram (in most Hindu traditions, the idol is a living embodiment of a god). In preparation for this duty, he followed an eleven-day regime of ritual purification.[200] Modi's performance of a religious role, seemingly in his capacity as Prime Minister, appears troubling to Western eyes. Yet strangely, his mainstream Indian critics hardly mentioned it, with strenuous objections being relegated to fringe media.[201] Modi's main political opponents were, for the most part, more upset about his exploitation of the event for political gain than about any potential slide into state endorsement of religion.[202]

Lord Ram is one of the most important Hindu deities, worshipped widely throughout India and the world. But for many Indians—and not only for Hindu fundamentalists—he is also the symbol of a just nation, as much a cultural icon as a Hindu god.[203] In some ways, the use of Ram as a national symbol is analogous to the widespread Western use of the blindfolded Greek goddess Themis as the personification of justice, holding the scales of judgement and sword of retribution. An illustration of Ram appears at the head of the charter of fundamental rights in the official 1950 manuscript of the Indian Constitution. Mahatma Gandhi himself spoke of the ideal state as a *Ram Rajya* or 'Ram State', writing that 'the ancient ideal of Ramraj is undoubtedly one of true democracy in which the meanest citizen could be sure of swift justice.'[204] When laying the cornerstone for the Ram Mandir in 2020, Modi explicitly cited this Gandhian formulation.[205]

There have been only scattered objections in the Indian commentariat to Modi's use of the *Ram Rajya* metaphor to support an aspirational goal for good governance. Nonetheless, it is perhaps only a thin line that separates Modi's goal of a *Ram Rajya* from his critics' accusations that he is in fact setting up a *Hindu Rajya* or Hindu state in India. At the Ram Mandir consecration, Modi repeatedly blurred that line with exhortations like:

> My countrymen, the worship of Lord Shri Ram should be special for us ... this worship should transcend the ego and be for us as a community. ... We need to present Lord Ram with the offerings of consistent valour, effort, and dedication. By consistently worshipping Lord Ram in this manner, we will be able to make *Bharat* [India] prosperous and developed.[206]

In using such language, Modi directly connected the worship of Lord Ram to the health of the Indian state. This kind of rhetoric is new to India, where religious sensibilities run high. But to put his comments into perspective, the international community hardly batted an eye in 2010 when Germany's Chancellor Angela Merkel said that her country needed more focus on 'our Judeo-Christian tradition ... then we will also be able to bring about cohesion in our society.'[207] Her political party, the Christian Democratic Union, went on to pass a resolution stating that German culture is based on the 'Christian-Jewish tradition' and declaring that 'Germany does not benefit from a minority that refuses to integrate, does not want to learn our language, and denies participation and advancement to their children.'[208] The context made it clear that the minority referred to in the resolution was Muslims.

Similarly disparaging language has also been used by leaders in other Western European countries. But if religion is a controversial topic in Europe, it is a deadly force in India, where the last major episode of mass religious violence was presided over by none other than Narendra Modi. Back in 2002, in a prior role as chief minister of Gujarat, Modi failed to prevent communal riots that resulted in the deaths of 1,025 people, according to official figures. Roughly 80 per cent of them were Muslim.[209] The riots were intimately connected with the Ram Mandir movement: they were sparked by a fire that claimed the lives of fifty-nine Hindu pilgrims on a train returning from Ayodhya. The official investigation found that the fire had been set by a Muslim mob, which proceeded to pelt the pilgrims and even the firefighters with stones.[210] Hindu mob retribution swept out of control, and although allegations that Modi orchestrated or condoned the violence have been examined and dismissed, there is no escaping the fact that he proved unable, or as his critics assert, unwilling to stop it.[211]

Communal violence and command responsibility

'There will either be a divided India, or a destroyed India.'[212] This was the message of Direct Action Day: Friday, 16 August 1946. On this day, the All-India Muslim League opened a campaign of terror that led inexorably to the partition of India along religious lines almost exactly one year later. Muhammad Ali Jinnah, the League's longtime president, said that direct action meant 'we bid good-bye to constitutional methods.'[213] The League's general secretary Liaquat Ali Khan (1895-1951) ominously explained that direct action 'can take any form,' including 'disobeying laws.'[214] But one thing is certain, or as near as can be when dealing with such febrile times: it was not Jinnah (who in one year would become the undisputed father of an independent Pakistan) or even Khan (who would become Pakistan's first Prime Minister) who said that India would either be 'divided' or 'destroyed.' The unhappy phrase is near-universally attributed to Jinnah, even in academic works, but he was never publicly reported in contemporary sources to have uttered it.

Instead, 'divided' or 'destroyed' was actually the inflammatory vow of Jinnah's close associate Abdur Rab Nishtar (1899-1958).[215] When the headline reporting Nishtar's portentous words was printed in the *The Times of India*, a photograph of Jinnah happened to appear immediately underneath. In the attached article, the threatening words were unambiguously attributed to Nishtar. Jinnah, however, is not reported to have raised any objection—with the result that history has perhaps correctly judged him the auteur of the phrase, even if he was not in fact the author. It was only on the eve of Direct Action Day itself that Jinnah finally issued a statement clarifying that there should be no violence on 16 August. Somewhat confusingly, he explained that 'August 16 is not for the purpose of resorting to direct action in any form.'[216] But whatever Jinnah's true intentions may have been, there were many calls for violence on August 16 by the Muslim press and by local Muslim League politicians.[217]

The Muslim League chief minister of Bengal, Huseyn Shaheed Suhrawardy (1892-1963), controversially declared Direct Action Day a public holiday, presumably in order to facilitate street protests. The *New York Times* correspondent in Calcutta sympathetically concluded that 'Mr. Suhrawardy lit a match hoping for at least a small explosion to demonstrate the Muslim League's potentialities – and was unable to check the ensuing conflagration.'[218] But Suhrawardy, who addressed an estimated crowd of 100,000 Calcutta Muslims on the day, seems to have been deeply implicated in inciting violence against Hindus, ensuring a lethargic police response, and delaying the intervention of the army to restore order.[219] Consensus estimates are that between 5,000 and 10,000 people were killed in Calcutta over the extended weekend of 16-19 August 1946.[220] It is widely assumed that most of the victims were Hindus.

As news of the killings spread, Hindus staged anti-Muslim pogroms north of Calcutta, in rural Bihar province, which may have been abetted by the Hindu Mahasabha.[221] Including all of these incidents, the riots on and after Direct Action Day may have killed tens of thousands of people, led to thousands of women being raped, and resulted in the displacement of more than 100,000 refugees. Much of this has been forgotten in the wake of the even more horrific violence that accompanied the partitioning of India along religious lines one year later. But the events of Direct Action Day drove the political narrative that led to that outcome. They formed the backdrop for the disentangling of Hindu and Muslim communities that occurred in anticipation of the British withdrawal, with ethnic cleansing reinforcing a pattern of residential segregation that exists to this day. There were many serious outbreaks of widespread intercommunal violence in India before 1946, but Direct Action Day was perhaps the first time that political leaders of a major party directly instigated the attacks.

Even as the violence raged, negotiations for the transition of India from British rule to self-government were ongoing. Earlier in 1946, a 'Cabinet Mission' had been sent from London to negotiate the terms on which the United Kingdom would withdraw from India. The Indian National Congress (INC), dominated by Mahatma Gandhi and his protégé Jawaharlal Nehru, wanted the British to grant independence to a united India, which would then elect a Constituent Assembly to determine its own destiny. The Muslim League, led by Jinnah, wanted the partition of British India along religious lines into

Hindu and Muslim states, which would separately decide their own fates. Inevitably, the Cabinet Mission deadlocked, or rather, it was stillborn, for Jinnah had made clear before the Cabinet Mission ever left London that 'Muslim India will never accept any method of framing the Constitution of India by means of one Constitution-making body for all India.'[222]

Near-bankrupt after World War Two and eager to focus its limited resources on building a domestic welfare state, the post-war British Labour government was intent on withdrawing from India as soon as possible. That meant handing over power to a responsible local authority, whoever it might be. With the Muslim League refusing to participate in any all-India institutional mechanism for negotiating the transition of British India to responsible self-government, the Cabinet Mission reached the only conclusion it could. On 6 December 1946, it frankly admitted that:

> Should a Constitution come to be framed by a Constituent Assembly in which a large section of the Indian population had not been represented, His Majesty's Government could not of course contemplate ... forcing such a Constitution upon any unwilling parts of the country.[223]

This was in effect a decision to partition India along religious lines. If the British refused to impose any solution that Jinnah opposed, Jinnah would inevitably oppose any solution that did not meet his most extreme demands. The immediate result was the convulsion of liminal areas with mixed populations in a paroxysm of mass killing, arson, rape, forced conversion, and forced expulsion. This outcome should not have surprised a generation that had already witnessed the ethnic cleansing of the Balkans after World War One and was only just coming to terms with the Holocaust that accompanied World War Two. By publicly endorsing the principle of communal self-determination, the British Cabinet Mission fired the starting gun on a gruesome race toward genocide.

One, two, or many nations?

True to the Muslim League's demands, within one year of Direct Action Day—exactly 364 days later, India was partitioned. But that didn't stop the destruction. Quite the contrary. The separation of Pakistan from British India on 15 August 1947 saw the violence of Direct Action Day replicated on a much larger scale. Once again, no one knows precisely how many people were murdered, raped, assaulted, or forced out of their homes, but commonly cited figures suggest that 1 million people were killed and an additional 10 million displaced.[224] The violence was concentrated, naturally enough, along the dividing lines where the two states-in-formation intersected or overlapped. Bengal in the east and Punjab in the west were both divided along religious lines to create zones with clear majorities of one religion or another. These two provinces where the Muslim proportion of the population was just over 50 per cent became the killing fields of Partition.

Any meaningful analysis of the challenges facing Indian democracy today must begin with the partition of India in 1947. Originally appearing in contemporary accounts as a lower-case noun, the partition of India has come to be regarded as an event of such historical importance that it must be capitalised: Partition. Like the Holocaust, it may have been an event too horrific to be fully comprehended by those who lived through it. Thus what was described at the time as the 'partition of India' became for a later generation simply 'Partition.'

Incredibly, the legal documents associated with the end of British rule in India describe the birth of two nominally secular nations, one that happened to have a Hindu majority and the other a Muslim majority. A more realistic account of history (and long the dominant one) tells of a secular India gaining its independence only at the price of accepting the secession of two Muslim-majority territories carved out of its eastern and western flanks to form the new Islamic state of Pakistan. Another, more emotive version of the same story suggests that if Pakistan had to be created as a homeland for India's Muslims, then obviously what remained of India should be acknowledged to be civilisationally Hindu. These two latter accounts of Partition form the basis for two competing claims about the meaning of Indian nationhood. In their broad outlines they represent, respectively, the contrasting world-views of contemporary India's two leading political parties, the INC and the BJP.

The INC world-view implies that India is and was always destined to be a secular country, but one from which tens of millions of Muslims inexplicably seceded—withdrew—in 1947 under the influence of Jinnah and his Muslim League. The BJP world-view implies that India is and has always been a Hindu civilisational state, albeit one that these days magnanimously hosts the millions of Muslims (and other minorities) whose ancestors chose to remain loyal to *Bharat Mata* ('Mother India'). The tension between the formal inclusivity of the INC's rhetoric of civic pluralism and the more solidarist Hindu universalism that characterises BJP rhetoric is a direct legacy of Partition. These two competing ideologies represent incompatible visions for Indian nationhood, both historically grounded but neither historically complete. The question of which vision is correct is a political question, not a historical one. The answer depends on which of the many available histories one chooses to accept.

Academic historians tend to organize their work around the countries that exist today, but they understand that those countries are themselves products of history. Nationhood is a flexible and malleable concept, and it is an elementary error of historiography to backdate today's national identities to eras before the idea of nationalism had taken hold. In other words, it is a mistake to assume that people felt attached to nations that did not yet exist. For example, as late as 1931, many of Burma's independence leaders argued for the continued inclusion of their country in an Indian federation, and opposed Britain's plans to separate Burma from India, of which it had been a part for almost eight decades.[225] If these particular nationalists had had their way, there would have been no Myanmar, and most Burmese people would probably consider themselves an ethnicity within India. That may also be the situation of most of the tribal peoples of northeast India today.

To paraphrase the Danish philosopher Søren Kierkegaard (1813-1855), national histories are generally constructed backwards, but they must be lived forwards. Today's nations did not exist from time immemorial. They were created by activists and intellectuals who argued passionately for their creation. Some of those nation-builders succeeded, but most failed, and history is littered with the record of would-be nations. India's nation-builders, succeeded—or at least, they succeeded in creating a country called India. None of them imagined that their heirs would inhabit an India with the borders that modern India has today. Some of India's nation-builders had much more expansive views for the shape an independent India should take. A common view was that India should include all the land between the Himalayas and the sea.[226] Yet even as late as the

1870s, local-language Indian books on geography and history still treated the regions of India as consisting of disparate peoples with distinctive histories, customs, and national stereotypes.[227]

The partition of India in 1947 was the end result of half a century of wrangling over what form post-British India would take. British India was never a single colony or unitary state; it was an irregular agglomeration of possessions and spheres of influence. The island of Ceylon only became the independent state of Sri Lanka because it was acquired directly by the British Crown in 1802, and was not part of the inheritance transferred from the privately-managed British East India Company in 1858. The Maldives in turn were governed from Ceylon, but are now independent. The territory of Burma—present-day Myanmar—was governed as a kind of dependency of British India from 1853 until 1937, when it was hived off into a separate colony. Farther afield, the Malaysian city of Penang and the Yemeni city of Aden were at various times governed as colonies of British India.

More than 560 princely states maintained a nominal independence inside British India. Meanwhile on the Himalayan frontier, the British client states of Nepal and Bhutan retained their independent national identities, but both entered into special relationships with British India that continue with modern India. These South Asian neighbours of India now celebrate their own national histories, but they could have, under slightly different historical circumstances, ended up as states of the modern Indian nation. By contrast, the French colony of Pondicherry, the Portuguese colony of Goa, and the British protectorate of Sikkim—all candidates for independent statehood—were integrated into independent India, voluntarily or otherwise, between 1954 and 1975. India became the country it is today because Britain first amalgamated India, then partitioned it.

Divide and rule?

By the time of Partition, debates over the future of British India had coalesced around the lands that now make up India, Pakistan, and Bangladesh. These lands accounted for more than one-sixth of the world's population, and more than a quarter of the world's Muslims. The British government at that time also ruled over another quarter of the world's Muslims in its other colonies that included the holy cities of Mecca, Medina, and Jerusalem, a fact that made global Muslim sentiment a major consideration for British policy in India.[228] The population of British India had been 20 per cent Muslim at the time of the 1891 census, but by 1941, that proportion had risen to 24 per cent and was growing fast.[229] The British Indian Army was roughly 35 per cent Muslim in 1947.[230] If the Muslims of British India demanded a nation of their own, they were bound to get one.

The formal process that led to this point had kicked off as early as 1928, when a British parliamentary commission arrived in India to inquire into 'the working of the system of government...and the development of representative institutions, in British India.'[231] The Indian Statutory Commission, known as the Simon Commission after its chairman, landed in Bombay, present-day Mumbai, to the jeers of protesters waving black flags and calling on the British to leave India immediately. The INC refused to cooperate with the commission, instead empaneling a committee of its own to draft a constitution for an independent India. This committee was chaired by Motilal Nehru (1861-1931), father of Jawaharlal Nehru, who served as secretary to the committee.[232] The Nehru committee proposed a roadmap for a unitary India, with some parliamentary seats specially reserved for Muslims for the first ten years of independence. After that, all bets were off.

The Muslim League flatly rejected the Nehru Report, as it came to be known. Jinnah formulated his 'Fourteen Points' response of 1929.[233] He insisted that India, once independent, should be a loose federation, with a high degree of regional autonomy. All legislatures, both federal and state, should have seats divided by religion. Muslims should be guaranteed at least one-third of the seats in the federal legislature, and one-third of the ministerial positions in all legislatures, regardless of their relative population—including in states where Muslims made up only a sliver of the population. Muslim legislators, and those of other religious groups, should have an effective veto over any legislation, and Muslims would have reserved places in the civil services. Finally, each individual state should have the power to veto any future constitutional changes.

These demands were clearly unworkable, and indeed were not endorsed at the Muslim League's 1929 meeting. But the sentiments they expressed later became the basis of Muslim League policy from then until Partition. At the League's 1930 session, the incoming president Muhammad Iqbal (1877-1938) gave a fiery speech in which he rejected the proposition that it was 'possible to retain Islam as an ethical ideal and to reject it as a polity, in favour of national polities in which religious attitude is not permitted to play any part.' He further rejected 'the construction of a polity on national lines, if it means a displacement of the Islamic principle of solidarity,', saying that it was 'simply unthinkable to a Muslim.' He claimed that 'the Muslims of India are the only Indian people who can truly be described as a nation in the modern sense of the word,' saying that Hindus had 'not yet been able to achieve the kind of homogeneity which is necessary for a nation.'[234]

From 1930 onwards, the Muslim League's hardening

position was that Muslims could only live in a post-British independent India if they, acting as an organised community, had political control over areas where they formed the majority and a political veto where they were in a minority. Of course, the League took it for granted that the organised community of India's Muslims could only be represented by the Muslim League. It consistently maintained this position notwithstanding the fact that it lacked any mass mandate. The League's performance in provincial elections conducted under limited suffrage in 1937 was abysmal, especially in the Muslim-majority provinces that it saw as the core of a future Muslim state (and which now form the independent state of Pakistan). Out of 285 seats up for grabs in Muslim-majority Punjab, Sind, and the North West Frontier Province, it won only one.

In the wake of the 1937 election fiasco, Jinnah set about rebuilding the Muslim League, both popularising it, and radicalising it. He coopted Muslim public opinion by committing the Muslim League unambiguously to the partition of India along religious lines. In this, Jinnah, the practical politician, may have been following, not leading, the opinion of important Muslim Indian intellectuals of the 1930s. Islamic nationalism was on the rise throughout the British Empire, and India was no exception. Thus, Jinnah decided to seize the future with both hands. In his famous 'Two Nations' speech at the 1940 Muslim League conference in Lahore, he declared that India's 'Mussalmans are not a minority. The Mussalmans are a nation by any definition.' He explained that:

> It is extremely difficult to appreciate why our Hindu friends fail to understand the real nature of Islam and Hinduism. They are not religions in the strict sense of the word, but are, in fact, different and distinct social orders; and it is a dream that the

> Hindus and Muslims can ever evolve a common nationality; and this misconception of one Indian nation has gone far beyond the limits and is the cause of more of our troubles and will lead India to destruction if we fail to revise our notions in time.[235]

Jinnah's clear dog-whistle for an independent Pakistan accomplished its immediate goal: popular support for the Muslim League surged, and many Muslim politicians who had formerly remained aloof from the League joined its ranks. But Jinnah's warning that the imposition of a 'common nationality' would 'lead India to destruction' was meant as much for the British as for Indians. He was speaking during the opening days of World War Two in Europe, after the fall of Poland but before the Battle of France. Britain was at war, with many Muslims serving in its Indian Army. The last thing that the British wanted was a second Indian Mutiny. Even more ominous, a Muslim mutiny in India had the potential to grow into a pan-Islamic uprising against British rule all across the Arab world.

It is often said that the United Kingdom pursued a 'divide and rule' strategy for subduing its Indian empire, and at a tactical level, that was certainly the case.[236] Some have made more expansive claims, suggesting that the British strategically encouraged the partition of India to promote their post-colonial ambitions for continuing dominance over the Muslim Middle East.[237] But whatever the role played by Britain in enabling or encouraging communal tensions in its Indian empire, it may not have made any difference in the end. The violence of Partition was horrific, and may have been avoidable. The fact that British India would be partitioned, however, was almost certainly inevitable—and most of the prominent participants in India's independence struggle knew it.

The riddle of Partition

Jinnah opened his bid for an independent Pakistan at the beginning of World War Two, and by the end of the war, he had beaten both the INC and the British occupiers into acquiescence. But he had to bypass the laws of logic to make Partition make sense. There was a conundrum at the heart of the Pakistan project that Jinnah never addressed—that even after the creation of an independent Muslim-majority Pakistan, the Hindu-majority remnants of British India would still retain a massive Muslim minority. Rajendra Prasad (1884-1963), who would later become the first president of independent India, noted this as early as 1940.[238] It was also obvious to the father of the Indian Constitution, the great Dalit leader B R Ambedkar (1891-1956). In 1945, he pithily observed that 'the scheme of Pakistan does seem to concern itself with the Muslim majorities who do not need protection and abandons the Muslim minorities who do.'[239]

Nehru considered the looming partition of India in detail in his 1946 book, *The Discovery of India*, succinctly summarizing the conundrum in the following terms:

> Any division of India on a religious basis as between Hindus and Moslems, as envisaged by the Moslem League today, cannot separate the followers of these two principal religions of India, for they are spread out all over the country. Even if the areas in which each group is in the majority are separated, huge minorities belonging to the other group remain in each area. Thus instead of solving the minority problem, we create several in place of one.[240]

The challenge of partitioning India along religious lines had a fractal-like geometry: every possible division to create regions with clear Hindu and Muslim majorities would spawn new minority problems within the areas that had just been divided. These new minorities should presumably have the same rights to independent nationhood as the original minority, *ad infinitum.* Moreover, the long historical coexistence (and even integration) of Hindus and Muslims in India militated against any partition at all. In his own book on partition, Rajendra Prasad had made these issues crystal clear:

> If the Muslims who constitute 75 per cent or even less of the population in some regions can justly and fairly demand and enforce separation from India of the regions where they predominate why cannot the non-Muslims who are 76.2 per cent in India as a whole ... with equal justice and fairness refuse to submit to separation, particularly in view of long historical association in administration, if in nothing else?[241]

Ambedkar, however, acknowledged that the time for a united India was running out fast, if it had not already passed. In his 1945 book on the prospective partition of India, he wrote that 'Hindu-Moslem unity up to now was at least in sight although it was like a mirage. Today it is out of sight and also out of mind.'[242] He followed this proposition with twenty-five pages detailing the intercommunal violence of 1920-1940. Retrospective documentaries about the violence of the actual 1947 Partition of India are full of testimony (mostly from people who were children at the time) that before the violence of Direct Action Day, Indians of all religions lived side-by-side in intercommunal harmony. Ambedkar's exhaustive recitation of the history of Hindu-Muslim violence during the interwar years puts paid to that notion. His hard-nosed analyses led Ambedkar to the only possible conclusion: whatever the merits of the case for Partition, 'if the Musalmans (Muslims) will not yield on the issue of Pakistan then Pakistan must come.'[243]

By April 1946, even Mahatma Gandhi had accepted the inevitability of partition due to the irreconcilability of his doctrine of non-violence with Jinnah's increasing demands, and it was at that point that Jinnah concluded that if he could show Muslim popular support for Pakistan, it was only a matter of time before he achieved his goal.[244] The demonstrations on Direct Action Day and the violence of the ensuing months proved to Gandhi and the rest of the INC leadership that resistance to Partition was futile. Thus when, on 6 December the British Cabinet Mission had implicitly accepted that a partition of India was Britain's only practical exit strategy, the British faced only tepid resistance from the INC. On 8 March 1947, with Punjab already in a state of civil war, the INC working committee practically acceded to Jinnah's demands, and accepted that an independent, Muslim-majority Pakistan would be carved out of Britain's Hindu-majority Indian empire.

Many leading politicians of the day attempted to put on a brave face despite the violence that had already broken out. Some called for mutual trust between majorities and minorities in the future India and Pakistan; others espoused the 'hostage theory' that Hindu India and Muslim Pakistan would keep on good behaviour because of the threat that their co-religionists in the other country might be slaughtered by their hosts. In the event, few Hindus, Sikhs, or adherents of other religions proved willing to risk their lives as religious minorities in Muslim-majority Pakistan. All hopes that the partition of India might solve, rather than exacerbate, intercommunal tensions turned out to be fantasies. Rajendra Prasad was one of the few to recognise this truth. Even as the British boundary commissioners were poring over the government's maps and census tables in a vain attempt to engineer a clean break, he foresaw the decades of hostility to follow. In 1947, he wrote that:

> One thing is certain: partition is not likely to be attained with the goodwill of those most concerned, and this illwill is bound to persist on both sides, even if the proposal succeeds, even after the separation is effected. Distrust which is the basis of the proposal is bound to grow and any hope that after separation things will settle down and the independent states will soon become friendly will have been built on sand.[245]

Within a week of Partition, Pakistan launched an invasion of the nominally independent princely state of Jammu and Kashmir; in response, its Hindu maharaja brought the Muslim-majority territory into independent India. Nearly all of West Pakistan's (and most of East Pakistan's) Hindus fled to India as Pakistan moved toward Sharia law in 1949 and launched an unsuccessful bid to put itself at the head of a new pan-Islamic caliphate. Meanwhile, independent India's Muslims, who today number more than 200 million, continued to live as a minority community within a Hindu-dominated democracy, subject to many of the same intercommunal tensions that were used to justify the partition of India in the first place. Partition may have been inevitable, but it never made sense, and its legacies continue to shape India (and even more so, Pakistan and Bangladesh).

Three movements for national liberation

Partition transformed India from a colony into a country, and at the same time, transformed politics from a struggle for independence into a competition for votes. Most of the political organisations that played major roles in India's independence struggle were not created to be political parties. The INC, the Muslim League, and the Hindu Mahasabha had all, at various times, contested elections, as did many regional organisations. But as long as India was occupied by the British and ruled from London, these organisations were primarily concerned with contesting the terms under which British India would be transformed into one or more independent countries. They were movements for national liberation, not parties involved in responsible governance, and they were differentiated not so much by disagreements over practical politics as by disagreements over exactly what 'nation' it was that they wanted to liberate.

The INC was, and to some extent remains, a classic Third World national liberation movement. It is often identified as India's sole national liberation movement, despite the fact that much of the nation it aspired to liberate ended up in Pakistan and Bangladesh. Like other national liberation movements all around the world, the INC viewed itself as an umbrella organisation consolidating all strands of its country's independence activism under one roof. It aimed to be the sole, authoritative voice of the nation-in-formation, and as such the sole intermediary between the colonised and their colonisers. In principle, the many factions of the INC should have dissolved their alliance at the stroke of independence and entered into competitive party politics, presenting alternative policy platforms and running against each other for the privilege of leading their shared nation. Yet like national liberation organisations everywhere, after independence was achieved, the INC sought instead to remain united and in sole possession of political power.

Anyone who wonders why so many post-colonial states fell prey to single-party rule need look no further than the routine manner in which national liberation organisations like the INC sought to turn themselves into ruling political parties. Mahatma Gandhi himself seems to have recognised this danger: he suggested toward the end of his life that the INC had 'outlived its use' as an organisation and should withdraw into social welfare work after achieving Indian independence.[246] That was never likely to happen, but any home that independent India might make a smooth transition into multiparty politics was dashed when Gandhi was assassinated on 30 January 1948. His murder gave Nehru and the INC he led an ideal excuse to suppress the few remaining autonomous opposition groups. They made mass arrests of political opponents, stoking a moral panic that led to the lynchings of many people associated with the Hindu Mahasabha and other Hindu nationalist organisations.[247]

Looking back from the present, a reader relying on standard histories of India might come to believe that the INC was the country's sole national liberation movement organisation. But that is to view history with the omniscience of hindsight. Pakistan, Bangladesh, and Myanmar all share roots in British India, but the INC is not remembered in any of these countries as their national liberation movement. Had India disintegrated further, it is unlikely that an independent Bengal, Hyderabad, Maharashtra, Punjab, or indeed Kashmir would give pride of place to the INC. Contemporary accounts of India's independence struggle did focus on the INC, but considered both the Muslim League and the Hindu Mahasabha as major ideological opponents offering alternative visions of competing nationalisms. Nehru himself acknowledged that the main Hindu nationalist organisation in India was not the INC, but 'the Hindu Mahasabha, the counterpart of the Muslim League.'[248]

The colonial-era INC offered (and the modern INC still offers) a secular vision of India as a pluralistic nation composed of many identity groups who share, in Nehru's words, 'a common land and a common culture' in a united India.[249] Meanwhile the Muslim League under Jinnah advocated the 'two-nation' theory that Hindus and Muslims formed distinct nations within the geography of British India.[250] Echoing this, the longtime leader and intellectual lodestar of the Hindu Mahasabha, Vinayak Damodar Savarkar (1883-1966), expounded the parallel theory that India's Hindus constituted a nation of their own—a nation that had a right to the whole of British India.[251] The aspirations of the Muslim League and the Hindu Mahasabha for national liberation were not exactly parallel, but the critics of these organisations saw a clear resonance between them. As Ambedkar quipped, 'Mr. Savarkar and Mr. Jinnah instead of being opposed to each other on the one nation *versus* two nations issue are in complete agreement about it.'[252]

That captures the spirit of India's competing nationalisms, but it was not quite true. Jinnah may have denied the dignity of nationhood to India's Hindus, but he did accept the geographical fact of their preponderance in large swathes of British India. Savarkar, by contrast, denied the dignity of nationhood to all of India's Muslims, whom he considered only a religious minority.[253] Savarkar held that although Muslims could become legal citizens of an independent India, they could not be accepted as members of the Hindu nation on which it was to be based.[254] This was not, however, simply a political manifestation of a militant Hindu chauvinism, as it is often portrayed today.[255] In the wake of the Holocaust, the idea that a minority group might be denied a place in the nation has become an anathema, but it is historically disingenuous to judge the past on the morality of the present.

Savarkar did not develop his ideology of Hindu nationalism

in a vacuum. Far from it. He was inspired by, and his views were generally consistent with, the most modern Western intellectual and legal theories of his era. A British-educated barrister, Savarkar published the first edition of his major political work *Hindutva: Who Is a Hindu?* in 1923, in the immediate aftermath of World War One. As a lawyer, Savarkar was well-equipped to grasp the legal technicalities of the interwar 'minority treaties' that carved up the collapsing Austro-Hungarian and Ottoman empires into the new countries of central Europe and the Balkans.[256] In those treaties, the Western victors of the war recognised some groups as 'nations' and others as 'national minorities'—granting sovereignty to the former and no more than civil rights to the latter.[257] Savarkar's historical crime was to apply these formerly accepted principles to the Indian context. It is perhaps not his fault that the West later evolved a new morality of nationhood.

Hindutva as national self-determination

The result of the 1919 Treaty of Versailles and its associated pacts was a series of near-genocidal inter-ethnic conflicts all across the Balkans, Eastern Europe, and the Near East. These included the Armenian genocide, the Greco-Turkish war, and the suppression of what was intended to become an independent Kurdistan. Protecting the rights of the German minority in the Sudetenland would later become the justification for Adolf Hitler's demands at the 1938 Munich Conference. The enforceable minority provisions guaranteed under the Minority Treaties were the legal basis on which Britain, France, and Italy agreed to dismember Czechoslovakia. The Western liberal promotion of national self-determination with national minority rights may have been well-intentioned, but it incentivised minority intransigence and majority ethnic cleansing across a wide swath of Europe and the Near East.

Back in India, Savarkar was keenly aware of the mass intercommunal violence that accompanied the 1921 Moplah Rebellion, an event that was directly connected to the breakup of the Ottoman Empire and the consequent British occupation of Mecca and Medina.[258] This incident in what is now the southwestern Indian state of Kerala saw Muslim farmworkers rise against their predominantly Hindu landlords, murdering hundreds (estimates vary wildly) and forcing thousands to convert to Islam.[259] The unlikely goal of some of the leaders of the rebellion seems to have been to establish an independent Islamic state on the Malabar coast, acting on the promise of national self-determination made by US President Woodrow Wilson (1856-1926) at the end of World War One.[260] One particularly extreme Muslim nationalist of the 1920s, F K Khan Durrani, actually argued on Versailles principles that all of India should become an Islamic state.[261]

Nearly everyone involved in the debates over Indian independence, the partition of India, and the construction of Indian national identities (Hindu, Muslim, and secular) referenced the Minority Treaties that followed the end of World War One in support of their claims. These treaties implicitly defined a 'nation' in terms of 'race, language, and religion,' guaranteeing protections to minority groups who differed from the majority nation in any of these aspects. The idea that a nation is a group of people who share a common race, language, and religion probably derives from a naive misreading of the nineteenth century political philosophy of John Stuart Mill (1806-1873). In a widely quoted passage from *Considerations on Representative Government* (1861), Mill asserted that:

> A portion of mankind may be said to constitute a nationality if they are united among themselves by common sympathies which do not exist between them and any others–which make them co-operate with each other more willingly than with other people, desire to be under the same government, and desire that it should be government by themselves, or a portion of themselves, exclusively. This feeling of nationality may have been generated by various causes. Sometimes it is the effect of identity of race and descent. Community of language and community of religion greatly contribute to it. Geographical limits are one of its causes. But the strongest of all is identity of political antecedents; the possession of a national history, and consequent community of recollections; collective pride and humiliation, pleasure and regret, connected with the same incidents in the past.[262]

This famous definition of nationality would have been known to nearly every participant in the Versailles conference, and certainly to Wilson, the political science-professor-turned-president who put national self-determination at the centre of his programme for postwar peace. In fact, Wilson directly cited the importance 'of race, of language, and of religion' in the building of national identity in his 1898 political science textbook.[263] Of course, Mill's actual point was that race, language, and religion were not the most important markers of national identity. But the reduction of Mill's fulsome formulation to such a simple formula is just the sort of thing that happens when brilliant thinkers are misremembered or misunderstood by second-rate scholars.

India's independence leaders tended not to cite Mill directly. Instead, they cited a textbook written by the liberal intellectual

James Bryce (1838-1922), who among other qualifications had served as president of the American Political Science Association at a time when Woodrow Wilson was teaching political science at Princeton University. Bryce argued that among Mill's criteria for national identity 'the chief ... are Racial sentiment and Religious sentiment, but there is also that sense of community which is created by the use of a common language.'[264] This very passage was quoted by Rajendra Prasad, who wrote emphatically of the '*trinity of the Minority Treaties: race, language and religion.*'[265] As Prasad saw it, the conflation of nationality with the right to an independent state was 'due to the setting up of National Self-determination as an absolute dogma according to which every cultural group *ipso facto* is entitled to claim a separate independent State for itself.'[266]

A straight line can be drawn from Mill through Wilson and Bryce to Jinnah's demand for a Muslim state and Savarkar's demand for a Hindu one. The insistence that India should be a Hindu *rashtra* (nation) formed the core of Savarkar's doctrine of Hindutva, a doctrine that is still influential in India today. A parallel logic sat at the centre of the Muslim League's demand for an independent Pakistan. It is impossible to accept Jinnah's argument for a Muslim Pakistan without also accepting Savarkar's argument for a Hindu India—but the practice of politics is rarely logical. In the sweepstakes of history, Jinnah came to be celebrated as the father of his nation, while Savarkar came to be marginalised (at least in intellectual circles) as an exclusionary religious nationalist. Meanwhile nearly everyone has forgotten that both based their political philosophies directly on the most advanced Anglo-American liberal thought of their era, however outdated that thought may seem today.

Hindustan or Englishstan, India or Bharat?

Gandhi, Nehru, Jinnah, and Savarkar, all aspiring fathers of countries, may have been ideological opponents, but they shared similar positions in Indian society. They were all British-educated lawyers (although Savarkar was arrested for revolutionary activities before he could be called to the bar). Similarly, Ambedkar, Iqbal, and Liaquat Ali Khan were all British barristers, as were the prominent INC leaders V K Krishna Menon (1896-1974) and Vallabhbhai Patel (1875-1950). The Indian revolutionary Subhas Chandra Bose (1897-1945) studied at Cambridge; his brother Sarat Chandra Bose (1889-1950) was another British barrister. These titans of the Indian independence struggle were no ordinary Indians. They were fluent in English, internationally educated, trained in British law, and plugged into global political networks.[267] In the memorable words of historian and colonial administrator Thomas Macaulay (1800-1859), these men formed 'a class who may be interpreters between us and the millions whom we govern—a class of persons Indian in blood and colour, but English in tastes, in opinions, in morals and in intellect.'[268]

Taken as a class, these men constituted what some sociologists call a 'comprador' elite. When the Portuguese opened regular trade between Europe and India in the 1500s, they needed local go-betweens who could help them acquire goods they wanted to purchase for their annual trading fleets. These interlocutors were called *compradores* or 'buyers'. The term later came to be used by other Europeans throughout maritime Asia; for example, the Cantonese businessmen who facilitated British trade with China were also known as compradors. In the centuries since, the term has come to stand broadly for those native elites who had the skills and connections needed to act as intermediaries between foreign occupiers and colonised populations. And in India, as Macauley understood, the one foundational skill on which all others depended was the ability to communicate in English.

India's independence struggle was not unique in being led by members of an English-speaking comprador elite. Malaysia's first Prime Minister, Tunku Abdul Rahman (1903-1990), studied at Cambridge University, then went on to become a British barrister. Singapore's Lee Kuan Yew (1923-2015) followed the same trajectory. Ghana's Kwame Nkrumah (1909-1972) held two master's degrees from the University of Pennsylvania and undertook postgraduate studies in anthropology and law in London. Tanzania's Julius Nyerere (1922-1999) earned his master's degree from the University of Edinburgh. Kenya's Jomo Kenyatta (1897-1978) studied in Moscow before earning a master's degree in anthropology from the London School of Economics. All of them, like Gandhi in India and Jinnah in Pakistan, came to be known by the sobriquet 'father of the country.'

But in India, unlike in most other colonial societies, there existed a second stratum of highly educated, politically engaged individuals who posed a robust alternative to the comprador elite. Its members lacked international experience, but nonetheless possessed substantial intellectual and financial resources. This 'national' elite in colonial India consisted of local business families, middle-class professionals, bureaucrats, engineers, scientists, and others who developed their careers and their ideas entirely or almost entirely within the local Indian milieu. Most of them were competent in English, but they wrote and conversed primarily in Indian languages, and their networks were mainly colonial, not imperial. They formed the rank-and-file of the INC and India's other national liberation movements, but they were largely excluded from decision-making at the highest levels.

The social division between the comprador and national elite is not highlighted in standard histories of India, but it is nevertheless visible to those who look for it. For example, at the midnight ceremony proclaiming India's independence, five people had the privilege of addressing India's Constituent Assembly—in order of speaking: Rajendra Prasad, Jawaharlal Nehru, Sarvepalli Radhakrishnan, the Muslim League representative Chaudhry Khaliquzzaman (1889-1973), and the All India Women's Conference representative Hansa Mehta (1897-1995). Nehru and Mehta had strong imperial connections and British postgraduate educations. They spoke in English. The other three had completed their education entirely in India. Radhakrishnan, a native Telugu speaker, spoke in English, reflecting not a class distinction, but the north-south linguistic divide that remains a salient fault line in India today. Prasad and Khaliquzzaman, however, spoke in Hindustani, the former *lingua franca* of northern India from which Hindi and Urdu are both derived.

In India's constitutional debates, the question of what would be the official language of independent India was one of the most contentious issues, with the Constituent Assembly deadlocking on the choice between English and Hindi. The compromise solution was to appoint a committee to consider the question over a period of fifteen years. The now-permanent Committee of Parliament on Official Language continues its work to this day. A parallel controversy arose over what should be the official name of the new country. Many people had simply assumed that the Hindu counterpart to Muslim Pakistan would be called Hindustan. The drafting committee for the Indian Constitution, chaired by Ambedkar, opted for 'India,' but in the debates that followed, less luminary members of the Constituent Assembly argued passionately for the Sanskrit-derived term *Bharat*. A final compromise was reached on the quizzical formulation 'India, that is Bharat.'

These competing understandings of India, always present in the background, have now come to the fore as the chief fault line in Indian politics today. It operates alongside the north-south linguistic division, which operates as a complicating factor. The formerly shunned Hindu nationalist 'Veer' Savarkar has been rehabilitated by 'Bharat' advocates as an ideological champion of Hindutva thought, and a statue of the armed revolutionary Subhas Chandra Bose has been installed at the centre of the National War Memorial. Some of the more conservative icons of the independence-era INC have even been appropriated by the BJP as Hindustani patriots. In 2018, Narendra Modi unveiled a 600-foot statue of 'Sardar' Patel deep in the countryside of his home state of Gujarat. Called the 'Statue of Unity,' it represents for one segment of society an unredeemed claim on history.

Yet there is still a comprador 'Establishment' in India that is deeply uncomfortable with such crass displays of nationalism as the Netaji Subhas Chandra Bose memorial and the Patel Statue of Unity. Echoing their internationally minded independence-era forbears, its members worry that India is being transformed into a majoritarian Hindu nationalist state. They fret that Narendra Modi is leveraging the populist rhetoric of a *Hindu Rashtra* or Hindu Nation in a bid to transform India into a *Hindu Rajya* or Hindu State. They revere the country's Nehruvian inheritance, and are deeply pessimistic about the direction India is heading under a newly self-confident national elite. Internationalist by instinct, members of the Establishment are much more closely connected to global English-language academic and media networks than are members of the national elite, and thus their viewpoint dominates international discourses about India. Within India itself, however, they are becoming increasingly marginalised—and they know it.[269]

Toward a 'community of recollections'

In his 15 August 1947 'Tryst with Destiny' speech at the birth of modern India, Nehru spoke of 'the soul of a nation, long suppressed' that would awaken 'at the stroke of the midnight hour.'[270] The trope of national awakening is a common one, but social scientists have long argued that the modern nations that are recognised today were not actually 'awakened' from history, but invented in the present—or, to use the memorable formulation of the political scientist Benedict Anderson, 'imagined' into existence. Anderson defined a nation as a construct that is imagined as being limited in scope, sovereign in authority, and forming a horizontal community.[271] This is true (so far as it goes), but nations cannot be imagined out of thin air. Every successful nation is built, as Mill suggested, on a 'community of recollections'—that is, on a shared history.

Social scientists tend to be sceptical of the actual role played by history in the formation of national identity, or to reduce that role to the indoctrination of impressionable young students via school textbooks. But Mill was right to emphasise that shared history, not race, language, or religion, is the most stable foundation for nation-building. The scepticism of social scientists arises from the fact that national historical memories tend to be so highly selective as to border on the arbitrary. That is to miss the main point. National histories are not 'imagined', as

Anderson would have us believe. They are chosen. To use a term from John Stuart Mill, from among the many available 'political antecedents' of a present-day society, some are selected as the favoured antecedents of the modern political nation. Others fall out of favour and are discarded. They continue to exist in history, but they are written out of the history of the nation.

At the close of World War One, 'India' stretched from Karachi to Rangoon, and no one had ever heard of Pakistan. There were strong nationalist sentiments in Bengal, Kashmir, Maharashtra, Punjab, Madras (present-day Tamil Nadu), and other regions, and in the 1920s it was not a foreordained outcome that a postcolonial India would be a unified state. After all, the polyglot Austro-Hungarian, Ottoman, and Russian empires had just been split into a multitude of new nations, mainly on the basis of language. As things turned out, the British hived off Buddhist Burma into a separate country (now Myanmar), created Muslim homelands in West and East Pakistan—now Pakistan and Bangladesh, respectively—and allowed the princely state of Hyderabad to declare independence, prompting a five-day war with newly independent India, which promptly occupied the would-be nation.

Of course, history always turns out as it turns out. Each of the successor states to British India settled on a version of its national history to serve as its official origin story. In constructing its own national story, modern India had the opportunity to choose from a wide menu of historical memories of 'collective pride and humiliation, pleasure and regret, connected with the same incidents in the past,' to again use the words of John Stuart Mill. Alone among the postcolonial successors of British India, modern India's independence leaders chose to identify their country with British colonial history, calling their country

'India' and adopting the history of British India as its own. Again, something that has become obvious in retrospect was not so obvious at the time. It has been reported that Jinnah was reportedly 'absolutely furious' that Nehru had opted for the name 'India,' thus implicitly laying claim to the historical memory of the pre-Partition colonial whole.[272]

Geographically speaking, modern India is not the same country as British colonial India. Today's India is 1947 British India, minus Pakistan and Bangladesh, plus the princely states, plus Pondicherry, Goa, and Sikkim, minus the far northwestern zones that are currently under Pakistani and Chinese control. To claim for this particular collection of territories a "community of recollections ... connected with the same incidents in the past" is a challenge, to say the least. But seen from the perspective of nation-building, that may not matter. The most important factor determining the stability of postcolonial nation-states is not the historical accuracy of the national story, but its future viability. As the social theorist Jeffrey Prager explains:

> The principle problem faced by new nations has been to create a new sense of community corresponding to the new forms of social organization accompanying independence: to create new bonds of solidarity between members of the society consistent with the transreligious, transethnic, transregional, and transfamilial character of the new society.[273]

Prager's emphasis is on the fostering of an organic social solidarity, not a merely mechanical social agglomeration. Applied practically in the Indian setting, this implies that to be stable, India's national identity must transcend religion (as indeed it does), but need not necessarily incorporate minority religious sensibilities. Prager suggests that 'while inclusion remains an important variable in the construction of democratic stability,' it is not the most decisive factor.[274] In Prager's formulation, the crucial factor for stability is that the political system embody mechanisms for transforming the particular into the universal while protecting the political autonomy of the individual citizen. Individual participation in the democratic nation, not group participation in state institutions, is the basis of democratic governance.

Many qualities are desirable in a well-functioning liberal democracy, but the only certain prerequisite for democracy is that there exist a shared political community within which democracy can operate. There are many non-democratic nations, but there are no democracies without nations. As Prager put it, 'we know of no society that achieves stability when the feeling of connectedness and attachment to the nation is absent.'[275] Perhaps the best example of this is post-independence, pre-breakup Pakistan. In united Pakistan's first and last direct popular election (1970), the Bengali-dominated Awami League won every seat in East Pakistan or present-day Bangladesh, but not a single seat in West Pakistan or present-day Pakistan. Lacking a shared sense of national identity, postcolonial Pakistan fractured at the polls along preexisting proto-national lines. It could not simultaneously remain a single state and a democracy.

Having developed a shared sense of national identity, postcolonial India did survive—not only as a unified nation-state, but as a democratic one. There seems no reason to believe that a future *Hindu Rajya*, should one arise in twenty-first century India, would be undemocratic. After all, many legally Christian states are democracies. Sri Lanka is an officially Buddhist democracy, while the world's only Jewish state is a democracy. Few would dare argue that the world's many Islamic republics could never evolve into democracies. The proper question to raise about Modi's overt official religiosity is not whether it threatens India's democracy, but whether it threatens India's national unity. The long-term health of India as a democratic society requires that Indians of all religions believe that they are equal participants in the Indian nation.

The Hindu-centric rhetoric of Narendra Modi and the BJP may not threaten the citizenship rights of Muslim Indians, but it must, in the long run, diminish their sense of belonging. Formal citizenship rights are not enough to ensure that a community participates fully in the life of a nation. The fact that the Muslim citizens of India are usually referred to as 'Indian Muslims' illustrates the tenuous status of Muslim Indians in the Indian national community, despite their possession of full citizenship rights. In purely grammatical terms, Indian Muslims are Muslims who happen to be Indian. The more inclusive term 'Muslim Indians' refers to Indians who happen to be Muslim. It uses their Muslim religion to describe them, but not to define them. Hindu nationalism can coexist with a democratic Indian state, but it inevitably threatens the cohesion of Indian society.

An Extraordinary Democracy

Rabindranath Tagore (1861-1941) famously declared in his 1917 essay on 'Nationalism in India' that 'Our real problem in India is not political. It is social.'[276] That sentiment both reflected and inspired the conventional wisdom of India's nation-builders. Major political figures like Mahatma Gandhi, B R Ambedkar, and V D Savarkar campaigned against social ills like caste-based discrimination, female illiteracy, poverty, and disease even as they campaigned for an independent India. Such social reforms were certainly dear to Tagore, but if one reads all three of his essays on nationalism (Western, Japanese, and Indian), it becomes clear that he saw India's social divisions as deriving from something much more fundamental than mere disadvantage or discrimination. He repeatedly suggested that 'from the beginning of history' India's problem has been 'the race problem.'[277]

Like his contemporaries in Europe, Tagore did not imbue the word 'race' with the genetic or skin colour meaning that it has in the United States, though he did identify the integration of African-Americans and Native Americans as America's own 'race problem.' In the Indian context, Tagore used 'race' alternately as a shorthand for caste, region, and religion. He viewed the American and Indian national challenges as 'parallel': both called for the 'welding together into one body various races.'[278] Exactly what such a body might look like, Tagore didn't say. He did not want to see either the American or the Indian challenge solved by nationalism.

Tagore was 'against the general idea of all nations,' declaring that 'nationalism is a great menace' and 'the particular thing which for years has been at the bottom of India's troubles.'[279] By that, he meant that British nationalism was troubling India, but he did not see a countervailing Indian nationalism as any solution to that particular problem. Writing in the middle of World War One, he emphasised the need for social unity, and recognised the impossibility of political peace without it. Tagore's hope was that India could offer an open-ended, spiritual model of social unity to a world beset by closed-minded nationalist rivalries. He contrasted his aspirations for India with Japan's embrace of European-style militarism, upbraiding the Indian nationalists of his day for prioritising political power over social reform.[280] Tagore thought that the goal of humanity should not be nation-building, but society-building.

For Tagore, as for many idealists, nationalism was a degenerate form of social solidarity. But the romantic notion that people should form abstract attachments to the societies in which they live without embracing any particular sense of nationhood remains little more than an internationalist ideal. In the real world, people have proven willing to make serious personal sacrifices only for the benefit of an exclusive national community, not for the general betterment of all of humanity. Tagore characterised the nation as a society organised for competition with other nations, and he worried that such international competition would always drive countries to prioritise national goals over social ones.[281] He may have been right.

Nonetheless, time and again over the last two centuries, states that were not nation-states have either developed into nation-states, or disintegrated into nation-states. The second half of the nineteenth century saw the coalescence of modern nation-states in Italy, Germany, and Japan. Then in the aftermath of World War One, the multinational Russian, Austro-Hungarian, and Ottoman empires collapsed or were broken into a panoply of nation-states based on real or imagined national communities. The world-spanning British Empire lost most of Ireland to an aggressively anticolonial Irish nationalism in 1922, and the far-flung dominions of Australia, Canada, New Zealand, and South Africa developed separate national identities. When communism fell in the multinational states of Yugoslavia and the Soviet Union, both broke up along national lines. For good or for bad, the nation-state seems to be the only stable form of modern governance.

Moreover, although many nation-states have experienced spells of non-democratic government, it is difficult to find a multinational state that has ever been a democracy. The European Union may someday fulfil that promise, but for now, pan-European democracy remains more a project than a reality. Arguably, the success of that project depends on the creation of a new pan-European nationalism. The widely held idea that nationalism is a threat to democracy, a basic assumption of informed political commentary today, flies in the face of history. It might more accurately be said that nationalism is a necessary (though not a sufficient) condition for democracy. The French 'father of sociology' Émile Durkheim (1858-1917) defined democracy as 'a system where the State, whilst remaining distinct from the mass of the nation, is closely in communication with it.'[282] He considered democracy to be virtually synonymous with the concept of the nation-state.

India's independence leaders had seen the disintegration of the great European multinational empires in their lifetimes, and were well-aware of the ongoing devolution of the British Empire into self-governing dominions. When Mahatma Gandhi's influential 1909 tract *Hind Swaraj* was published in English as *Indian Home Rule*, his contemporaries would have immediately identified the title with Ireland and the 'Home Rule' movement for Irish independence. Gandhi was careful not to mention Ireland anywhere in the book, but the British banned it all the same. When the American president Woodrow Wilson later declared in 1918 that 'national aspirations must be respected' and peoples may be 'governed only by their own consent,'[283] aspiring revolutionaries around the world took note. It was against this backdrop that India's independence leaders came to believe that nationalism was the solution to their social divisions, and democracy their only path to 'home rule.'

India beat the odds to become the only poor, postcolonial society to remain a democracy because its nation-builders broke down the multitude of petty religious hierarchies that had previously dominated Hindu society and replaced them with a web of cross-cutting national associations. As a result, India early on developed a modern civil society that connected people of many different backgrounds and beliefs. Unlike in Western countries, however, civil society in India was built mainly by faith-based groups that put social responsibility at the core of their missions, not by individual people seeking personal fulfilment through voluntary participation in affinity groups.

Had the Hindu faith remained socially hierarchical, as it was before the mid nineteenth century, Indian democracy probably would have failed soon after independence. All postcolonial societies embraced nationalist ideologies, but only in India was the social structure underlying nationalism strong enough to support a lasting democracy.

No bourgeoisie, no democracy

In 1959, in one of the most-cited papers in the history of the social sciences, the American political sociologist Seymour Martin Lipset wrote that 'economic development involving industrialization, urbanization, high educational standards, and a steady increase in the overall wealth of the society, is a basic condition sustaining democracy.'[284] Judged against these expectations, modern India is by far the world's most extraordinary democracy. It is 'extraordinary,' not because it is better than other democracies, but because India is by far the poorest country in the world to have become and remained a democracy. Independent India has an unbroken record of open elections in which the party in government has never refused to cede power on defeat. National elections have been delayed only once (in 1976), and even that delay was conducted legally, in accordance with India's own constitutional procedures—although not without controversy. When elections were duly held one year later, the Prime Minister who had ordered the delay was resoundingly defeated and peacefully stepped down.

No other democracy outside the developed West can match India's record of seven decades of constitutional democratic rule. In Asia, the only country that comes close is Israel, with a national income level that is more than twenty times that of India. In fact, India is the only stable democracy on the

Eurasian mainland between Israel in the West and South Korea in the East. In that tough neighborhood, India has remained a democracy despite experiencing multiple invasions of its territory from Pakistan and China and dealing with multiple armed insurgencies sponsored at different times from Pakistan, Sri Lanka, and Myanmar. Indian democracy has been subjected to serious criticisms, many of them legitimate, but no comparable country can point to a comparable record of competitive elections with peaceful transitions between opposing political parties. India's record in this regard is truly extraordinary.

The standard story of democracy taught in political science classes around the world is that democracy emerges when a rising middle class demands a greater say in politics. The political sociologist Barrington Moore Jr famously summarised this thesis in 1966 when he wrote in a book cited even more often than Lipset's famous article that 'a vigorous and independent class of town dwellers has been an indispensable element in the growth of parliamentary democracy. No bourgeoisie, no democracy.'[285] Concurring with this view, Lipset was less concise, but more explicit:

> Only in a wealthy society in which relatively few citizens lived at the level of real poverty could there be a situation in which the mass of the population intelligently participate in politics and develop the self-restraint necessary to avoid succumbing to the appeals of irresponsible demagogues. A society divided between a large impoverished mass and a small favored elite results either in oligarchy (dictatorial rule of the small upper stratum) or in tyranny (popular-based dictatorship).[286]

Yet India is a poor country, and was extremely poor at the birth of its democracy in 1947. Although it is now seeing the emergence of an educated middle class, it remains, to echo Lipset, 'divided between a large impoverished mass and a small favored elite.' Even today, only 13 per cent of the working-age population holds a university degree, while 78 per cent have a ninth-grade education or less.[287] Countries like India aren't supposed to be capable of maintaining meaningful democracies. In the first major quantitative analysis of the long-term relationship between democracy and development, the comparative political scientist Adam Przeworski and his colleagues concluded in 2001 that, statistically speaking, 'the odds against democracy in India were extremely high.'[288]

The ordinary patterns of democratic development coincide to such an extent that (statistically speaking) it can be difficult to differentiate between the characteristics of democracies and the characteristics of rich, Western (or Westernised) countries. India is the lone Third World exception to biologist Joseph Henrich's 'WEIRD' rule that democratic countries are necessarily Western, educated, industrialised, and rich.[289] India possesses none of these other characteristics. The obvious conclusion is that although the WEIRD rule describes most existing democracies, it does not define democracy itself. India is the exception that disproves the rule.

Put simply, the highly developed countries of North America, Western Europe, and the Pacific Rim are ordinary democracies. India is different. Born in poverty, beset by war within months of achieving independence in 1947, and initially committed to a disastrous path of Soviet-style modernisation, India has always been an unlikely democracy. All through independent India's first twenty years, it wasn't clear if India would remain a democracy at all. India's founding Prime Minister never yielded power; soon after his death, he was succeeded by his daughter, establishing a family dynasty; when her rule was threatened, she declared a state of emergency and suspended elections. But miraculously—or seemingly miraculously—India pulled through this crisis. Instead of becoming just another Third World dictatorship, India returned to democratic governance in 1977 and never looked back.

The robustness of democratic principles in such a poor, embattled, postcolonial country as India is one of the great mysteries of social science. Apologists for empire ascribe the success of India's democracy to its legacy of British institutions, but no other country that inherited British institutions—and there were many—replicated India's democracy. In terms of Third World democracy, India really is *sui generis*. Thus some Indian nationalist authors attempt to link modern Indian democracy to the practices of ancient republics, to traditions of elected village councils, or to the tenets of the Hindu faith. But today's Indian democracy bears no resemblance to that of the *janapadas* or 'people's realms' of the fifth century BC. Moreover, nearly all agricultural societies have traditions of village councils, and democracy is no more Hindu than it is Christian. Such facile explanations do not suffice.

If there is a solution to the mystery of Indian democracy, it is to be found in modern India and in India's distinctive path to nationhood. In contrast to most other postcolonial states, India did not win its independence on the battlefield, notwithstanding the BJP's recent attempts to manufacture precisely such a martial myth. Nor, like its neighbours Pakistan, and later Bangladesh, was India born as an antithesis to another nation-state. Instead, India's modern national identity was built, consciously and painstakingly, by a wide array of civil society organisations, each of them working to inculcate a sense of national unity in a traditional but rapidly modernising population. These organisations had and still have different aspirations for Indian nationhood, but one value that nearly all of them share is that a sense of duty to the nation is fundamental to what it means to be a citizen of India. Civic duties, not civil rights, are at the core of Indian nationhood.

Just another Third World dictatorship?

The first thirty years of Indian democracy were not particularly extraordinary. The country's dominant national liberation movement organization, the INC, transformed itself into a political party and assumed the reins of power. Although the INC had been a 'big tent' collaborative movement throughout India's independence struggle, its leader Jawaharlal Nehru became the unchallenged party strongman after independence. Four months before India went to the polls in its first-ever democratic elections, Nehru amended the Constitution to limit freedom of speech and of the press. In that first election, he won a commanding majority in parliament, capturing 364 of the 497 seats available in the Lok Sabha. The INC's nearest competitor, the Communist Party of India, won only sixteen seats. Nehru went on to win overwhelming majorities in the next two elections, maintaining an essentially unchallenged dominance over national politics until he died in office in 1964, at the age of seventy-four.

Nehru's successor as Prime Minister Lal Bahadur Shastri (1904-1966), did not last long. He died nineteen months after taking office, while on a trip to the Soviet Union. He was only sixty-one years old. The cause of death was recorded as heart failure, and Shastri was reported to have been in ill health.[290] Nonetheless, the circumstances were mysterious, and his family never accepted the official accounts of his death.[291] Upon Shastri's passing, Nehru's forty-eight-year-old daughter, Indira Gandhi, won the internal INC election to become the party's Prime Ministerial nominee, and given the party's dominance in the Lok Sabha, she became the country's third Prime Minister a mere twenty months after her father had passed away.

Indira Gandhi was Nehru's only child. She had acted as India's unofficial 'first lady' throughout Nehru's seventeen years in office, and was thus well-accustomed to the corridors of power. In later years, she may even have been the true power behind her father's throne. Writing a year before Nehru's death, the chief India correspondent for NBC News perfectly pegged her future as it was about to unfold. In his 1963 book *After Nehru, Who?*, Putnam Welles Hangen not only predicted that Shastri would most likely be Nehru's immediate successor, but also that 'Shastri's days would be numbered.' Hangen thought that the key question was actually 'after Nehru's successor, who?' His answer was Indira Gandhi.[292]

Hangen's chief source for this prescient analysis was reportedly Mrs Gandhi herself![293]

Indira Gandhi's accession may not have been predetermined. History never is. But like so many other national liberation movements in so many other postcolonial societies, the INC devolved into a family fiefdom. The leadership of the INC was passed down from Nehru to his daughter Indira, then to her son Rajiv Gandhi, and after his death to his Italian-born wife Sonia Gandhi and their son Rahul Gandhi. Although the post-independence Gandhi family is no relation to Mahatma Gandhi, they are all related to Jawaharlal Nehru, who was himself the son of the two-time INC president Motilal Nehru. The charge of 'dynastic politics' remains the most potent criticism against the INC to this day.

India was not exceptional in seeing political power pass from a broad national liberation movement to a particular family dynasty. On the contrary: the descent into dynasticism is the general pattern of postcolonial democracies. In country after country, national liberation movements turned into dynastic political parties that refused to accept electoral defeat. Corrupted by power, the leaders of these movements were easily seduced by their own messianic rhetoric into believing that only they could deliver peace and prosperity to their countries. To quote, perhaps unfairly from Nehru's famous speech at the birth of independent India, they all believed that they had a 'tryst with destiny' to lead their countries.[294] Cincinnatus-style leaders like George Washington have been thin on the ground in the postcolonial world.

Nehru may have ruled India autocratically, but he was no dictator. Although many questions can be (and have been) raised about his commitment to liberal democratic norms, the esteem accruing to him from his role in the independence struggle and his legacy as the Mahatma's chief lieutenant was sufficient to ensure his continued tenure in office for as long as he chose to remain as India's Prime Minister. His daughter, however, possessed no such charisma. She was unpopular with the INC old guard, who in 1969 had her expelled from the party on charges of 'gross indiscipline,' 'fostering a cult of personality,' and posing 'grave threats ... [to] the traditions of democracy that we want to build up in this country.'[295] Mrs Gandhi rode out the crisis, reconstituted a new INC around her loyalists, and won a renewed parliamentary mandate in 1971—amidst widespread electoral fraud.[296] Immediately on winning reelection, she pushed through a series of constitutional amendments that seriously reduced individual rights and judicial oversight.

Finally, in 1975, India came very close to following the well-worn path from post-independence strongman democracy to one-person dictatorial rule when Indira Gandhi engineered the declaration of a state of emergency. The ostensible grounds were that 'the security of India is threatened by internal disturbances,' but the immediate prompt was an Indian Supreme Court ruling questioning the legitimacy of her election to parliament. The state of emergency empowered Mrs Gandhi to suspend elections, disregard civil liberties, and outlaw all political opposition for almost two years. More than 100,000 people (including 30 MPs) were detained on political charges.[297] Mrs Gandhi promulgated five more constitutional amendments, including one (the 42nd) that made major changes to the structure of the Constitution itself.

The Emergency of 1975-1977 was the bifurcation point of India's political development, the crossroads between democracy and dictatorship. It is a testament to the robustness, not of India's national institutions (which largely complied with Indira Gandhi's diktats)[298], but of India's unique political culture, that the country chose the road less travelled: the road toward genuine democracy. At the very moment of India's independence in 1947, Sarvepalli Radhakrishnan had exhorted his fellow parliamentarians to observe the 'unimportance of the individual and the supreme importance of the unfolding purpose which we are called upon to serve.'[299] That spirit of service to society is the spirit that pulled India through the Emergency and placed its democracy on a firm foundation for the future. But it wasn't inborn in the Indian psyche. It had to be instilled, nurtured, and stiffened over the course of decades to become strong enough to keep such a fractious country as India on the democratic path.

A democracy of duties

The historical trajectory of Indian democracy diverged from the path taken by nearly every other postcolonial state on 18 January 1977, when Indira Gandhi took to All India Radio to announce elections for a new parliament. No one knows for certain why she decided to go to the polls. The simplest explanation may be the correct one: in the opinion of Granville Austin, the leading American historian of the Indian Constitution, 'Mrs Gandhi called the elections because she thought she would win.'[300] On the opposite side of the debate, many of her boosters believe that she called elections because of a genuine faith in democracy, and cite multiple examples of her confiding to advisors that she expected to lose.[301] How much faith one should put in these protestations is irrelevant now. Although Gandhi called elections, she held them amidst continued press censorship, and without ending the Emergency.

Nonetheless, when Indira Gandhi lost the elections—spectacularly losing even her own Lok Sabha seat of Raebareli in Uttar Pradesh—she did step down.

The new government promptly ended the Emergency, released political prisoners, restored most of the civil liberties that had been stripped out of the Constitution, and put India on the liberal democratic path that it has pursued ever since. Two highly symbolic changes to the constitution, however, were retained. The first was Indira Gandhi's insertion of the words 'socialist' and 'secular' into the preamble of the Constitution, thus enshrining two of the INC's core political positions in the text of the Constitution itself. This decision remains highly controversial; the BJP in particular seems to abhor it.[302] The words were probably allowed to stand as a matter of compromise. Although the coalition that unseated Mrs Gandhi included many long-time opponents of the INC, it included the organisational rump of the INC that had expelled her, and its figurehead and Prime Minister was the octogenarian INC stalwart Morarji Desai.

The second symbolic change that the new government allowed to remain in the Constitution was Indira Gandhi's insertion of a charter of ten 'Fundamental Duties' of the citizen. Most written constitutions (including India's) have charters of fundamental rights. Among truly democratic constitutions, few contain charters of fundamental duties. Most other charters of duties are perfunctory, and derived from the constitution of the Soviet Union (and thus not to be taken seriously). India's charter of duties, while for the most part unenforceable, is truly aspirational; it includes the duties to 'value and preserve the rich heritage of our composite culture,' to 'protect and improve the natural environment,' to 'develop the scientific temper,' and to 'strive toward excellence.' In 2002, a later government added the duty for parents to 'provide opportunities for education' for their children.

The charter of Fundamental Duties has proven relatively (though not entirely) uncontroversial in India. The duties of the citizen is a favourite theme of the current Prime Minister, Narendra Modi, but it was also a favourite of Mahatma Gandhi in the decades before India's independence.[303] Modi himself cited Mahatma Gandhi's philosophy of duty in a *New York Times* article celebrating the Mahatma's birth sesquicentenary.[304] The principle that citizens have duties as well as rights may be unfamiliar to the Anglo-American mind, but it is commonplace in continental European political thinking.[305] The European Union's Charter of Fundamental Rights emphasises that the 'enjoyment of these rights entails responsibilities and duties with regard to other persons, to the human community and to future generations.'[306] Against the critic's suggestion that duties are emphasised by authoritarian regimes 'to erect a mask over violations of citizen's [sic] rights' may be placed the Mahatma's assertion that 'real rights are a result of performance of duty.'[307]

Obviously, India's constitutional charter of duties is not literally enforceable. But in 2022, the then Chief Justice of India N V Ramana told the Supreme Court Bar Association that 'the fundamental duties are not merely pedantic or technical. They were incorporated as the key to social transformation.'[308] In other words, they speak to the aspirations of Indian society—or at least, of a large segment of Indian society—to formulate a specifically Indian path to modernity. The 'essential reciprocity' of rights and duties is to be found everywhere in Gandhian thought,[309] but the traditional Indian conceptualisation of the relationship between the individual and society is perhaps better expressed by the Indian nationalist philosopher Sri Aurobindo Ghose (1872-1950). He wrote that:

> It has been said that democracy is based on the rights of man; it has been replied that it should rather take its stand on the duties of man; but both rights and duties are European ideas. *Dharma* is the Indian conception in which rights and duties lose the artificial antagonism created by a view of the world which makes selfishness the root of action, and regain their deep and eternal unity.[310]

For Sri Aurobindo, the reciprocity of rights and duties was not a transactional relationship (individuals earn their rights by performing duties), but a holistic one (individuals fulfil their *dharma* by exercising their rights in such a way as to perform their duties). Prefiguring the spirit of Indira Gandhi's

Fundamental Duties, Sri Aurobindo taught that the ultimate goal of Indian nationalism should be the promotion of a greater human welfare. He taught that Indians 'must live as a nation' in order to 'live as a nation for humanity': just as 'a man must be strong and free in himself before he can live usefully for others, so must a nation.'[311] Like all ideals, these Indian ideas about nationhood may be most often honoured in the breach, but they are nonetheless entirely at odds with Western theorisations of the nation.

In the Anglo-American tradition reflected in the writings of Thomas Hobbes and John Locke, the state is conceptualised as a transactional commonwealth of individuals who have banded together for mutual benefit. There has always been much philosophical angst over whether an individual's membership in society is voluntary or involuntary, but the fundamental assumption is that individuals only owe duties to society because they receive benefits from society. In the continental European tradition reflected in the writings of Jean-Jacques Rousseau and Johann Herder, the nation is conceptualised as a kind of super-organic collective being, whether civic (Rousseau) or ethnolinguistic (Herder) in nature. Social solidarity demands that individuals discharge their duties to society as a generalisation of their duties to family and friends.

In India, Anglo-American individualism is entirely a twenty-first century import, and the European model of the nation-state is a non-starter in a country with twenty-two officially recognised regional languages. Other forms of nationalism, like China's imperial Confucian tradition or the Soviet Union's totalitarian modernism, presume the existence of a strong central state, something that India has always lacked, and which the Indian constitution militates against. The obvious foundation for Indian nationhood—the construction of India as an explicitly Hindu state—was rejected by India's nation-builders, despite their own attachment to the Hindu faith. They sought inspiration from Hindu religious thought and drew language from Hindu scriptures, but they were enlightened enough not to attempt to build an explicitly Hindu state. Perhaps they knew that, lacking any central authority, the Hindu faith could only inspire a nation's people, not support authoritative state institutions.

Why no coup?

Modern India's constitution was ratified by the country's Constituent Assembly on 26 November 1949. The president of the assembly, Rajendra Prasad, gave a long speech on the occasion. He expressed his faith in universal adult suffrage, which in effect meant that illiterate 'people of the village' would 'constitute the bulk of this vast electorate' and that 'their sturdy commonsense will enable them to see things in the right perspective.'[312] India's villagers are now mostly literate, but that has not diminished the 'sturdy commonsense' of their traditional values. Even today, the majority of Indians still hold values that would be considered extremely traditional by the standards of Western democracies. For example, more than 95 per cent of Indians believe that to be 'truly Indian' it is important to respect the army, to stand for the national anthem, and (most of all) to respect elders.[313] Less than 0.05 per cent of Indians report having no religion.

Traditional village values like these are not generally associated with the development and persistence of democracy. Nor are supposedly 'authoritarian' values like a commitment to law and order. From the time the World Values Survey was first administered in India in 1990 through to the most recent survey in 2012, Indians consistently rated 'maintaining order in the nation' as their top national priority, far ahead of 'protecting freedom of speech' or 'giving people more say in government decisions.'[314] Western political theorists might read into such values a proclivity for dictatorship, and indeed in the Western context it may be true that 'prospects of democracy are bleak where emancipative [non-traditional] values remain weak.'[315] But the Indian context is different from the Western context. When Indians rejected the Emergency of 1975-1977, it wasn't because Indira Gandhi trampled on freedom of speech or took away people's say in government decision-making. It was because they considered Mrs Gandhi's assumption of emergency powers a betrayal of her duty to the nation. There is even some evidence that she felt that way, too.

In the final analysis, India pulled through the Emergency because Indians refused to accept a transition to dictatorship. That simple proposition may seem almost tautological, but in light of the available historical evidence, it is much more complicated than it sounds. Perhaps inspired by Gandhian principles of non-violent non-cooperation, Indians offered no systematic armed opposition to Indira Gandhi's personal rule. There were some serious demonstrations against the Emergency, particularly in Bihar, where the revolutionary agitator Jayaprakash Narayan (1902-1979) led a socialist student movement in mass protests. State governments in Gujarat and Tamil Nadu initially refused to implement many of Mrs Gandhi's extrajudicial orders, but both governments were dissolved and the states subjected to direct central authority. None of these tokens of resistance rose to the level of organised opposition to her rule, let alone armed rebellion against it. Strangely, although relatively few people seem to have supported Indira Gandhi's emergency government, no one seems to have done much to overthrow it.[316]

Not even the military. Had India followed the path of most other traditional societies characterised by high levels of respect for the army and a strong preference for law and order, the Emergency would have been the signal for a military take-over. India might at least have seen a competition for power between civil and military authority. But India's senior military officers steadfastly refused to be drawn into any form of action regarding the Emergency, for or against.[317] When Indira Gandhi asked the Army leadership simply to provide drinking water for the crowd at one of her political rallies, they refused.[318] India's armed forces remained steadfastly aloof during the Emergency, taking no position for or against. They prioritised their duty to the nation over their own opportunities for personal advancement under the Gandhi regime, or indeed the opportunities they might have gained had they ousted Mrs Gandhi and substituted their own regime in its place.

The contrast with Pakistan is striking. Post-1947 Pakistan, which comprised both West and East Pakistan, inherited the same British institutions as post-1947 India. This included its military institutions, with individual British Indian Army regiments earmarked for either the Indian or Pakistani army, with many Muslims leaving Indian-designated regiments to join Pakistani ones and most Hindus and Sikhs leaving Pakistani-designated regiments to remain in India. In the immediate aftermath of Partition, more British officers stayed on with Pakistan's army than with India's, and some British officers even served with Pakistani units during their 1947 invasion of Kashmir.[319] Yet it was the Pakistani army that seized control of the country in 1958, and arguably never afterward fully relinquished it.

The difference here in historical trajectories between independent India on the one hand and Pakistan and Bangladesh on the other is due neither to differences in institutions, nor even in religion. While it may be tempting to see the problems of civil-military relations in independent Pakistan as typical of the problems of the Muslim world, the two Buddhist-majority countries that emerged out of British rule in South Asia—Myanmar and Sri Lanka—have had similar histories of military involvement in politics. Lest it be surmised that the Hindu religion is responsible for India's relatively benign civil-military relations, one need only look north to Hindu-majority Nepal, where the military has always been deeply involved in business, government, and society, from the British client-state past right through to the democratic present.[320]

India is the only major South Asian country where the military has never meddled in politics. The prominent scholar of civil-military relations Zoltan Barany finds it 'remarkable that in India the state's control of the military has remained virtually unshaken,' even though India ticks multiple risk factors, including especially the routine use of the military to quell internal insurgencies.[321] But India's military, or at least its officer corps, has always respected civilian rule. Barany's fellow political scientist Aqil Shah attributes this to the 'normative restraints on military officers' built up over years of professional socialisation that acted as 'a bulwark against potential praetorian tendencies even when the broader political structure [became] permissive.'[322] In other words, future army officers are not born embracing democratic behavioural norms. They are socialised into them.

Education for nationhood

What is true of the military is true of society in general. People are not born embracing their duties as citizens in a democratic society. They are socialised into democracy, whether through public education as in the United States or through parliamentary debates as in the United Kingdom, or even through the propaganda of an occupying power as in postwar Japan. In India, informed opinion crystallised around democracy through the pamphlets, newspaper articles, magazines, and books published by Indian nationalists throughout the first half of the twentieth century; no country in the world has such a voluminous independence literature as India. But at the time of India's independence struggle, those writings were accessible only to an educated few.

Prasad's sturdy villagers did not learn democracy from the editorial pages of the country's elite English-language newspapers. They were socialised into democracy by those who ventured out into the villages to teach it. In the earliest stages of a germinating Indian nationalism, these were primarily the followers of Hindu reform movements like the Brahmo Samaj and its many offshoots, the Arya Samaj, and the Ramakrishna Mission. These organisations did not explicitly teach democracy. According to the American Indologist Gerald James Larson, they shared 'a primary focus on developing among the people of India a self-confident national awareness that will provide a solid foundation for India as a modern nation-state.'[323] Even as the INC and other national liberation organisations were working to shape the future Indian state, Hindu reformers were working to shape the future Indian citizen.

Muslim reform movements were also active in British India, but most of them promoted transnational connections to the wider Muslim world. As a result, instead of contributing to the formation of India's national identity, they fostered a future Pakistan's orientation toward the Arab Middle East. But both

Hindu and Muslim religious reform movements played key roles in integrating the fragmented, traditional, intensely local social networks of Indian villages into an emerging modern society. In Western countries, and in Japan, this transition was accomplished through urbanisation and industrialisation, yet by the time of independence, India was still overwhelmingly rural and agricultural. In India, the emergence of modern society resulted from the work of religious reform movements.

India's Hindu reform movements sought to unify Hindu society by teaching the intrinsic unity of diverse religious experiences, promoting a sense of shared cultural heritage based on works like the *Ramayana* and the *Bhagavad Gita*. They also worked hard to reduce caste distinctions and end caste-based discrimination. Crucially, their work penetrated to the very base of society, cutting across the social barriers that traditionally separated different strata of Hindu society. Though they were (for the most part) not directly involved in India's national liberation movements, they nonetheless prompted a 'reconstruction of nationalism, a necessity if the movement were to penetrate beneath the English-educated intellectual groups and an Indian rather than a neo-Western nation were to be created.'[324]

The reconstruction of Hindu society undertaken by India's nineteenth century Hindu reform movements thus constituted a kind of education for nationhood. These organisations did not explicitly promote the development of an Indian nation, Hindu or otherwise, but they did help create the conditions under which a single, unified Indian nation—or at least a unified Hindu nation—could emerge. At the time of the 'mutiny' or 'independence war' of 1857, it really was true that, as Winston Churchill later remarked, India was 'a geographical term ... no more a united nation than the equator.'[325] By the time the independence struggle kicked off in earnest after World War One, India was a nation-in-formation. It was not yet clear what exact form the Indian nation would take—indeed, the character of the Indian nation is still hotly contested—but it was clear that India would be a nation. And in the 1920s, a new social movement arose to usher it into existence.

National rejuvenation movements have emerged in many places besides India. They have a particularly well-documented history in Europe. The academic archetype of the national rejuvenation movement is the German *Turnverein* (Gymnastics Association), established in 1811 by a patriotic high school teacher named Friedrich Jahn (1778-1852). In the United States, Jahn is best remembered as the 'father of gymnastics,' and he is generally credited with inventing most of the standard equipment that gymnasts still use today. But Jahn's purpose in establishing the *Turnverein* was not the development of a new sport, but the rejuvenation of the German nation. Jahn incorporated physical fitness as only one aspect of an intensely patriotic programme targeted at young men. He laid out his vision of a rejuvenated Germany in an 1810 book, *Deutsches Volksthum* (German Folkways), in which he advocated for a politically unified Germany with a national school system that would provide 'a democratic education aimed at the creation of a new citizenry.'[326]

Inevitably, nineteenth century German nationalists have come to be associated in people's minds with the rise of twentieth century Nazism, but in his own time, 'Father' Jahn, as he was called, was considered a leading liberal, inspiring young Germans to resist both the military occupation of Germany by the troops of Napoleonic France and the authoritarian rule of Germany's fractious 'princely states'. Directly or indirectly, his *Turnverein* was the model, or at least the precursor, for Giuseppe Mazzini's Young Italy, China's Society of Righteous and Harmonious Fists (the Boxers), Czechoslovakia's Sokol public exercise movement, and Hassan al-Banna's Egyptian Muslim Brotherhood. All of these movements emphasised the importance of physical exercise and traditional values in preparing young men for a life of service to the nation-in-formation. They all embraced social welfare missions, emerged in countries under foreign domination, and sought to free their countries by organising society in the cause of an incipient nationalism.

In the wake of World War One, the principle of national self-determination became the accepted basis of future state-formation. Many organisations sought to define the future Indian state in line with their own visions of nationhood. But only one organisation sought to remake the Indian nation itself: the Rashtriya Swayamsevak Sangh (RSS), or National Volunteer Organisation. Founded in Maharashtra in Nagpur in 1925 by the medical doctor K B Hedgewar, the RSS recruited its initial cohorts from among the students of traditional Hindu *akharas* or martial arts gymnasiums.[327] Knowingly or not, Hedgewar effectively duplicated the program of Friedrich Jahn, with the British occupiers of colonial India replacing the French occupiers of 1811 Germany. He founded the RSS to be a nationalist organisation of the Hindus, awakening them from the 'deep slumber' through which India had in his view lost nearly one-third of its population to foreign religions.[328]

If the INC was the key social movement organisation of India's national liberation movement, the RSS was its counterpart in the movement for national rejuvenation and would quickly grow to become 'the most potent organised Hindu cultural group of the twentieth century'.[329]

The RSS and the organisation of Hindu society

The US Library of Congress catalogue entry on the RSS describes it as 'a right-wing Hindu nationalist, paramilitary, volunteer, and allegedly militant organization in India.'[330] This description is grossly misleading, and seems to have been cribbed from Wikipedia. It is true that the RSS is a volunteer organisation, and it is thoroughly nationalist. But the epithet 'right-wing' is applicable to it only to the extent that religious conservatives are routinely denounced as such by their opponents, and it is 'militant' only in the strict sense of the word when used as an adjective, not a noun. The RSS is militant in its pursuit of Indian national rejuvenation on its own, uncompromising terms. But it absolutely is not an organisation composed of militants: i.e., armed combatants. The only 'weapons' training received by RSS members or 'volunteers' (*swayamsevaks*) consists of drills with *lathis*, long bamboo sticks that are used in martial arts exercises.

Similarly, the RSS is absolutely not a 'paramilitary' organisation, at least not under any ordinary dictionary definition of the term. The organisation has never engaged in terrorism, and has never been known to stockpile firearms or explosives. The label seems to have been applied simply because RSS *swayamsevaks* wear uniform khaki pants and white shirts at formal meetings. It is true that some individuals associated with the RSS have been involved in deadly riots, and much invective has been mustered to assert that the murderer of Mahatma Gandhi was a 'member' of the RSS—though this has little more practical relevance than the fact that the assassin of the American president Abraham Lincoln was a member of the Episcopal Church. Gandhi's assassin, Nathuram Godse (1910-1949), reportedly attended RSS gatherings, but there seems to be no evidence of him having ever had any ongoing role in the organisation. Violent criminals have passed through the doors of every inclusive community organisation, and participation in RSS events is open to all Hindu men.

The RSS is often described as a 'Hindu nationalist' organisation, even sometimes by the RSS itself, but even that description is not as straightforward as it sounds. The organisation has always maintained that 'the word Hindu ... is tantamount to the word Indian,' to quote its longest-serving *Sarsanghchalak* (Respected Leader) M S Golwalkar (1906-1973).[331] At a surface level, the RSS is a Hindu nationalist organisation in the same sense that continental Europe's postwar Christian democratic parties were Christian nationalist organisations. These parties were founded and staffed by people of Christian faith who took it for granted that their countries were Christian in culture, even though they were not tied organisationally to any particular church. At a deeper level, although the RSS does espouse a specifically Hindu construction of Indian nationhood, the country's extraordinary religious diversity precludes their identification of Indian nationhood with any particular strand of Hindu belief. The organisation assiduously promotes the consolidation of India's Hindus into a single national identity while defining the nation itself in purely geographical terms.

There is no doubt that the RSS is seen as and sees itself as a Hindu organisation. The challenge is that the precise Hindu quality of the RSS is sometimes difficult to pin down. It is the parent organisation of the Vishva Hindu Parishad (VHP), or World Hindu Council, but this is a studiously non-sectarian organization. The RSS and its wider network of related organisations, known informally as the Sangh Parivar or organization family, do not work within any particular Hindu tradition. This ambiguity is further complicated by the inherent openness of Hindu worship. Specific Hindu traditions can be distinguished from one another, but their adherents often cannot. In contrast to the Christian world, most Hindu traditions do not require exclusivity of their worshippers, with the result that many Hindus do not 'belong' to a single tradition. Thus, when the RSS works toward the rejuvenation of the Indian nation through a revival of Hindu culture, it does so only in very general terms. The RSS does embrace a specifically Hindu identity, but it is a very diffuse form of Hindu identity indeed.

In this, the RSS represents a kind of secularisation of the old Hindu revival movements. In effect, the RSS continued the nation-building functions of those movements by adopting a lowest-common-denominator definition of Hindu worship: one so broad that it considers Sikhism, Jainism, and Buddhism to be varieties of an all-encompassing Hindu faith.[332] The current RSS *Sarsanghchalak* Mohan Bhagwat has even gone so far as to implicitly include Muslims and Christians under the Hindu tent:

> Ideologically, all Bharatiyas [Indians] are Hindus and Hindus mean all Bharatiyas. All those who are in Bharat [India] today are related to Hindu culture, Hindu ancestors and Hindu land, nothing other than these.[333]

This unsolicited ecumenicalism has often been the cause of much consternation among adherents of other religions, but it is fundamental to the RSS worldview—and the meaning of 'Hindu nationalism' when applied to the RSS. Whereas non-RSS commentators tend to construe the term 'Hindu nationalism' as exclusionary, RSS intellectuals prefer to construe the term inclusively. That is not to say that the majority of RSS *swayamsevaks* or even full-time activists or 'organisers' (*pracharaks*) behave in ways that are consistent with this inclusive model of Indian nationhood. There is much evidence that they do not. But there is also much evidence that it is the ideal toward which the organisation strives.

The RSS has always maintained that it is not a political organisation, but the current Prime Minister, Narendra Modi, built his career working as a *pracharak* for the RSS and is still closely associated with it. So is his political party, the BJP, which is, in effect, the political arm of the RSS. Fear of its potential political influence prompted the official suppression of the RSS both before and after India's independence. The organisation was temporarily banned by Nehru in 1948 after the assassination of Mahatma Gandhi, then banned again by Nehru's daughter Indira Gandhi in 1975. Of the twenty-six organisations outlawed on the first day of the Emergency, only the RSS was considered important enough to be mentioned by name in the *New York Times* report of the decree.[334]

Among the other civil society organisations that were banned, only three warranted attention in the more detailed *The Times of India* coverage: the Muslim service organization Jamaat-e-Islami Hind (widely considered to be the South Asian analog of the Muslim Brotherhood), the Hindu spiritual society Ananda Marga, and the social wing of the Communist Party of India (Marxist-Leninist), or CPI-ML.[335] Of the banned organisations, the RSS was by far the largest, and alongside Jamaat-e-Islami Hind, was one of only two that had a truly national footprint. According to the commission set up in 1978 to document the excesses of the Emergency, RSS volunteers were detained even in states where the RSS presence was and still remains weak: they constituted 15 per cent of all political detainees in Kerala, 14 per cent in West Bengal, and 7 per cent in Tamil Nadu.[336] Just fifty years after its founding, the RSS had already spread from its strongholds in the north and west of India to establish a meaningful presence everywhere except in the far northeast of India. It was and remains India's dominant civil society organisation.

Civil society and the democratic nation

In the internal mythology of the RSS, the organisation claims to have been the 'backbone' of the underground resistance to Indira Gandhi's Emergency government.[337] The political opponents of the RSS, of course, dispute this.[338] Since the RSS was formally banned at the time, the true scope of its activities during the Emergency may never be known. From the perspective of the historian or the ideologue, this is unfortunate, but for the purpose of understanding the political sociology of Indian democracy, it may not matter. It may be that the most important role the RSS played in preserving Indian democracy was not what it did during the Emergency, but what it did in the decades before it. Through its Sangh Parivar of social, cultural, economic, and spiritual affiliates, the RSS was instrumental in building a unified Hindu society in India. The RSS did little to integrate Muslims into broader Indian society, but it did seek to unite the many disparate strands of Hindu society around a shared affirmation of Indian nationhood.

The RSS has always been, first and foremost, a nationalist organisation. It is undeniably Hindu in culture and in politics, but it understands itself specifically as a Hindu 'movement for national reconstruction.'[339] The idea of a shared nationhood is something that always seems obvious in retrospect, but it was often less obvious to those who were living before the birth of the nations that we recognise today. Viewed from the perspective of the pivotal years of India's independence struggle, the RSS mission of mobilising Hindu society in support of the unity of an independent India was a key precursor of the formation of the modern Indian nation. Although the RSS did not attempt to unify all Indians, it did work to unify India's majority community across multiple geographical, linguistic, and even political divides, including in the independent princely states. Through its Sangh Parivar network of social, cultural, economic, and spiritual affiliates, the RSS was instrumental in building a unified Hindu society that could form the basis for a unified Indian nation.

In a deeply religious country like India, it was inevitable, perhaps even indispensable, that national identity should have been underpinned by the support of faith-based civil society organisations. During the independence struggle, the RSS had a Muslim parallel in the Jamiat Ulama-i-Hind (JUH) or Council of Muslim Theologians of India, which staunchly opposed the creation of Pakistan. Had the JUH been as successful in mobilising Muslim society around support for a unified India as the RSS was in mobilising Hindu society, India might never have been partitioned. But the JUH and other Muslim organisations that opposed Partition were unable to gain broad Muslim support for a united independent India. Eventually, British India was divided into a secular but Hindu-dominated India and a Muslim faith-based Pakistan, not at the instigation of Hindu nationalists in the RSS, but at the demand—backed up by violence—of the Muslim League. The question of whether colonial India should have been divided along religious lines is debatable, but it seems perverse, almost bordering on the absurd to fault the RSS for organising Hindus at a time when all organisations, including the INC were organising communities along religious lines.

To expect that colonial India's disparate civil society movements should have been united along interfaith lines would be to impose a twenty-first century Western morality in a time and place to which it is wholly foreign. Mahatma Gandhi made repeated, often ostentatious attempts to appeal for Hindu-Muslim unity in the nationalist cause, to little avail. Yet in a supreme twist of historical irony, modern India emerged as a secular country because diverse Hindu civil society organisations subscribing to different and often conflicting doctrines embraced an overarching Indian national consciousness. The RSS played a major though by no means a determinative role in aligning these organisations by recruiting Hindu men to join their own organization regardless of caste and supporting Hindu organizations regardless of sect. The RSS did not create Hindu civil society, but it did increase the density and national connectivity of Hindu civil society networks, while at the same time promoting—some say 'fanatically'—a shared sense of Indian national identity.[340]

A shared sense of nationhood will not, by itself, call forth a democratic society, but it is almost certainly a necessary condition for the maintenance of democracy. The fact that India's independence leaders chose a democratic form of government for their country was no surprise. Nearly every newly independent country has adopted a democratic constitution. The surprise is that India's democracy survived its initial decades of single-party dominance, and even more so that it survived the crisis of the Emergency. On the basis of macro-level social indicators like average incomes, education levels, literacy, and urbanisation, twentieth century India should never have been able to sustain a democracy. The persistence of Indian democracy is a testament to the strength and unity of India's civil society.

Effective nation-building weaves civil society organisations into a mass of tangled roots that can keep democratic institutions firmly anchored even in the thinnest soil. It is no insult to India to observe that it did not, and in many ways, still does not possess the conditions under which democracy easily takes root and flourishes. But it is, nevertheless, a testament to the patient toil of India's nation-builders that they were able to cultivate a society strong enough to sustain a democracy under extremely challenging conditions. Their success illustrates a central methodological flaw in democracy theory. The standard account of the rise of democracy draws a straight line from a prosperous urban middle class to demands for a democratic system of government. But this standard account glosses over an important intermediate variable: the strength of civil society.

Many scholars have pointed out the importance of dense civil society networks for the robustness of democracy, most famously the American political scientist Robert Putnam.[341] Putnam's key case study involved a comparison of civil society in northern versus southern Italy. But northern Italy, possessing a stronger civil society, had been wealthier than southern Italy for at least a thousand years before the dawn of Italian democracy in the late nineteenth century. No major theorist seems to have envisaged that a poor country with limited resources could short-circuit the path to democracy by jumping in at the intermediate stage by building a strong civil society without the benefits of a prosperous middle class. A rich, urban, educated, literate middle class may offer fertile soil for the development of civil society networks, but it is not an absolutely necessary condition for building civil society networks. India is the exception that proves this rule.

How democracy survives

Every country has a civil society, but the structure of civil society can differ dramatically across countries, or even across regions within a country. In his work on Italian civil society, Putnam stressed the importance of strengthening 'horizontal' ties among 'agents of equivalent status and power' in contrast to 'vertical' ties 'linking unequal agents in asymmetric relations of hierarchy and dependence,' in the belief that 'networks of civic engagement that cut across social cleavages nourish wider cooperation.'[342] Such horizontal ties are exactly what Hindu reform movements began to foster in the late nineteenth century, and what they and the RSS continues to foster today. These groups put decades of effort into breaking down the vertical ties that had characterised traditional Hindu society, in particular the scourges of caste hierarchy and untouchability. At the same time, they dramatically expanded the horizontal ties that connected Hindus across sectarian, linguistic, and geographical divides.

The modern Indian nation forged by the RSS, its Sangh Parivar, and related Hindu reform movements is a web, not a pyramid. This dense web knits Indian society together at the all-India level. It does, however, incorporate one obvious drawback when considered as a social foundation for modern Indian nationhood—its omission of a meaningful role for non-Hindus in the life of the nation. That is both a moral failing and a potential political opportunity. But in an imperfect world full of challenges, the Indian nation has done better than most in preserving its country's governing institutions and preventing a collapse into arbitrary rule. During Indira Gandhi's Emergency, it was arguably India's densely-interwoven Hindu civil society that kept the country and its democracy on course. It is difficult to provide direct empirical evidence that this was the case, but social theory strongly supports the existing circumstantial evidence that India owes its continuing democracy to the strength of its Hindu civil society.

In an influential 1994 article on the role of civil society in democratisation, the British political scientist Gordon White identified four theoretical 'expectations about the role of civil society in democratization':

> First, a growing civil society can alter the *balance of power* between state and society in favour of the latter .... Second, it is argued a strong civil society can play a *disciplinary role in relation to the state* by enforcing standards of public morality .... Third, civil society plays a potentially crucial role as *an intermediary or (two-way) transmission-belt between state and society* .... Fourth, civil society can play a *constitutive* role by redefining the rules of the political game along democratic lines.[343] [italics as in the original]

India's Hindu civil society played all four of these roles before and during the Emergency. It acted as a strong pole of social organisation that balanced against the power of the state by offering safe harbour to opposition activists, financing and provisioning opposition movements, and providing meaningful venues for non-state, though not explicitly anti-state activism. It disciplined the state by placing moral limits on the levels of violence that Indira Gandhi could exercise without attracting the censure of wider society. It intermediated between the state and society by repeatedly offering to negotiate pathways through which Mrs Gandhi could exit the Emergency. This flexibility later formed the basis for much criticism of the role played by the RSS in the Emergency. It also perpetuated the national myth that India remained a democracy despite Indira Gandhi's engineered state of emergency, reinforcing the notion that elections were only delayed, not abolished forever.

Contrary to self-serving RSS narratives of its own heroism during the Emergency, the survival of Indian democracy cannot be attributed solely, or even primarily to the actions of the RSS at the time. That is not to downplay the heroism of individual RSS *swayamsevaks* and *pracharaks*, many of whom faced loss of civil rights, loss of income, and even imprisonment during the Emergency. Nor is it to downplay the role played by the RSS in helping organise the opposition vote that ultimately drove Indira Gandhi from office. It is merely to recognise that if RSS opposition had been the only factor preventing a slide into dictatorship, the organisation could have been much more ruthlessly suppressed by Indira Gandhi—just as for example, the Muslim Brotherhood was nearly wiped out in Egypt after the country's brief flirtation with democracy in 2011-2012. For that matter, Mrs Gandhi might never have called the election of 1977 that the RSS proved so instrumental in winning for the opposition.

The real contribution made by the RSS to the survival of Indian democracy was its patient, decades-long work building horizontal linkages across Hindu civil society. A more vertically organised civil society would have been much easier for Indira Gandhi to divide and rule. Examples of this were seen in two important states, Kerala and Maharashtra, where hierarchically organized groups did in fact form alliances with Mrs Gandhi's government. In Kerala, the staunchly atheist Communist Party of India (CPI) maintained a power-sharing agreement with Indira Gandhi's INC, while in Maharashtra, the local potentate Bal Thackeray (1926-2012) reached a *modus vivendi* with Mrs

Gandhi that gave his party primacy in local politics while allowing her free reign over national policy.

In most of the rest of India, at the grassroots level, the horizontal web mostly held firm. In Western countries like the United States, that web would have been composed of a wide variety of mostly secular voluntary associations formed by individuals to serve their own personal interests. Western civil society organisations are formed for a multitude of different purposes. Some are churches, unions, and political parties, but civil society also includes parents' associations, homeowners' associations, ethnic associations, veterans' groups, hobbyist groups, fraternities and sororities. Putnam's archetypical civil society organisation was the bowling league. Obviously, India also has organisations like these. But India's many Hindu faith communities are far stronger and more widespread than its secular associations. Unlike religious communities in Western societies, these have overlapping memberships, embedding people in a web of intersecting affiliations instead of in a series of vertical denominational silos.

The structure of India's Hindu civil society is thus more akin to that of the secular than of the religious civil societies of Western countries, and it seems to play a similar role in supporting democratic institutions. Western theorists are accustomed to thinking of religious institutions either as authoritatively hierarchical, like the Catholic, Orthodox, and Lutheran churches in Europe and Latin America, or as self-contained communities, like the many Evangelical Protestant denominations in the United States. As a result, they have overlooked the potential for intersecting and overlapping faith-based civil society institutions to knit society together. It is true that there are communal tensions in India that divide Hindu civil society from Muslim, Christian, and sometimes Sikh civil society, but with Hindus accounting for around 80 per cent of the population, it is Hindu civil society that determines the general character of Indian civil society as a whole, and through it, the character of Indian nationhood.

Muslims in a Hindu Nation

According to V-Dem's historical database, there were only five democratic countries at the dawn of the twentieth century: Australia, Belgium, and Switzerland, which were classified as full 'liberal democracies', plus New Zealand and France, which were rated somewhat lower, as mere 'electoral democracies'.[344] The United States was classified as an 'electoral autocracy'. In V-Dem's estimation, the country that fought World War One to make the world safe for democracy did not itself become a democracy until 1920, and did not become a full liberal democracy until 1969. At the 1919 Paris Peace Conference that ended World War One, the most democratic of the major powers involved in the negotiations was the victorious United Kingdom, which was rated as a liberal democracy and ranked number 6 in the world for that year, followed closely by the vanquished Germany, an electoral democracy that was ranked at number 9. Both must have been quite upset to be dictated terms by a non-democracy like the United States, but history is full of such ironies.

Quantitatively, the main reason for 1919 America's low

V-Dem score was its lack of women's suffrage, as women were not guaranteed the vote until 1920. But qualitatively, the United States was also a racially segregated country in 1919, and remained so for much of the twentieth century. Race was the most important fault line in American nationhood from the very beginning. In the original text of the United States Constitution, representation in Congress was 'determined by adding to the whole Number of free Persons, including those bound to Service for a Term of Years, and excluding Indians not taxed, three fifths of all other Persons.'[345] With this language, the shame of slavery was swept under the carpet, with enslaved African-Americans alluded to as 'other Persons.' Native Americans 'not taxed' (i.e., living tribally) were excluded from the nation entirely. Americans fought a race-based civil war over slavery to decide the character of their nation, and a series of race-based frontier wars to determine its extent. In later years, race-based immigration laws would prevent many Asians and others from becoming part of the American nation, giving preference to Europeans until well into the twentieth century.

Race remains a dividing line in America today, often the most important dividing line. Other countries have different dividing lines, like nationality in the United Kingdom, language in Belgium and Switzerland, and dialect in China. In India, the key dividing line is religion, and although there are many religions in India, the one religious division that really matters is the one between Hindus and Muslims. The roughly 15 per cent of the Indian population that is Muslim can be thought of in some ways as occupying a place in the national imagination that is analogous to that occupied by the roughly 15 per cent of the American population that is of African descent. The parallels are far from exact. In contrast to African-Americans, Muslim

Indians were never enslaved. Nothing could be further from the truth as Muslims historically arrived in India as conquerors. They do not face serious economic disadvantage, as their average social indicators are broadly similar to those of Hindus. But the role played by Muslims in India's national identity since independence is, in some meaningful ways, reminiscent of the role of African-Americans in the American story.

Due to the carving of Pakistan out of India and the accompanying violence of Partition, the role of Islam in Indian nationhood has always been fraught with controversy. It is also a focus of current politics. The received wisdom is that although 'Hindu majoritarianism is ascendant' under BJP leadership in India, this is a new phenomenon, since:

> Thanks to the political dominance of the Congress Party and with due deference to the country's extraordinary diversity, secular nationalism came to define India's post-1947 identity. Under the tutelage of the country's inaugural Prime Minister, Jawaharlal Nehru, India's postcolonial leadership embarked on an ambitious project of nation-building by refusing to privilege any one religion above all others.[346]

This is a carefully parsed but thoroughly misleading account of history. Muslims have never been well-integrated into the Indian nation. From the beginning of the independence struggle, the INC was unsuccessful in its attempts to integrate the country's Muslim leadership into its big tent national liberation movement. In particular, the INC singularly failed to attract Muslim votes in the crucial 1945 elections that determined the makeup of the Constituent Assembly that wrote independent India's republican Constitution. The 1945 elections were held under British administration with voting limited to a small elite with separate electorates set aside specifically for Muslims. The Muslim League led by Muhammad Ali Jinnah won every single one of the seats reserved for Muslims ... and not a single one of the seats that were open to candidates of all religions. The INC was unable to secure a single Muslim-designated seat. Provincial elections the following year generally confirmed this lopsided result.

Although no one can know for certain the political opinions of ordinary Muslims in pre-Partition India, it is a fact that in 1945, the majority of elite Muslims—an astonishing 86.5 per cent across the 30 seats reserved for Muslims—voted for the Muslim League and its explicit call for Muslim separation from India.[347] All told, 80 Muslims were among the 296 delegates initially elected or selected to participate in the Constituent Assembly; at its first sitting, only four attended.[348] The Muslim League had called for Muslim representatives to boycott the assembly, and although more Muslims later attended as it became clear that the parts of the country they represented would remain in India and not be assigned to Pakistan, Muslim attendance was never high.[349] In the Constituent Assembly, proposals to set up separate electorates for Muslims in independent India's parliament were debated and rejected. Both the INC leadership and the Constituent Assembly embraced the view that a secular state should not have constituencies defined by religion.[350]

Although the majority of the Constituent Assembly took it for granted that independent India would be a secular democratic republic, a proposal to include the word 'secular' in the Constitution was soundly defeated. The word was only inserted three decades after independence by Indira Gandhi during the Emergency. Nonetheless, India was born and remained a secular state. That said, the Indian nation has never been a secular nation, and the Indian state has always had to reckon with the intense religiosity of its citizens. Indian law assumes and demands in practice that every Indian be associated with a recognised religion. This is a legacy of British and indeed Mughal times that has only recently been successfully challenged.[351] Interfaith marriage remains rare in India, and when one partner is Muslim, generally seems to involve the conversion to Islam of the non-Muslim (usually female) partner. Equivocations like 'generally' and 'seems' are necessary because data on this topic is either not collected or, when collected, not published.

Politically correct pieties notwithstanding, Indian nationalism has always had a distinctively Hindu character. Historically, the acceptance of Sikhs, Buddhist, and Jains as full participants in the Indian nation has been mostly, but not always, unproblematic. The status of Christians has tended to be more controversial, but their small numbers, relatively high incomes, and geographical concentration in peripheral and tribal areas have tended to defuse tensions. Among all the religious minorities in India, it is Muslims who have historically posed the greatest challenge for the construction of an inclusive Indian nationhood, a challenge that has never been satisfactorily resolved. Legally, Muslim Indians have absolute equality with all other Indians, but socially, culturally, and politically, Muslims are often 'othered' in India and treated as a distinct group outside the mainstream. Is it not obvious how that othering can be reversed, or even whether Muslim Indians want to reverse it. What is obvious is that the long-term health of Indian democracy depends on the successful integration of Muslims as full participants in the Indian nation.

Reports of repression

The freedom and security of Muslims in India is a major concern of international human rights organisations, Western governments, and indeed the international community as a while. When the United Nations Office of the High Commissioner for Human Rights conducted its fourth Universal Periodic Review of India in 2022, it reported that 'the proliferation of hate speech and violence against religious minorities is a concern.'[352] Its panel of experts went further, sounding 'the alarm over reports of attacks on minorities' and calling 'for urgent corrective action.'[353] Independent human rights organisations joined in the criticism. According to Human Rights Watch, in 2022 India's 'BJP-led government continued its systematic discrimination and stigmatization of religious and other minorities, particularly Muslims.'[354] Amnesty International reported in 2024 that the BJP 'advocated hatred and violence against religious minorities with impunity, particularly Muslims, marking a rise in hate crimes'.[355] Many more such ominous warnings and exhortations could be cited.

Nonetheless, while acknowledging the validity of many of the specific allegations that underlie these conclusions, it can sometimes be difficult to know just how seriously such condemnations should be taken. For comparison, the corresponding United Nations High Commissioner's report on human rights in the United States cited 'racial discrimination, racial profiling, impunity for human rights violations, police brutality, extrajudicial killings, restrictions on freedom of assembly, and the 'criminalization of poverty,' and many other violations.[356] Human Rights Watch believed that Joe Biden's America was characterised by 'entrenched, unequal power structures—largely based on racism, white supremacy, and economic inequality.'[357] Amnesty International found that Americans 'experienced excessive violence based on their actual or perceived sexual orientation or gender identity, especially transgender people from racialized groups' in 2023.[358] Those were just the headline findings. Similarly dire accusations are routinely levelled against other well-established Western democracies.

Clearly, a more systematic approach to measuring human rights is needed. On the status of religious minorities like India's Muslims, there is really only one standard global data source: the Pew Research Center's annual reports on 'Global Restrictions on Religion.' Since 2009, these reports have tracked two annual indices of religious repression, the Government Restrictions Index (GRI) and the Social Hostilities Index (SHI). These two indices are designed to be 'quantifiable, objective measures' of religious persecution.[359] The GRI focuses on 'government actions, policies and laws' that restrict religious practice, while the SHI focuses on 'hostile acts by private individuals, organizations and social groups' against people of other religions.[360] The GRI and SHI are compiled for 198 countries based on twenty questions for the GRI and thirteen questions for the SHI, with some questions including multiple sub-questions. Although Pew does not explicitly spell out the connection, it is implied that the social hostilities tracked by the SHI are attributable to the failure of governments to protect members of religious minorities.

Ever since its first report in 2009, which was based on data for 2006-2008, Pew has rated India as being 'high' in government restrictions on religion, consistently ranking it among the worst 20 per cent of countries on the GRI. In every single year, Pew has rated India as 'very high' in social hostility toward religion, consistently placing it among the world's ten worst performers.

India was rated the second-worst country in the world for social hostility to religion from 2006-2008 through 2011, temporarily improving to third-worst in the world in 2012, then falling back to second-worst in 2013. These were all years of INC government at the national level. India's situation improved slightly in 2014 and 2015 under the BJP, when it was ranked fourth and seventh worst in the world, respectively. It then nosedived to absolute worst in the world for the entire period from 2016-2020, before improving marginally to second-worst in 2021 (the latest year for which data are available), when it was just pipped by Nigeria for the bottom spot.[361]

It is tempting to read into these results the assumption that India exhibits widespread Hindu persecution of Muslims, either facilitated by government negligence or exacerbated by government repression. In the absence of any further details, that would be the default interpretation. But by a fortuitous coincidence, a detailed examination of the reasons for India's poor performance on the GRI and SHI was published in the methodology section of the 2009 Global Restrictions on Religion report.[362] This documentation is revealing, to say the least.

In that report, sample exercises were worked through to illustrate the coding of one question for each of the two indices. For the GRI, the exercise focused on a question about 'Incidents of Government Force Toward Religious Groups.' Five out of the six examples of government repression involved the repression of Christians, not Muslims. The one example involving the use of force against a Muslim was the arrest of a Muslim man who 'eloped' with 'a Hindu female minor'. Pew's coders apparently did not realise that the protection of children from sexual exploitation is considered an appropriate use of police power in all civilised countries. For the SHI, Pew's sample coding exercise focused on a question about 'Incidents of Physical Abuse Motivated by Religious Hatred or Bias in Society.' Of the thirty-one incidents cited, twenty-five targeted Christians, three targeted Hindus, two targeted Muslims, and one targeted a Sikh. In other words, the coding exercise suggested that Muslims are not oppressed in India. If India is one of the worst countries in the world for religious freedom, it is supposedly because of the status of Christians.

To be fair, there is some degree of anti-Christian sentiment in India, but nowhere near enough to make India one of the world's most repressive countries for religious freedom. To quote the leading American authority on Christianity in India:

> ...relative to the size of their respective populations, the number of incidents of anti-Christian violence in India is lower than the number of hate crimes perpetrated against Muslims in the United States (according to FBI data), and would be well below the number of anti-Jewish hate crimes in the US *even if I were severely undercounting Indian incidents of anti-Christian violence.* [emphasis as in the original][363]

Anti-Christian sentiment also lacks the historical and cultural power that charges anti-Muslim sentiment in India. For example, the most prestigious undergraduate college in India is St Stephen's College, Delhi. It is impossible to imagine India's Hindu elite competing to send their children to a college named for a Muslim martyr. Christians make up only 2.3 per cent of the Indian population, and are concentrated in states where they either form the majority of the population or a politically powerful major minority.[364] Christians sometimes face challenges in India, but discrimination against Christians is not considered to be a major social policy problem. India's religious fault line simply is not Hindu-Christian. It is Hindu-Muslim. So why does Pew rely almost entirely on allegations of anti-Christian repression to substantiate its finding that India is one of the most hostile countries in the world for freedom of religion? Because just like democracy rankings, religious freedom rankings have become thoroughly politicised.

The weaponisation of bureaucracy

The peculiar results obtained by Pew's Global Restrictions on Religion project arise directly from the data that underlie Pew's two indices. Pew claims to compile data from nineteen different sources in constructing their indices, including government documents, human rights organisation reports, and United Nations reports.[365] But two sources in particular stand out: the annual reports of the United States Commission on International Religious Freedom (USCIRF) and the US State Department's annual International Religious Freedom reports (which provide the data for the USCIRF reports). Pew's two indices even mirror the structure of the State Department reports, which are divided into sections on 'Government Respect for Religious Freedom' and 'Societal Respect for Religious Freedom' corresponding to the GRI and SHI, respectively. All thirty-seven of the sample codings provided in Pew's inaugural 2009 Global Restrictions on Religion report were based on citations to these two sources. And both sources are concerned overwhelmingly with allegations of discrimination against Christians, not Muslims.

It should come as no surprise that these US government sources would be highly politicised and overwhelmingly focused on the treatment of Christians. Both the USCIRF and the State Department's Office of International Religious Freedom were created by the International Religious Freedom Act of 1998.

According to the *New York Times*, the Act was passed to meet the demands of the 'Christian persecution movement,' which succeeded in framing international religious freedom debates around the persecution of Christians despite the fact that 'what outsiders often label Christian persecution is often a complex brew of racial, economic, political, tribal and religious rivalries.'[366] Writing in the *Christian Science Monitor* immediately after the Act was signed into law, a retired Chief of Staff of the Senate Foreign Relations Committee explained that it represented 'special-interest politics at work.' He explained that the interest group involved was 'mainly evangelical Christians.'[367]

Such special-interest pleading is on full display in the US State Department's International Religious Freedom reports on India. The 2020 report (published in May 2021) documented twenty specific attacks on Christians, 7 on Muslims, and 5 on Hindus. It then went on to note submissions from no fewer than seven non-governmental organisations alleging 293, 279, 208, 200, 135, 75, and 49 attacks on Christians (respectively).[368] When documenting government restrictions on freedom of religion, the report highlighted the fact that 'ten of the 28 states in the country have laws restricting religious conversion.' Freedom to proselytise is a characteristically Christian concern, one that is not shared by adherents of most other religions. As the report notes, India's laws prohibit conversion by force, allurement, inducement, or fraud—restrictions that do not, at face value, seem unreasonable. The report also treats state laws against the slaughter of cows as a challenge to religious freedom. This too reflects an American cultural bias. To put things in perspective, many US states prohibit cat, dog, or horse slaughter, not because these animals are sacred to a majority of the country's population, but for no better reason than that many Americans like to keep these animals as pets.

In addition to political biases, the Pew methodology also suffers from population-size biases, reporting biases, and, ironically, biases arising from true religious pluralism existing in a free society. In particular, many of Pew's questions ask whether or not a particular infringement has ever occurred, not how often these occurred. For example, one of the SHI questions asks 'were there physical assaults motivated by religious hatred or bias?' Obviously, at least one such incident must occur somewhere every year in every country of the world. Amusingly, the most recent Pew report found that there were no religiously motivated assaults at all in Afghanistan—including in such troubled countries as Azerbaijan, Eritrea, Gabon, Mauretania, Turkmenistan, and Vanuatu. In India, a multifaith country of more than 1.4 billion people with an English language media that is free to report on religious conflict, the surfacing of at least one such incident every year is inevitable.

But the main problem with the GRI and SHI is that they rely disproportionately on highly politicised US government sources. In the early years of the indices, those sources mainly reflected the interests of Christian conservatives. That has since evolved, as other organised religious groups have recognised that they too could leverage the bureaucracy to their own ends. Multiple religious lobbies now compete to place commissioners on the USCIRF. They also seek to influence the policy narrative at the top. In addition to creating the USCIRF and mandating annual State Department reports, the International Religious Freedom Act of 1998 also established an Ambassador at Large to oversee both. The first three ambassadors appointed under the Act were closely connected with protestant theological seminaries. The fourth was a prominent Jewish rabbi. The fifth was the former US Senator Sam Brownback of Kansas, an outspoken Christian conservative.

The sixth United States Ambassador at Large for International Religious Freedom, appointed by President Joe Biden in January 2022, was an American of Muslim Indian descent: Rashad Hussain.[369] The first International Religious Freedom report to appear under his watch introduced a new contributor to the India report: the Indian American Muslim Council (IAMC).[370] The next year, the IAMC was cited three times—bizarrely, all three times it alleged violence against Christians in India.[371] By 2022, the State Department's India report was roughly twice as long as it was before Hussain's appointment. It documented seventeen specific attacks on Muslims, overtaking the fifteen attacks on Christians. It also cited a panoply of international human rights organisations that condemned India's treatment of Muslims. Reading the reports, it becomes clear that the Muslim agenda had overtaken the Christian agenda under Hussain's tenure. This leveraging of US government policy tools by Muslim campaigning groups is not necessarily inappropriate. But it does reflect the fact that the US government's international religious freedom reports have become weapons in other countries' political battles.

Hard data on religious discrimination

Fortunately, there is one truly reliable source of social science data on religious discrimination in India. It also comes from Pew. Between November 2019 and March 2020, just before the coronavirus pandemic made face-to-face interviews impossible, the Pew Research Center commissioned a major survey on religion in India. The research was carried out by RTI International, a not-for-profit contract research organisation based in North Carolina. The sample was nationally representative, covering the entire country except four small states and union territories that collectively comprised less than 0.5 per cent of India's population and a few insurgency-affected districts. A total of 29,999 households were surveyed in seventeen different languages. Incredibly, the survey achieved a response rate of 84 per cent in urban areas and 86 per cent in rural areas. The Pew team's headline takeaway from this mammoth survey effort was that:

> Indians of all these religious backgrounds overwhelmingly say they are very free to practice their faiths. Indians see religious tolerance as a central part of who they are as a nation. Across the major religious groups, most people say it is very important to respect all religions to be 'truly Indian.' And tolerance is a religious as well as civic value: Indians are united in the view that respecting *other* religions is a very important part of what it means to be a member of *their own* religious community.[372] [emphasis in the original]

Looking at the specific results for adherents of minority religions, 89 per cent of Muslim Indians and 89 per cent of Christian Indians said they were 'very free' to practise their own religions. Only 2 per cent of each group complained that they were 'not free' to do so.[373] Digging deeper into the survey, 24 per cent of Muslim Indians said that there is 'a lot of discrimination' against Muslims in India, compared to 72 per cent who said there is 'not a lot of discrimination', with the remainder declining to answer the question. The figures for Christians were similar: 18 per cent said there was a lot of discrimination against their community while 77 per cent said there was not. To put these figures into perspective, 16 per cent of Muslims and 14 per cent of Christians said that there was 'a lot of discrimination' against Hindus in India![374] When asked if they had personally experienced religious discrimination in the last twelve months, only 21 per cent of Muslim Indians and 10 per cent of Christians said 'yes' compared to 17 per cent of Hindus.[375]

Levels of self-perceived religious discrimination in India can also be benchmarked against levels of self-perceived racial discrimination in the United States. In March 2021, Pew surveyed 12,055 Americans about their impressions of racial discrimination, using the same questions that they had used in the 2019-2020 India survey. Pew found that that 80 per cent of African-Americans, 46 per cent of Hispanic-Americans, and 42 per cent of Asian-Americans believed that their groups faced 'a lot of discrimination' in the United States, levels far higher than those reported by members of minority religious groups in India.[376] In fact, Pew found that 39 per cent of Americans (not Muslim-Americans, but all Americans) believed that Muslims faced 'a lot' of discrimination in the United States, a figure far higher than the proportion of Muslim Indians who believe that Muslims face discrimination in India.

Even allowing for possible cross-cultural differences in survey responses, it seems clear that self-perceived levels of religious discrimination in India are dwarfed by levels of racial and religious discrimination in America. That comparison is intended neither to condemn the United States nor to exonerate India but to put claims of widespread religious discrimination in India, and specifically the claim that India is one of the worst countries in the world for religious freedom, into perspective. The best social survey data we have strongly indicates that nearly all Muslims and Christians who actually live in India believe that they are free to practice their own religions. Moreover, there is little scientific support for the widely disseminated view that India is a country riven by religious repression. Most of the anti-India evidence on this score is anecdotal, and much of it is highly susceptible to political interference. This is not to suggest that anti-Muslim discrimination does not occur in India; of course it does. On the contrary, it is to affirm that rates of repression and other forms of discrimination against Muslims appear to be relatively low.

Additional circumstantial, but no less scientific, evidence supports this conclusion. For example, although the 2019-2020 Pew survey found that adherents of every major religion in India considered intercommunal violence to be a major problem in the country, adherents of all major religions rated unemployment, corruption, crime, and violence against women to be bigger problems.[377] Muslims were not particularly more likely than members of other religious communities to be concerned with intercommunal violence, expressing slightly higher concern than Hindus and Christians, but less concern than Sikhs. Similarly, when Indians were asked whether or not politicians should 'have influence in religious matters',' 59 per cent of Muslims said yes, second only to Hindus at 64 per cent.[378] This strongly suggests that Muslim Indians are more likely to see the government as a force for preserving their religious rights than as a force of repression. An overwhelming 99 per cent of Muslim Indians report being 'proud' to be Indian (95 per cent of them 'very proud').[379]

This is not the profile of a country where Muslims face widespread and systematic religious persecution. Nor do socioeconomic statistics show much evidence of discrimination against Muslims in India. Unlike African-Americans, whose average levels of income and wealth are far below national averages, Muslim Indians exhibit economic outcomes that are roughly similar to those of majority Hindus, especially after adjusting for the region in which they live.[380]

In terms of specific indicators, a 2022-2023 large-sample survey conducted by the Indian think tank PRICE found that the average income of Muslim families (including government benefits) is 99 per cent of the average income of Hindu families.[381] Moreover, government survey data shows that Muslim households are slightly more likely than Hindu households to fall within the country's top two wealth quintiles, although admittedly these data are not very precise.[382] Muslim Indians lag seriously behind Hindus in education levels, but dramatically outperform Muslims in Pakistan and are roughly on par with Muslims in Bangladesh.[383] Only at the very top is there strong evidence of Muslim disadvantage in India, with Muslims being severely underrepresented among corporate executives and the super-wealthy.[384] This last difference, and the relative lack of Muslims among the national intelligentsia, can reasonably be attributed to the lasting effects of elite family migration during Partition.

Controversies surrounding Muslim immigration into India

Less scientific but nonetheless persuasive evidence that levels of anti-Muslim discrimination in India are much more moderate than human rights advocates claim can be found in population movements. India is bookended by the Islamic republics of Bangladesh in the east and Pakistan in the west. Bangladesh, in particular, has roughly the same level of national income as India as a whole, and borders states of India that are substantially poorer. Yet illegal Muslim migration from Bangladesh into the neighbouring states of India, as well as to the National

Capital Region surrounding Delhi, has caused major political unrest in India. The situation is complicated, with illegal Hindu migration from Bangladesh likely representing a much larger (and also controversial) proportion of the flow, and the statistics are murky. Although extravagant claims about hordes of Muslim Bangladeshis living illegally in India flourish online, in the press, and in parliamentary debates, the true numbers are fundamentally unknown.

Nonetheless, it is certain that a politically relevant number of Muslim Bangladeshis have chosen to live and work illegally in Hindu-majority India rather than remain in Bangladesh—enough to substantiate the inflammatory rhetoric of both populist politicians and human rights activists.[385] This was true even before the 2024 political unrest in Bangladesh. There are no reports of Muslim Indians moving in the opposite direction. The direction of migration flows is a blunt indicator, and it does not rule out the possibility of serious discrimination. For example, in Western Europe there are large inflows of Muslim migrants despite obvious discrimination against them. But in Europe, economic incentives arguably serve to override the deterrence effect of potential discrimination. There are no such disparities between India and Bangladesh. Whatever the true condition of Muslims in India may be, it is apparently not so dire as to deter Muslim illegal immigrants, nor is it sufficiently bad as to prompt Muslim Indians to seek refuge in Bangladesh, Pakistan, the Maldives, or Afghanistan.

It is thus ironic that some of the most trenchant accusations of anti-Muslim discrimination in India focus on the treatment of Muslim illegal immigrants. In 2019, India's BJP government passed the Citizenship Amendment Act (CAA), a law that provides a pathway to citizenship for illegal immigrants of

'Hindu, Sikh, Buddhist, Jain, Parsi or Christian' faith who arrived in India from the officially Muslim countries of Afghanistan, Bangladesh, and Pakistan before 31 December 2014. In one sense, the CAA makes complete sense: non-Muslims are subjected to serious persecution in all three countries, and it is possible to make a prima facie case that any member of a non-Muslim religious minority who flees one of these countries should receive permanent resettlement. It seems equally reasonable that although individual Muslim illegal immigrants from these countries may also qualify for asylum, they would not qualify on the basis of their religion alone. Seen from this perspective, the CAA is at the same time a generous gesture of refugee accommodation and a pragmatic solution to an otherwise intractable problem.

Yet critics of the CAA assert that the law 'violates the secular principles enshrined in the constitution' and labelled it as 'the greatest threat to Indian democracy today.'[386] Amnesty International called it: 'A blow to the Indian constitutional values of equality and religious non-discrimination.'[387] Human Rights Watch claimed that: 'the Indian government is creating legal grounds to strip millions of Muslims of the fundamental right of equal access to citizenship.'[388] The USCIRF gave credence to 'fears that this law is part of an effort to create a religious test for Indian citizenship and could lead to the widespread disenfranchisement of Muslim Indians.'[389] The United Nations Office of the High Commissioner for Human Rights stated in 2019 and reiterated in 2024 that the law 'is fundamentally discriminatory in nature and in breach of India's international human rights obligations.'[390] Political violence following the passage of the CAA led directly to the deaths of 'at least 76 people.'[391]

How could a law opening a pathway to citizenship for refugees spark such shrill condemnation and violent protests? Most of those warning that the CAA would be used to strip Muslim Indians of their rightful citizenship linked the CAA to India's pending National Register of Citizens, suggesting that while Hindus and others who could not document their citizenship would be smuggled in under the CAA, similarly undocumented Muslims would be deported. In a historically fluid border region like that between India and Bangladesh, it is certainly possible that some legitimate Indian citizens would be misidentified as Bangladeshi illegal immigrants. But most of the serious violence surrounding the passage of the CAA occurred in the National Capital Region, far from the Bangladesh border. The largest protests on the Bangladesh border occurred in Assam, an ethnically divided state where local Assamese groups were actually upset that the CAA might grant citizenship to millions of Hindu illegal immigrants from Bangladesh. Muslim illegal immigrants are more likely to live in and around Delhi.

While allegations that the CAA would be used to deny citizenship to millions of Muslim Indians have proven to be wildly overblown—with tragic consequences in loss of life—the controversy did not arise in a vacuum. The BJP only put forward the CAA after winning reelection with a reinforced majority in the 2019 elections. It was one of a suite of post-election policy initiatives that played mainly to its Hindu identitarian electoral base.[392] Although the BJP always maintains, with some credibility, that it governs in the interests of all citizens of India, there is no doubt that politically it appeals to a specifically Hindu, and implicitly Hindu nationalist, conceptualisation of India in its rhetoric, its policies, and even its iconography.[393] It is not the only party to do so, but it is the most prominent party to do so. When the BJP claims that it panders to no one, Hindu or Muslim, the unspoken implication is that it does not pander to Muslims. In this context, the CAA might be seen as a good policy arising from unnecessarily—and seemingly intentionally—divisive politics.

Hate speech, segregation, and social exclusion

Muslim Indians are not going to be disenfranchised by the Modi government, and the available empirical evidence strongly suggests that Muslims do not face high levels of overt discrimination in India. But Muslim Indians do experience endemic hate speech, widespread residential segregation, and obvious social exclusion. Hate speech incidents are widely reported, since they are eagerly picked up and publicised by an active critical media ecosystem. The Center for the Study of Organized Hate, a Washington-based NGO, claimed to have documented 668 'hate speech events' targeting Muslims in India in 2023.[394] The absolute number is meaningless in the absence of comparative data, and the report takes a very wide view of what qualifies as hate speech. More than 20 per cent of the reported incidents were committed by just five people. But some of the incidents cited represent clear attempts by Hindu, often BJP, politicians to gain favour by inciting anti-Muslim hatred.

Most incidents of anti-Muslim hate speech by public figures in India involve local politicians and low-level operatives. For example, one state-level BJP parliamentarian told a crowd: 'I want to tell the *landyas* [circumcised Muslims] involved in love jihad that they are already cut in half and we will cut them in whole.'[395] This particular politician was suspended at the time, but the fact remains that the BJP tolerates Islamophobia within its ranks, and arguably uses such less-prominent figures to test controversial stands while top party leaders maintain plausible deniability. This does not apply only to the BJP. Some of the most extreme anti-Muslim hate speech comes from politicians in regional parties, including Christian parties. There is also much anti-Hindu hate speech emanating from communist and Dravidian parties. Although anti-religious hate speech is illegal in India and 95 per cent of Indians say that 'to respect all religions' is 'important to be truly Indian', the use of provocative language to leverage religious animosities is widespread in political campaigning.[396] Inevitably, the brunt of these attacks falls on Muslims.

Intercommunal animosity is facilitated by the high levels of residential segregation between Muslims and other religious groups in India.[397] It is difficult to study residential segregation by religion, since the relevant census data are not made available to researchers because the topic is considered too sensitive.[398] One creative attempt to get around this embargo by laboriously compiling data from 'over two million' separate local-area census publications in multiple languages found that the urban residential segregation of Muslim Indians was roughly on par with that of African-Americans in the United States.[399] In a follow-up study using the same methods, it was found that levels of Muslim segregation in rural areas was only slightly lower than in urban ones.[400] Even these results may fail to capture the true level of segregation, since Muslims and others may reside in the same census enumeration area but still live very separate lives.

In 2024, Hindu residents of a public housing complex in Gujarat filed a police complaint opposing the allocation of a unit in their community to a Muslim family.[401] The petition was dismissed, but the point was made. According to the 2019-2020 Pew Religion in India survey, 36 per cent of Hindus said they would not be willing to accept a Muslim as a neighbour despite the obvious political incorrectness of such an answer.[402] A further 5 per cent refused to answer the question. On the same survey, only 16 per cent of Muslim Indians said they would not accept a Hindu neighbour. In fact, Muslim Indians are much more accepting of Hindus as neighbours than they are of Christians, Sikhs, Buddhists, or Jains. That may simply reflect the fact that Hindus, who make up 80 per cent of the population of India, are in effect the 'default' neighbours. Viewed more optimistically, it might represent an openness among most Muslim Indians to being included in the national mainstream, if only the implicitly Hindu mainstream will have them.

Although social exclusion is often conflated with poverty and as a result, measured using statistical indicators like income, education, and occupational attainment, it is in reality a much more nebulous concept. A group can face social exclusion without being materially disadvantaged; indeed, there are some examples of communities that experience social exclusion despite enjoying superior statistical indicators. For example, even though Asian-Americans have far higher average levels of income, education, and occupational attainment than most other Americans, they are underrepresented at all levels of American politics, as well as in the military and intelligence services.[403] Representation is only a blunt indicator of social exclusion, but it makes the point. Even statistics on residential segregation don't reveal how often people make friends with their neighbours, or how their neighbours feel about them. The reality of social exclusion is to be found in the subtle ways people are 'othered', or made to feel excluded from the national mainstream, or simply not included at all.

In an attempt to capture the elusive essence of social

exclusion, sociologists often turn to representation in film. This method has particular relevance in India, where Muslim actors generally cannot be distinguished from Hindu ones on the basis of physical traits, but Muslim characters are immediately identifiable on the basis of their names. Thus, the situation of Muslims in Indian films is different both from that of African-Americans in Hollywood, who are easily identified visually, and homosexuals in Hollywood, who are identifiable only if they 'out' themselves behaviourally. Muslim actors are widely believed to be substantially overrepresented in India's dominant Hindi-language film industry, though it is difficult to pin down any exact numbers. Yet despite the large number of Muslim actors in Bollywood, there are reportedly 'very few films based on Muslim protagonists'.[404] Where characters are represented as being Muslim, they tend to be stereotyped as Muslims facing challenges arising from their Muslimness, instead of being portrayed as ordinary Indians who happen to be Muslim.[405]

The supposedly negative portrayal of Muslim Indians in Bollywood films is a common trope of critical social science, one perpetuated by the strategic selection of films to analyse and the conflation of 'Pakistani' with 'Muslim' in the analyses. Obviously, in any Indian film portraying conflict between India and Pakistan, the enemies are bound to be Muslim. The real evidence for Muslim social exclusion isn't that separatists and terrorists tend to be portrayed as Muslim, or even that when Muslim actors play action heroes, their characters are often scripted as Hindu. Much more indicative of the social exclusion of Muslim Indians is the fact that when they are visible, they tend to be portrayed as Muslims dealing with Muslim issues in a majority Hindu country. Social exclusion means that the Muslim Indian is the 'other'; whether that 'other' is good or bad is less relevant than that the 'other' is a person marked out for special treatment distinct from the expectations that apply to the rest of society.

The institutional aftershocks of Partition

The separation of Muslims from mainstream Indian society is more than a matter of physical segregation and social exclusion. One of the biggest barriers to the full social inclusion of Muslims in India may be the persistence of colonial-era Muslim family laws under which Muslim Indians are governed by a set of laws that are different from the rest of society, marking them out as a distinct community and acting as a definite barrier to intermarriage. When Jawaharlal Nehru reformed India's family laws in the mid-1950s, he exempted Muslims and Christians from the new civil codes. Applying a terminology that echoed the pre-independence Hindutva rhetoric of V D Savarkar and the early RSS, Nehru's Hindu Marriage Act (1955), Hindu Succession Act (1956), Hindu Minority and Guardianship Act (1956), and Hindu Adoptions and Maintenance Act (1956) applied only to Hindus, Jains, Buddhists and Sikhs. Decades later, the INC still opposes the modernisation of India's Muslim and Christian family laws.[406] This opposition is widely viewed as a political sop to the patriarchal Muslim religious establishment.

It is inherently contradictory to argue that Muslims are equal citizens of India while at the same time maintaining that they require special and inherently regressive family laws. At the time of the passage of the Hindu code bills, the RSS had argued vehemently against them. But the organisation's affiliated political party, the BJP, later came to embrace the principle that India should have a uniform civil code, a policy position that was rebadged by Narendra Modi in August 2024 as support for a 'secular civil code.' Whether this change of heart was born out of a newfound commitment to secular liberal principles or out of petulant resentment over the loss of the traditional Hindu family laws, it has always been good politics. The BJP rightly argues that a uniform civil code for people of all religions would be a fulfilment of the Indian Constitution's aspiration that 'the State shall endeavour to secure for the citizens a uniform civil code throughout the territory of India' and a boon to Muslim women.[407] Meanwhile, critics of the BJP consider its advocacy of a uniform civil code to be a cynical anti-Muslim 'dog-whistle' to its voter base.[408]

Either way, the lack of a uniform civil code clearly reinforces Muslim 'otherness' in India. It also ties the image of Muslims in India to regressive social policy and family practices. India is the world's only liberal democracy where Muslim men are entitled to preferential treatment over Muslim women in divorce, inheritance, and child custody. In making a legal distinction between Muslims and other citizens of India, it perpetuates the logic of Partition and encourages the continuing characterisation of Muslim Indians as forming a separate political community within India. Indeed, much of the literature on Muslim underrepresentation in Indian politics focusses on the wide dispersion of Muslim voters throughout India, which results in a relative lack of Muslim-majority electoral districts.[409] The implicit logic is that Muslims form a separate community that should be represented by Muslims—the same logic that led to the creation of Pakistan.

The representation of Muslims in independent India's politics has always been low. Muslim candidates won only 4.4 per cent of the parliamentary seats in India's 2024 national elections, and the BJP has not had a Muslim member of parliament since it took the reins of government in 2014. But levels of Muslim representation were similarly low in the INC heyday of the 1950s-1960s, when Nehru could have placed as many Muslim members into parliament as he pleased.[410] In the 2024 elections, 38 per cent of Muslim Indians reported voting for the INC, implying that Muslims accounted for more than 25 per cent of all INC votes.[411] Yet only 7 of the INC's ninety-nine members of parliament are Muslim, far below its share of the Muslim vote. By contrast, only around 2.5 per cent of the BJP's voters seem to have been Muslim. While the complete lack of Muslims on the BJP's parliamentary benches may be striking, proportionally it is the INC that displays the bigger deficit.

The lack of Muslim representation in parliament reflects a broader lack of Muslim representation in all aspects of Indian political life. Outside of the Muslim-majority state of Jammu and Kashmir, which is now a union territory, there have only ever been six Muslim chief ministers of Indian states—and none since 1982.[412] The longest term served by any of them was only twenty-seven months. Of the eighty-seven national government department secretaries (chief civil servants) in mid-2022, only 2 were Muslim.[413] In 2023, the Indian Civil Services, which recruit based on highly competitive examinations, admitted only fifty-one Muslims in its class of 1,016 qualifying candidates (5.0 per cent).[414] Even that was a record year. The Muslim proportion was only 2.8 per cent in 2022 and 2.5 per cent in 2021. The situation is the same in the judiciary. As of mid-2024, only 6 per cent of independent India's Supreme Court judges have been Muslim, with similar proportions prevailing in lower courts.[415]

Viewed from a historical perspective, these statistics should perhaps come as no surprise. At the partition of British India in 1947, most Muslims living in the areas that would become part of independent India stayed in India. Those who migrated to Pakistan, however, were 'significantly more literate' and 'significantly less likely to be in agricultural professions'.[416] When the British Indian Army was divided in 1947, Muslims from areas that remained in India had the option to transfer to Pakistan; nearly all senior officers ultimately chose to do so.[417] The story for civilian colonial officers was equally lopsided. At the time of Partition, there were 101 Muslim officers in the Indian Civil Service and the Indian Political Service (the direct antecedents to today's Indian Administrative Service). Of these, at least '95 opted for service in Pakistan; the others remained in India or retired'. Forty-four of the 101 Muslim officers hailed from provinces that remained entirely in India, with most of the rest originating in the divided provinces of Bengal (eighteen) and Punjab (twenty-seven).[418] And of course, nearly all Muslim politicians opted for Pakistan.

Thus, although independent India remained roughly 10 per cent Muslim after Partition, a figure that has risen to nearly 15 per cent today, almost the entire Muslim political class had left the country. Many Muslim business families may have stayed, but the Muslim intelligentsia left—even those who lived in places like Delhi, Bombay (now Mumbai), and Madras (now Chennai), far from the borders of the new state of Pakistan. The after effects of this exodus are still apparent in India today, because occupations tend to run in families. For example, more than half of all Indian Civil Services candidates are themselves the children of government employees—though not necessarily of elite civil servants—with anecdotal memories suggesting that the proportion was even higher in the past.[419] The so-called 'social reproduction' of professions is not unique to India, but the statistical deficit of Muslims inevitably reinforces the notion that they form a separate and subaltern civic community, and that Muslims are not welcome in India's top state institutions.

The inflated rhetoric of activist scholarship

For all the controversies surrounding the status of Muslims in India, it does not play a direct role in the supposed deterioration in the quality of Indian democracy recorded in the flagship indices published by the major democracy rating organisations, although it does contribute a minor fraction to V-Dem's secondary Liberal Democracy Index. Not that you would know it from the press coverage; it is a widespread practice to conflate India's low V-Dem ranking with supposed discrimination against Muslims. Such confusion is sometimes promoted by V-Dem itself. In an article on religion and political polarisation in India, V-Dem lamented the stylized fact that 'authorities also deemed millions of Muslims ineligible to vote in the 2019 general elections because of a lack of documentation'.[420] The only citation provided in support for this bold statement was a link to an article appearing in the Qatar-based news portal *Al Jazeera*—hardly an unbiased source.

The *Al Jazeera* article itself references the claim to the leader of a non-governmental organisation called Missing Voters, who personally 'estimates that around 40 million' Muslim citizens are 'not on India's voting rolls'.[421] As of early 2025, the Missing Voters website was no longer operational, though many articles in the global media continue to reference the organisation's claims. When the Missing Voters website was operational, it attributed the 'around 40 million' claim to an article published in 2018, a year before the 2019 elections, that used creative statistical methods to estimate that 'nearly one quarter of Muslim adults in [the Indian state of] Karnataka were out of the electoral rolls'.[422] If you apply the figure 'nearly one quarter' to the Muslim population of 172 million recorded in the 2011, you can just about arrive at the estimate that 'around 40 million' Muslims were disenfranchised in the 2019 election

Even this figure is derived from a single study of highly questionable validity. The study relied on the extraction of data from scanned paper documents, finding that households in Karnataka with identifiably Muslim names matched with voter registration records at lower rates than households with non-Muslim names.[423] That is indeed provocative. But to complicate matters, electoral records in English had to be matched with household records in the Kannada language. It is quite possible that Muslim names translate less well into the Kannada script than native Karnatakan names. Many other reasons could be imagined for the differential matching rate of Muslim and other voters. It seems that no follow-up interviews were conducted to find out if anyone captured in the computer records was, in reality, not registered to vote.

The Election Commission of India registered 911,950,734 voters for the 2019 elections, substantially all of the estimated adult population at the time. If 40 million Muslims were missing, where were they? After every election, scattered reports emerge of people who went to vote but were denied a ballot. That said, 40 million people would certainly be missed, especially when they are members of a highly politicised minority. Much of the literature on the status of Muslims in India follows the same formula: serious social problems get lost amidst a forest of inflated claims, inflammatory rhetoric, and manufactured grievances. Shrill warnings like the assertion that 'the country is teetering at stage 8 (persecution) with the indicators of stage 9 (extermination) [of the 10 stages of genocide] becoming more and more visible' are worse than ridiculous.[424] Wash, rinse, and repeat, and it's not long before a liberal democracy has been turned into an electoral autocracy.

Extreme and often mendacious claims are found everywhere in relation to the status of Muslims in India. In particular, the broad convergence between Muslim and Hindu social indicators is often obscured by the intentional manipulation of statistics. It is a common practice to compare Muslim Indians specifically to 'upper' caste or 'general category' Hindus in India, instead of comparing them with the Hindu population as a whole. This comparison inevitably makes Muslims seem severely disadvantaged. In a similarly deceptive vein, a widely disseminated 2022 report from Oxfam attributed any unexplained differences between Muslims and other Indians to 'discrimination'. Even non-statisticians can tell that the Oxfam results are flawed when they read that 'discrimination' accounted for 21.9 per cent of the difference in employment levels between Muslims and non-Muslims in 2018-19, but only 3.7 per cent of the difference in 2019-20.[425] Either discrimination against Muslims virtually disappeared in the middle of 2019, or the entire analysis is meaningless.

Nor are such shenanigans limited to social activists. Academics engage in them too. For example, India's highly respected Centre for the Study of Developing Societies conducts large-scale surveys of the electorate before and after every parliamentary election called the National Election Studies (NES). In the 2024 post-poll questionnaire, they asked the provocative question:

> Some people believe that Muslims are treated unfairly by the state authorities, while others say that they are treated just like any other citizens of India. What is your opinion?[426]

Shockingly, 43 per cent of Muslim Indians agreed with this proposition. A study based on the survey interpreted this to mean that Muslim Indians experience 'a deep sense of insecurity'.[427] This study went on to warn that:

> 54% of the Muslim respondents consider that they are not 'as safe as any other citizen in the country' and 11% of them say that they are 'not safe at all'. This perception stands in stark contrast with those of the Hindus–whatever their caste–who appear in a rather complete denial of the Muslims' condition: 60%–62% of them claim that Muslims are equally safe.[428]

This must sound truly alarming—to people with no training in survey methodology. Any properly trained social scientist would realise that these figures mean very little in the absence of comparable data for Hindu and other Indians. It is very likely that many Hindus similarly feel that they are 'treated unfairly by state authorities', and that they are 'not as safe as' others. If the NES had asked these questions of Hindus, and large majorities had answered 'yes' to both, this likely would have been presented as evidence of Hindu majoritarian chauvinism. The narrative would have been that Hindu Indians bought into the Islamophobic narrative that their Muslim neighbours were dangerous criminals being shielded by an overindulgent state. Careful, sceptical, objectively-minded social scientists know better than to take statistics like these at face value.

The sad reality is that when it comes to India, many social scientists are not objective. They have transformed themselves from academics into advocates. A group of India-focused professors at prestigious Western universities has even banded together under the label, South Asia Scholar Activist

Collective.[429] When scholars become self-declared activists, it is difficult to have confidence in the impartiality of their research.

Nationhood as a work in progress

According to the rating system used by V-Dem to classify democracies, the United States was an 'electoral autocracy' until 1920 primarily because women were denied the vote, and only became a full 'liberal democracy' in 1969 when African-Americans achieved equality before the law. Such labels are easy to ridicule, as after all, by the criteria laid down by V-Dem, the archetype of all Western democracy, ancient Athens, would have been classified as a 'closed autocracy' on a par with its arch-rival, Sparta. Admittedly, V-Dem was not designed to be applied to ancient democracies. The example is only meant to illustrate the fact that labels can often be even more misleading than the statistics that underlie them. By any mainstream dictionary definition of the term, the United States has always been a liberal democracy. The problem is that, for nearly two centuries, it was a liberal democracy that excluded substantial sections of the national community from full participation in the democratic nation.

The relative lack of participation of Muslim Indians in India's national community is reminiscent of the situation of African-Americans in the late twentieth century. Like African-Americans in the United States, Muslims have full civil rights in India. In fact, they have always had full civil rights. But unlike African-Americans, Muslim Indians have not yet been brought into their country's national mainstream. In the twenty-first century, it has become common to see and hear African-American commentators speaking on all important issues. They are not restricted to commenting on race. Their participation in mainstream debates has become widespread despite the fact that African-Americans as a group continue to suffer much lower levels of education and income than other Americans. Whether this represents real progress or is merely the result of selective recruitment is irrelevant from the perspective of social inclusion. African-Americans may face disadvantage and even discrimination, but they are fully engaged—and seen to be fully engaged—in the country's national conversations. No one doubts their Americanness.

The same cannot be said for the 'Indianness' of Muslim Indians. In Pew's 2019-2020 Religion in India survey, 81 per cent of Hindu Indians said it was 'important' to be Hindu in order to be 'truly Indian'.[430] Perhaps even more concerning, 44 per cent of Muslim Indians agreed. Unfortunately, corrosive attitudes like these are promoted by politicians on all sides. The INC and its intellectual surrogates find it politically useful to stoke fear among Muslim Indians that they are in constant danger of disenfranchisement and potential expulsion from the country.[431] Meanwhile, the BJP and its intellectual ecosystem stoke equally damaging myths about Muslim Indian disloyalty and supposed support for Pakistan.[432] Many Western institutions are also strangely complicit in perpetuating the idea that Muslims can never be full participants in the Indian nation through their arguments that Muslim Indians should be represented by Muslim parliamentarians and through their support for Kashmiri separatism. Positions like these, in effect, endorse the 'two-nation theory' that led to the creation of Pakistan nearly a century ago.

Ultimately, however, neither India's politicians nor the international human rights community can tell people what to think. The challenge must be taken up by Indian society, and first and foremost by Hindu Indian society. In a country that is 80 per cent Hindu, Muslims will never experience full social inclusion unless Hindus actively work to invite them into the national mainstream. For Muslim Indians to be fully accepted as 'truly' Indian, Hindu Indians must come to accept them. That said, the Hindu nationalist argument that Muslim Indians must also come to the table is equally valid. The dogmatically liberal position that Muslim Indians bear no special responsibility to prove their loyalty is morally incontrovertible but sociologically illiterate. After all, Hindu Indians cannot be forced to welcome Muslim neighbours, or even to have Muslim neighbours at all. Pragmatically speaking, if Muslim Indians want to be accepted into India's national mainstream, they have to take positive steps to join it.

That means integrating instead of separating. The political scientist Maidul Islam suggests that the use of 'a defensive strategy by Indian Muslims has often led to issues of minority identity and minority affairs being confused with communal ones,' though he finds this internalisation of 'otherness' to be unsurprising in light of 'persistent socio-economic deprivation, educational backwardness, and the assertive Hindu-nationalist politics.'[433] His sentiments on self-othering are echoed by INC elder statesman K Rahman Khan, who argues that 'the migration of a large number of modern-educated Muslims to Pakistan in the wake of Partition created a massive leadership vacuum,' and that those who remained 'never worked out a roadmap of how to work together with the other communities and how to live amicably with them in a plural society.' According to Khan, 'promoting positivity, rather than merely denouncing negativity,' is the best route to greater Muslim integration into Indian society.[434]

Both Islam and Khan in their own ways distinguish between Muslim Indians who want to be free to practice their own religion while otherwise participating fully in the Indian mainstream and those who aspire to live separately in parallel Muslim-only habitats. Although neither would deny the right of individual Muslims to choose the second option, both doubt the wisdom of the entire community taking that course. Maidul Islam would like to see efforts to end Muslim social exclusion focus less on religious identity and more on socioeconomic and political representation. Rahman Khan believes that all Muslim children should be exposed to a secular education curriculum, even students who study in religious schools, and that Muslims should participate more fully in secular civil society institutions. Others, of course, disagree: Muslim Indians are just as diverse in their opinions as any other community. What is clear is that full Muslim integration into the Indian national mainstream will require both a meaningful effort by Hindu Indians to foster greater social inclusion and the willingness of Muslims to be included.

To appropriate a phrase from American history, Muslims can best be described, unironically, as a separate but equal minority community within India. Attributing this 'othering' to the legacies of Partition is a partially valid explanation, but a wholly unacceptable excuse. The fact that prior generations of Muslim intellectuals, most of whom left for Pakistan and all of whom are now dead, rejected inclusion in independent India does not imply that current generations of ordinary Muslims should be excluded from full membership in the Indian nation. For India to survive and thrive as a democratic nation-state, all parties, whether domestic or international, will have to accept that all of today's Indians are 'Indian', regardless of their religion, or even of their ancestors' loyalties. History is complicated, non-linear, and often unjust, but it cannot be undone.

Not Only Toleration

India has given the world many gurus. For most Westerners, Mahatma Gandhi immediately springs to mind, although inside India, his reputation as a guru or teacher is often overshadowed by his more substantial—and sometimes controversial—legacy as a practical politician. Others may think of Maharishi Mahesh Yogi (1917?-2008), who mentored the Beatles and promoted transcendental meditation throughout the world. But the quintessential guru of modern India is the Bengali monk Narendranath Datta (1863-1902), who is better known under his assumed name of Vivekananda ('taking pleasure in wisdom'). Although he died before reaching his fortieth birthday, Swami Vivekananda was one of the leading Hindu reformers of his era and an important proto-nationalist. He founded the Ramakrishna Mission, a major social service organisation headquartered in Kolkata that administers hundreds of non-denominational schools, hospitals, and orphanages across the country. Swami Vivekananda is near-universally revered throughout India not only for his wisdom, his teaching, and his service, but also for his patriotism.

The role played by Swami Vivekananda in the formation of India's national consciousness cannot be overstated. The French author Romain Rolland (1866-1944) wrote that 'the Indian nationalist movement smouldered for a long time until Vivekananda's breath blew the ashes into flame'.[435] The Indian political scientist Rajshree Dutta notes that 'the makers of the Constitution were deeply influenced by the socio-political thoughts of Vivekananda' and that even today, 'Constitutional developments are widely based on his ideas.'[436] Though Vivekananda studiously eschewed party politics, both the INC and the BJP compete to claim the mantle of his legacy.[437] The prominent INC intellectual Shashi Tharoor describes himself as a 'passionate follower' of the Swami, and Vivekananda's namesake Narendra Modi believes that the RSS was founded to fulfil the Swami's vision of a revitalised Mother India.[438] Legend has it that Rabindranath Tagore advised: 'if you want to know India, study Vivekananda. In him, there is everything positive and nothing negative.'[439]

Whether or not the Tagore quote is genuine, the important thing is that no one seems to question it. Modern India has produced no more inspiring spiritual teacher than Swami Vivekananda. Despite his relative youth and early death, Vivekananda was extraordinarily successful in translating the highly refined arguments of Hindu theologians into workaday lessons that ordinary people could understand. He is also remembered in the United States, where he founded Vedanta Societies in New York and San Francisco and influenced a generation of progressive Harvard intellectuals. The first major milestone of his public life was a speech at the 1893 Chicago Parliament of the World's Religions, which became the first entry in his collected works. In Chicago, Vivekananda introduced the American public to 'a religion which has taught the world both tolerance and universal acceptance,' proclaiming that Hindus 'believe not only in universal toleration, but we accept all religions as true'.[440]

This concept of the unity of all religions was indeed at the centre of Vivekananda's ministry, both in India and in the West. He told the Chicago Parliament that the 'wonderful doctrine' preached in the *Bhagavad Gita* was that:

> *Whosoever comes to Me, through whatsoever form, I reach him; all men are struggling through paths which in the end lead to me.*[441] [emphasis in the original]

This is drawn from a verse in the *Gita* in which Lord Krishna tells the warrior Arjuna that 'people follow my path in all places', assuring Arjuna that he appears 'whenever there is a decline in *dharma*.'[442] Vivekananda repeatedly stressed this message that different forms of worship ultimately led to the same God, though he was well aware that Muslims and Christians generally did not accept this principle. Of course, Vivekananda did not speak for all Hindus, and many strains of Hindu practice remain parochial and exclusionary to this day. But his message was broadly representative of the thinking and practice of the Hindu reform movements of the nineteenth and early twentieth centuries.

Despite his short life, Swami Vivekananda undertook two global lecture tours in 1897-1899 and 1899-1902. One of his standard lines on these tours seems to have been that Hindus 'hold that religion embraces all religions.' He emphasised: 'We tolerate everything but intoleration.'[443] In expressing this sentiment, Vivekananda anticipated Western liberal thinking by more than half a century. Philosophically minded readers may recognise in Vivekananda's maxim the seeds of the 'paradox of tolerance' famously described by Karl Popper (1902-1994) in his 1945 book *The Open Society and Its Enemies*:

> Rationalism ... implies the recognition of the claim to tolerance, at least of all those who are not intolerant themselves. [...] If we extend unlimited tolerance even to those who are intolerant, if we are not prepared to defend a tolerant society against the onslaught of the intolerant, then the tolerant will be destroyed, and tolerance with them.[444]

Popper proclaimed 'in the name of tolerance' that intolerance should be criminalised, and like 'incitement to murder, or to kidnapping, or to the revival of the slave trade' be 'placed outside the law.' The secular liberal hero would, by this standard, have outlawed much provocative speech, and sent many a firebrand Christian or Muslim preacher to prison. Popper was very clear about this:

> I do not imply ... that we should always suppress the utterance of intolerant philosophies .... But we should claim the *right* to suppress them if necessary even by force.[445]

By comparison, Swami Vivekananda's tolerance was much more humane. He was aware that tolerance could not be imposed on an unwilling interlocutor, and sought a more accommodative path toward inclusion. He understood that 'the word "toleration" has acquired an unpleasant association with the conceited man who ... looks down on his fellow-creatures with pity' and considered this 'a horrible state of mind.' Emphasising the universality, not only of religion, but of the human experience *tout court*, he taught that:

> We are all travelling the same way, towards the same goal,

> but by different paths made by the necessities of the case to suit diverse minds. We must become many-sided, indeed we must become Protean in character, so as not only to tolerate, but to do what is much more difficult, to sympathise, to enter into another's path, and feel *with him* in his aspirations and seeking after God.[446] [emphasis in original]

That is to say, while each pursuing our *sva* (own) *dharma*, we are all pursuing *dharma*. The implication that people should thus embrace 'the idea, not only of toleration, but of sympathy' was a theme that Swami Vivekananda returned to again and again in his sermons.[447] It contrasts sharply with Popper's approach. Both Popper and Vivekananda believed that intolerance could not be tolerated, but while Popper would oppose it with the force of state institutions (if necessary), Vivekananda would oppose it with 'acceptance, and not exclusion.'[448] That may be easier said than done, but the difference in attitude between Popper and Vivekananda is emblematic of the difference between Western and Indian responses to the challenge of peaceful coexistence in a pluralistic society.

Hindu and Muslim ideals of reform

Swami Vivekananda was famous for promoting 'the idea, not only of toleration, but of sympathy,' but he was hardly the first Indian to do so. In India, the rhetoric of religious tolerance is as old as the stones themselves. In the third century BC, Emperor Ashoka the Great ruled over most of what would later become modern India. He reigned nearly a millennium before the birth of Islam, but already India was riven by religious strife. In Emperor Ashoka's time, this involved multiple Hindu, Buddhist, and Jain sects in continual competition for scholarly prestige and imperial favour. Ashoka sided first with one, then with another of these sects, before adopting a policy of 'ecumenism.'[449] Repeatedly citing the 'gift of *dharma*,' Ashoka had carved into the living stones of his kingdom, a set of edicts proclaiming the idea, not only of toleration, but of sympathy. The most famous of these edicts, Rock Edict XII, reads in part:

> One should honour another man's sect, for by doing so one increases the influence of one's own sect and benefits that of the other man; while by doing otherwise one diminishes the influence of one's own sect and harms the other man's. [...] Therefore, concord is to be commended, so that men may hear one another's principles and obey them.[450]

Ashoka's edicts are amenable to multiple translations, and not all translations of Rock Edict XII represent its message in such clearly religious terms. Even accepting that Ashoka sought to promote 'concord' among sects (religions), the edict admits of a reading in which an exasperated king simply commands his subjects to stop bickering and keep the peace. And, of course, there is no way to know for sure the extent to which the enlightened rhetoric of Ashoka's edicts was reflected in the actual governance practices of the Ashokan state. All of these caveats notwithstanding, the important point for understanding modern Indian nationhood is that Indians have chosen to present the image of a tolerant Ashoka as the very model of ancient kingship. The Lion Capital of Ashoka is the state emblem of India, and the *chakra* or wheel of Ashoka appears on the Indian flag.

Other narratives for the foundation of a new nation were available, even from the edicts of Ashoka. In Rock Edict XIII, Ashoka noted that after he conquered the neighbouring Kalinga kingdom:

> People deported from there numbered 150,000; those killed there totalled 100,000; and almost that many died [of other causes]. Thereafter, now that the Kalingas have been secured, the intense study of dharma, love of dharma and instruction in dharma occupy the Beloved of Gods [i.e., Ashoka himself].[451]

It probably gave little comfort to the Kalingas that their extermination afforded the 'Beloved of the Gods' the leisure to focus on the contemplation of *dharma*. Hindu fundamentalists might have taken from this edict a license to murder for the establishment of *dharma*. Almost any religious text can be used as the basis for holy war. Hindu Indians chose instead a humane interpretation of their own religion, setting their country on a tolerant course.

This was not inevitable. In British colonial India, there were spiritual leaders of all religions who actively promoted religious intolerance, distrust, hatred, and separation, while some even engaged in forced conversion, sanctified rape, and mass murder. Wistful elite memoirs recalling a bygone era of intercommunal harmony in the decades before Partition are flatly contradicted by the historical record. During the independence struggle, Muslim League leaders in particular emphatically did not call for religious tolerance. Instead, when the critical moment arrived, they called on their Muslim followers to take 'direct action' against their Hindu neighbours. Obviously, horrific acts were committed on both sides in the cataclysm of Partition. The difference is that while the country's most prominent Hindu leaders were publicly pleading for restraint, its most prominent Muslim leaders were vigorously stoking the flames of violence.

That too was a choice. There were Muslim reformers in late nineteenth and early twentieth century India who taught religious tolerance and 'acceptance, not exclusion.' The most notable of these was the Sufi philosopher and musician Hazrat Inayat Khan (1882-1927). In many ways, Inayat Khan's career paralleled that of Swami Vivekananda, who was his near contemporary. Both preached the unity of all religions; both embarked on extensive ministries to the West; both died young. Hazrat Inayat Khan paid homage to a succession of religious 'Masters' running from Adam through Krishna and Jesus to Mohammed. He quoted parallel passages from the Bible, the *Bhagavad Gita*, and the *Quran* to teach that all four were manifestations of 'one single Master,' and that it was only through ignorance that people 'clung to the name, forgetting the true being.'[452] Insisting that 'the Sufi in his tolerance allows everyone to have his own path,' he concluded that:

> Therefore the Sufi concerns himself little with the name of the religion or the place of worship. All places are sacred enough for his worship, and all religions convey to him the religion of his soul. 'I saw Thee in the sacred Ka'ba [the holy Kaaba of Mecca] and in the temple of the idol also Thee I saw.'[453]

Such liberality, particularly with regard to idolatry, never gained much traction in India, and Hazrat Inayat Khan is today mainly remembered in the West. India's most successful Muslim reform movements took a very different turn. The puritanical Deobandi movement that was founded in 1866 excluded many Muslims from the community of believers—to say nothing of Hindu 'idolators.'[454] Among the thousands of *fatwas* issued by Deobandi scholars were rulings that 'discouraged social and business intercourse with Hindus ... and deemed illegitimate the appearance of being Hindu, whether in dress, hair style, or the use of brass instead of copper vessels.'[455] The Deobandis' fiercest competitors, the Barelvi movement inspired by the Sufi scholar Ahmed Raza Khan (1856–1921), was similarly intolerant. In 1902, Raza Khan issued a fatwa to the effect that 'all those scholars who did not believe in his ideas' were 'devils and heretics.'[456]

The most famous Muslim reformer in the history of British India, Sir Sayyid Ahmad Khan (1817-1898), founded the Aligarh movement to promote modern scientific education. At the centre of this movement was the creation of the Aligarh Muslim University, whose scholars provided the intellectual case for the partition of India, spawning the establishment of the Muslim League and leading to the creation of Pakistan.[457] Jinnah left the bulk of his estate to educational institutions founded by followers of Sir Sayyid Ahmad Khan, though the Pakistani courts did not allow the portion due to Aligarh Muslim University to be paid out.[458] The university that had played such an outsized role in Partition itself ended up in India.

Reform movements like these were never going to form the basis for a tolerant and inclusive postcolonial society, and proved difficult to integrate into the mainstream of what was, inevitably, a majority Hindu nation. Their institutional heirs in India today include organisations like the Deobandi Jamiat Ulema-e-Hind (Council of Scholars of India), its missionary cousin the Tablighi Jamaat (Preachers Society), and the fundamentalist Jamaat-e-Islami Hind (Society of Islam of India) come across as sullen and reluctant participants in the pluralistic society that is today's India. They publicly express their loyalty to the Indian Constitution and rightly insist on the legal status of Muslim Indians as equal citizens of the Indian state. But they seem wholly uninterested in inculcating among Muslim Indians the 'feeling of connectedness and attachment to the nation' that the sociologist Jeffrey Prager said was an indispensable prerequisite for democratic stability.[459]

The Establishment's tryst with history

Finding a place for Muslims in the Indian nation means finding a role for Muslims in India's national story. Muslim Indian civil society has, for the most part, shown little interest in taking up that challenge. Before Partition, the overwhelming majority of Muslim Indian intellectuals sought instead to define themselves as Indian Muslims: not as Muslim members of the Indian nation, but as Indian members of the Muslim nation. Note the specific juxtaposition of adjective and noun. Over the last hundred years, the use of 'Indian Muslims' has consistently predominated over that of 'Muslim Indians' in English language books by a ratio of approximately twenty-five to one.[460] The construction 'Hindu Indians' is also more common than 'Indian Hindus,' but by a ratio of only two to one. Even allowing for differences in meaning and context, it is clear that English language writers tend to treat Muslim Indians as Muslims first and foremost. Yet if both international commentators and Muslim Indians themselves agree that the primary identity of Muslim Indians is 'Muslim,' can Hindu Indians be blamed for taking the bait?

Of course, not all Indians have accepted this othering narrative. Ever since independence, the main responsibility for integrating Muslim Indians into the country's national story has been taken up by INC and Marxist intellectuals, most of them Hindus and all of them educated in English. This resolutely secularist remnant of colonial India's old comprador class lives on as the 'Establishment,' a loose assemblage of elite individuals who are more readily identified by their cultural shibboleths than by their membership in any particular organisation. To be a member of the Establishment means to be liberally educated, fashionably socialist, a native English speaker, a reader—or better, a writer—of serious books, an atheist (or at least an agnostic), a drinker of alcohol in a country that is mostly dry, an eater of beef in a country where many venerate the cow, and of course, a child of a member of the Establishment. The self-acknowledged Establishment intellectual Pavan K Varma memorably described this group as the kind of Indian who when asked a question in Hindi, answers in English.[461]

There is no real Establishment in India, but it is a convenient cultural shorthand that everyone understands. A close synonym is 'Lutyens' Delhi' or the 'Lutyens' elite'—referring to the heavily policed government district laid out in the waning decades of the British Empire by the architect Edwin Lutyens (1869-1944).[462] A more pejorative term, made famous by Narendra Modi in a 2019 election interview, is 'the Khan Market Gang.'[463] The Khan Market is a sophisticated shopping area that lies roughly one mile south of the ceremonial centre of New Delhi, sandwiched between the Delhi Golf Club and the lush Lodhi Garden. It has the highest retail rents of any commercial district in India.[464] It is said to have been named for the Muslim INC politician Dr Abdul Jabbar Khan, one of the few prominent Muslim leaders who had opposed Partition. Khan, whose wife was British, later became a cabinet minister in Pakistan. Had he instead remained in India, his children would certainly have become members of the gang that bears his name.

A London-trained physician, Dr Khan Sahib, as he was known, was a true comprador, acting initially as an intermediary between the British and the Pashtun tribes on the Afghan border, and later as an intermediary between the Pashtuns and the government of Pakistan. By all accounts, he was an honourable politician who promoted good relations among practitioners of all religions and harboured no ill will toward India. But the naming of a prominent Delhi landmark after a potential Muslim role model was no accident. It was part of a conscious effort by Nehru to construct a new national story for India in which Muslim Indians could participate as equal partners.

At the forefront of Nehru's programme was the reconnection of the modern Indian capital with its Muslim imperial past. Conveniently, the Mughal Empire (1526-1857) had fought the British, been ruled by Muslims, and had Delhi as its capital. It offered a glorious and highly visible antecedent polity to which the history of independent India could be traced. It was in this context that, as the art historian Santhi Kavuri-Bauer put it, 'the Mughal monuments were radically and singularly reframed as sites of national heritage.'[465] The clearest indication of Nehru's intentions was his choice of Delhi's Red Fort for the symbolic first raising of independent India's new flag. Built during the reign of Shah Jahan (1592-1666), the Red Fort was the former seat of the Mughal emperors. Following Nehru's example, it has become a tradition for the Indian Prime Minister to address the nation from the ramparts of the Red Fort every year on the morning of 15 August.

The choice of the Mughals as independent India's national antecedents was supported by Establishment intellectuals and validated by Establishment historians. Generations of academics, archeologists, and aesthetes toed the party line, whether INC or Marxist, to construct a national story that linked modern New Delhi with Mughal old Delhi.[466] The most prominent historian of modern India, Ramachandra Guha, even went so far as to open his 2007 book *India After Gandhi* with a eulogy for the

Mughals.[467] As a historical narrative that could unite Hindus and Muslims in what John Stuart Mill called a 'community of recollections,' it was credible.[468] The challenge was to make it palatable. After all, the first Mughal emperor was Babur, a central Asian descendant of Genghis Khan. It is that very Babur who stands accused of building a mosque (the Babri Masjid) over the birthplace of Lord Ram in Ayodhya. That alone would, in the eyes of Hindu Indians, disqualify him as a viable candidate to serve as the symbol of communal harmony in a pluralistic modern India.

Babur's grandson Akbar (1542-1605), however, was a more attractive prospect. He is widely celebrated for his Sufi religious syncretism. In a much-repeated anecdote, Akbar is said to have commented that 'the wisdom of the Vedanta [ancient Hindu teachings] is the wisdom of Sufism.'[469] Much wishful history rests on this single unsourced dictum recorded by a now deceased historian, Annemarie Schimmel (1922-2003). The absence of a citation for the quote even leaves its meaning open to question: was Akbar perhaps being ironic, implying that there was as little wisdom in either? Non-experts have no way to verify this, and the experts simply cite Schimmel. The religious historian Wendy Doniger (citing Schimmel) turns the quote into a proclamation 'universalizing the two great universalizing religions by equating (which is to say universalizing) them.' Yet it is thin evidence for her conclusion that 'Akbar the Tolerant' was 'by far the most pluralist of the Mughal rulers (indeed of most rulers anywhere and anytime in history).'[470]

Of such stuff are nations made. The legend of Akbar's open-minded religious pluralism sits at the centre of a Gandhian 'discourse on composite culture' that portrays modern India as the heir, not of the British colonisers, but of an enlightened

Mughal realm in which Hindus and Muslims lived side by side as equal subjects of an enlightened emperor.[471] Nehru argued in *The Discovery of India* that Indian culture had always been 'composite' in nature, 'even with reference to the distant past,' and that even less in the present should it be described as distinctively Hindu. He wrote in this vein that Akbar was 'the great representative of the old Indian ideal of a synthesis of differing elements and their fusion into a common nationality.'[472] That may have been true, seen from one point of view. But in the wake of Partition, it required aggressive intellectual policing to prevent alternative points of view from emerging.

From 'composite culture' to 'Hindu civilisation'

The proposition that India possessed a 'composite culture' that was equally Hindu and Muslim was a difficult sell even before Partition. In the immediate aftermath of Partition, with streams of Hindus and Sikh refugees fleeing persecution in Pakistan and independent India's remaining Muslim minority reduced to less than 10 per cent of the total population, the writing of a new national story that celebrated a thousand years of intercommunal harmony and cultural exchange took heroic effort—or a repressive programme of historical falsification, depending on your point of view. Akbar offered a promising focal point, but even Akbar's supposed syncretism could only be pushed so far. For example, the colonial era historian Vincent Arthur Smith (1848-1920) described Akbar's religious synthesis as a 'political sham religion' that 'consisted essentially in the assertion of his personal supremacy over things spiritual as well as things temporal.'[473] Such views can readily be discredited as serving the political purposes of the British administration, but they are not so easily disproven or dismissed.

In any case, Akbar's purported religious tolerance—whether enlightened or merely self-serving—did not survive him. The emperor who, in the words of the Establishment historian S A A Rizvi (1921-1994) 'fully realised that the Empire could stand only on the basis of complete toleration,' was followed by an unbroken succession of sixteen orthodox emperors who governed Delhi for another 252 years.[474] The most notorious of these was Akbar's great-grandson, Aurangzeb. Rizvi lamented that in 1669, Aurangzeb issued 'a general order to demolish temples and Hindu centres of learning,' which Rizvi claimed 'made success impossible for him.'[475] Notwithstanding these missteps, over the next three decades Aurangzeb was able to push the Mughal Empire to its greatest historical extent. At his death in 1707, it covered essentially all of south Asia except Sri Lanka and the southern tip of India.

If independent India was to trace its history to the Mughals, Aurangzeb had to be rehabilitated. The problem was that the evidence of Aurangzeb's desecrations and demolitions of Hindu temples is extensive, well-documented, and widely known. It is clearly visible to any casual visitor to Varanasi in Uttar Pradesh, where he built a mosque on the very foundations of one of the holiest temples in India, with (in the words of American historian Audrey Truschke) 'part of the ruined temple's wall incorporated into the building.'[476] But Establishment historians persisted in propping up Aurangzeb, extoling his virtues and excusing his excesses. A famous example occurred in a 1986, when a group of Establishment historians wrote to the *The Times of India* to protest its 'recent tendency ... to give a communal twist' to coverage of dispute over a holy site in Mathura, Uttar Pradesh, where Aurangzeb had destroyed an important temple in 1670 and built a mosque on the site. The historians wrote that the temple 'was extremely popular and acquired considerable wealth.' That's why:

> Aurangzeb had this temple destroyed, took the wealth as booty and built an Idgah [outdoor worship space] on the site. His actions might have been politically motivated as well. It should be remembered that many Hindu temples were untouched during Aurangzeb's reign, and even some new ones built. [...] Acts of intolerance have undeniably been committed in India by followers of all religions, but they have to be understood in their context. It is a debasement of history to distort these events for present-day communal propaganda.[477]

Such a tone-deaf position was bound to prove untenable in the long run. As the newspaper editor and later BJP politician, Arun Shourie wryly observed in a 1998 book ironically titled *Eminent Historians*: 'the litmus test of whether you are committed to secular history-writing is whether you are prepared to stand up for Aurangzeb!'[478]

Though there were many outsider challenges to the Establishment's narrative that a composite Hindu-Muslim culture had peacefully flourished in India for a millennium or more, the metaphorical dam broke in 2021 with the publication of Pavan K Varma's *The Great Hindu Civilisation*. The very title of the book was provocative, and meant to be so. Varma characterised the composite culture thesis as 'a concerted, organised and deceitful attempt to gloss over the facts of history in the false belief that this will be in the interest of preserving secularism in India.' While conceding that 'Hindu and Muslim cultures enriched each other' in many ways, he argued that it was wrong to treat 'this cultural exchange as the dominant feature of the Muslim conquest in India with the deliberate aim of glossing over its documented destructiveness, its religious intolerance and the massive damage it caused to Hindu temples and civilisation.' Accepting the need to include Muslims in India's national story, he contended that:

> The sane alternative is to accept history as it happened, acknowledge the traumatising impact of the Muslim destruction of Hindu civilisation, recognise the inestimable loss that it caused to the collective assets–physical and intellectual–of a very significant part of our history, and accept that a great deal of the destruction was due to the religious fanaticism of the Islamic rulers.

Though he believed that the 'advent of Islamic rule broke the continuity and evolution of a great civilisation,' he nonetheless embraced a secular understanding of India's national identity, concluding that 'true secularism can only arise from a reconciliation with history, not suppression of truth.'[479]

There had been many criticisms of Establishment historiography before Varma wrote his book, but they had mostly been written by outsider intellectuals and published by fringe presses. Some of them, like the sensationalist 1990 exposé *Hindu Temples: What Happened to Them?* compiled by Sita Ram Goel (1921-2003), were widely discussed. These books, however, easy to dismiss, both because of their authors' lack of formal credentials and on account of their frankly low standards of editing, scholarship, and presentation. Varma's book was different, coming as it did from a well-respected member of the Establishment and self-confessed scion of Lutyens' Delhi who grew up a stone's throw away from the Khan Market.[480] Moreover, Varma, a polished former diplomat, was an outspoken political opponent of Narendra Modi and the BJP. For him to attack the 'composite culture' consensus of India's most reputable historians—and worse, to approvingly cite, and thereby legitimate, the writings of many of their outsider critics—signalled a shift in the limits of acceptable elite discourse in India.

It is, perhaps, no coincidence that Varma, long an introspective critic of the Establishment's dominance of Indian cultural discourse, should have so decisively broken ranks at the beginning of the 2020s. Modi's direct assault on the legitimacy of the 'Khan Market Gang' had, after all, been the closing argument of his 2019 reelection campaign. The unexpected victory of the BJP with an enhanced parliamentary majority demonstrated that their success in 2014 had been no mere fluke, and suggested that the old Establishment no longer wielded the cultural authority that it once had. In the new dispensation that was taking form, new arguments were needed to counter the growing influence of the Hindu-centric ideology of an emerging cadre of 'New India' intellectuals. Although Varma's book was written to oppose the manipulation of history by the Establishment, it also scathingly criticised the weaponisation of history by the BJP and the RSS.[481]

The 2019 election rang the death knell on the Nehruvian concept of the Indian nation and the place of Muslims in it. Varma, citing Vivekananda, Ashoka, and the Hindu poet Tulsidas, whose death is recorded in 1623, wanted to replace it with a humane vision of a capacious Hindu civilisation founded on 3,000 years of tolerance and acceptance.[482] Other, less humane authors had different ideas.

New India's civilisational state

In *The Great Hindu Civilisation*, Varma implied that modern India was the heir to a fundamentally Hindu civilisation, and argued that only an honest engagement with this heritage would allow Hindus 'to build, along with all the other great faiths that have a home in this ancient land, a modern India that is democratic but also rooted in the great wisdoms of its past.'[483] His claim that India was indeed home to a great Hindu civilisation, though controversial in Lutyens' Delhi, would (outside of narrow academic circles) be considered self-evident to most Westerners. Establishment Indians and their Western supporters have, however, historically avoided such conclusions out of a fear that their work might be used to undermine the old Nehruvian consensus on Indian nationhood. As the religious studies scholar Diana L Eck frankly admitted of her 2012 book, *India: A Sacred Geography*:

> I was discouraged about the writing of it, fearing that somehow the image of a sacred geography enlivened by the presence of the gods and interlinked through the circulation of pilgrims would further feed the fervor of an exclusive new Hindu nationalism.[484]

This kind of intellectual boycott can only hold for so long. Lacking the honest guidance of conventionally credentialed historians and social scientists, Indians have turned elsewhere for fresh perspectives. These emerging 'New India' intellectuals are in many cases highly credentialed professionals in their own fields, but are generally not formally educated in the humanities and social sciences. They are, in effect, 'gentleman scholars' on the model of Karl Marx, John Stuart Mill, and Herbert Spencer—amateurs, perhaps, but amateurs to be reckoned with.

By far the most prominent of the New India intellectuals is a constitutional lawyer, J Sai Deepak. His breakout book was the wildly popular *India That Is Bharat*, published in 2021 just a month after Varma's *Great Hindu Civilisation.* The book's title echoes the stylised formulation given for the name of India in the preamble to the Constitution. In the book, Sai Deepak rigorously interrogates the scholarly literature on colonialism and indigeneity to establish that India actually suffered from two waves of colonialisation: European, of course, but also an earlier wave of 'Middle Eastern' colonialism.[485] In this formulation, 'Middle Eastern' is clearly a euphemism for 'Muslim.' Sai Deepak argues, in all seriousness, that independent India's Constitution made the postcolonial state responsible for the welfare of an indigenous Hindu culture called 'Bharat,' and that since India 'is the only natural homeland for the Indic [i.e.: Hindu] consciousness, the Indian State has the civilisational duty to ensure that this space remains as such.'[486]

In Sai Deepak's reasoning, Hindus are the indigenous people of India, and the modern Indian state has a moral and legal responsibility to ensure their cultural survival. On this basis, Sai Deepak criticises the Indian state for posing:

> ...A serious and existential challenge to the long-term survival of the Indic consciousness since those worldviews [i.e.: Muslim] which have historically displayed a marked inability to peacefully coexist with the Indic consciousness have been afforded greater freedom to preserve their societal groupings and institutions with almost no interference by the Indian State, ostensibly in the name of advancement of the rights of 'minorities'.[487]

This is radical left wing social science taken to its logical right-wing conclusion. Moreover, just as in the United States each Native American tribe maintains a distinct corporate identity vis-à-vis the American state, so too should each distinct

Hindu (or Sikh or Jain) group in India have corporate rights vis-à-vis the Indian state.[488] This characterisation of the Indian state as a postcolonial imposition on the indigenous peoples of India leads Sai Deepak to his coup de main. Having established that the Indian state presides over a 'federal civilisation with multiple sub-entities that are free to retain their identities but have remained culturally and politically bound for millennia,' Sai Deepak argues that India is indeed not a Hobbesian nation-state uniting a collection of individual citizens under a common government, but an Indic 'civilisation-state' bound together by the 'glue' of the 'Hindu religion' and bearing a responsibility to ensure the continued flourishing of that religion.[489] Q.E.D.

This is what happens when lawyers do social science. It is akin to African-American demands for the payment of reparations for slavery. It is tantamount to arguing that Hindu groups, too, should be entitled to open Indian casinos. There is nothing wrong with Sai Deepak's logic; the problem is with the social science on which it is based. Western societies accommodate radical theories like these only because their academic advocates are in no position to carry them out. Those same academics, faced with an intellectually naive but piercingly intelligent acolyte like Sai Deepak, are hoist by their own petards. All they can do is cry 'majoritarianism' and hope he goes away.[490]

The civilisation-state or civilisational state concept leveraged by Sai Deepak entered the popular consciousness in 2009, when the British journalist Martin Jacques applied it to China. In his bestselling book *When China Rules the World*, Jacques captured the millennial zeitgeist with the argument that China would soon, as the title suggests, rule the world. In order to understand our new overlords, it was crucial, according to Jacques to realise that China is not a conventional Western nation-state. In a pivotal chapter, Jacques describes China instead as a 'civilization-state' on the straightforward logic that 'China is not just a nation-state; it is also a civilization.'[491] In his 2012 second edition, Jacques suggested that the only other serious candidate for civilisation-state status was India. But he judged that India did not quite qualify, since "'India, as we know it today, was a relatively recent creation of the British Raj, its previous history being far more diverse than China's.'[492]

This was a red rag to the bull of Hindu nationalism. Indians responded with assertions of both the great antiquity and the fundamental unity of Hindu civilisation in India. Even the mainstream academic and journalist M S Prabhakara (1936-2022) took it for granted that:

> …from times immemorial, India has been a civilisational state, *Bharat Mata* ['Mother India'], mystically transcending the narrow legal definitions of European theorists of what constitutes the modern nation state.[493]

But Indian nationalists need not have been so concerned. A little bibliographic research would have revealed that the civilisation-state concept had actually been developed by an Indian, and with reference to India. The thoroughly Establishment historian Ravinder Kumar (1932-2001), a Director of the Nehru Memorial Museum and Library in Delhi whose research drew on 'liberal and Marxist traditions,' coined the term in 1989.[494] Nor did Kumar's coinage go unnoticed: the American Indologist Gerald James Larson built extensively on Kumar's characterisation of India as a civilisation-state in his 1995 book *India's Agony over Religion*.[495] From there, the concept seems to have bubbled along in Indian and Russian civilisational studies, particularly in the work of Aleksandr

Dugin, before resurfacing in Jacques' popular book.

Kumar's vision of the Indian civilisation-state was, however, rather different from Sai Deepak's. Believing that the civilisation-state concept 'holds out a prospect of tolerance and cohesion to the diverse cultural, linguistic and religious communities of modern India,' Kumar very much saw India's Islámic civilisational currents as flowing into the main stream of its civilisation. Kumar feared that pushing Indians to conform to a single 'national' identity would send 'tremors of alarm through wide swathes of the people, who look to their location in regional or local communities as the primary basis of their identity formation.' He thus preferred the idea of promoting a civilisational state 'resting upon a multiplicity of religious visions and drawing into its matrix the richness of the regional constituents of Indian society.'[496] That is surely a beautiful message. But it reflects a complete lack of understanding of what a state actually is.

Temples and mosques

The 'state' is defined by the Oxford English Dictionary as 'the body politic as organized for supreme civil rule and government.'[497] In the civilisation-state debate, it is Sai Deepak who actually has the correct understanding of the nature of the state as a system of administrative machinery wielded by a country's political leadership. What Kumar described was actually not so much a civilisation-state as a civilisational nation: 'diverse cultural, linguistic and religious communities' coming together to form a plural but nonetheless unified national identity. Given the numerical dominance of Hindus in India's population, a pluralistic Indian nation would necessarily have a Hindu centre of gravity, but it need not be exclusively Hindu. A truly civilisational nationhood in India would incorporate multiple strands of Hindu identity, but also absorb and ultimately assimilate Muslim and other minority identities. The 'reconciliation with history' called for by Varma is a necessary first step toward such a unified nationhood, but it would have to be followed by genuine acceptance and meaningful interfaith compromise.

The fact that Muslim emperors have in the past destroyed important Hindu temples need not be a barrier to the formation of such a multifaith civilisational nationhood. Consider the historical experience of the United States, where the majority European-origin population fought a series of savage frontier wars with Native American tribes throughout the nineteenth century—wars that were replete with brutal massacres on both sides. Nonetheless, even though Native Americans suffered egregious discrimination and dispossession, their martial valour was honoured and celebrated. When the American Tomb of the Unknown Soldier was consecrated in 1921, a mere three decades after the last major violence on the frontier, a Native American headdress was the final symbolic tribute placed on the grave. Despite the fact that Native Americans tribes are actually recognised in the United States as quasi sovereign entities with extensive rights of self-government, Native American histories have been fully subsumed within the larger narrative of American nationhood.

The merging of European and Native American civilisations into a unified American nationhood was made possible by a reciprocal exchange of concessions and esteem. Native Americans ultimately accepted the inevitability of living as a minority community in a society defined by customs and laws that were primarily European in origin. That may not have been just or fair, but it was a necessary prerequisite for their inclusion in the mainstream of American nationhood—a nationhood that would have, in any case, proceeded without them, had they not joined in. In exchange, the majority European origin community valorised traditional Native American culture as representing the peak of courage and nobility. Later, the majority community would also come to express regret for its past treatment of Native Americans. In any standard American history textbook, it is the Native Americans who are portrayed sympathetically and heroically, with the European colonists denigrated for their duplicity and aggression.

The historical accuracy of any of this is beside the point. Such rituals are not factual; they are functional. Their goal was and remains the peaceful incorporation of Native Americans into the country's national story on honourable terms that can be accepted by both sides. Similar exchanges have more recently marked the incorporation of African-Americans into the national mainstream, and still other minority groups await their turns. In the Indian context, a similar exchange between minority and majority might include concessions by Muslims on the highly sensitive issue of temple restitution, to be reciprocated by genuine Hindu participation in the valorisation of India's Muslim heritage. It will be as difficult for Hindu Indians to admire Babur's martial genius as it was for Muslim Indians to endure the destruction of Babur's mosque in Ayodhya, but such communal sacrifices are necessary if India is ever to build an inclusive national identity. The only alternative is a reluctant and irritable tolerance that occasionally breaks out into confrontation and intercommunal violence.

Unfortunately, neither side in this potential exchange shows much inclination toward reconciliation. On the Muslim side, every effort to restore a historical temple on a site now occupied by a mosque has been fought tooth and nail by a refractory religious establishment that seems to regard any hint of accommodation as a form of apostasy. To be clear: Muslim Indians have every legal right to fight for the retention of their places of worship. That said, in India there are multiple instances, most famously at Ayodhya but also in Varanasi and Mathura (all in Uttar Pradesh) where relatively nondescript local mosques sit on the ruined foundations of some of the holiest shrines in the Hindu faith.[498] These sites are not trapped in fundamentally irreconcilable disputes over religious belief, like the Temple Mount in Jerusalem. With goodwill, they could be solved through civil agreements to relocate the mosques with compensation, in the form of both money and gratitude. But many Muslim civil society organisations maintain that mosques 'cannot be gifted, sold or shifted.'[499]

Such intransigence is perhaps understandable in light of the inflated claims for restitution put forward by some New India ideologues. For example, the media savvy molecular biologist-turned-political commentator Anand Ranganathan believes that 'reclaiming demolished, destroyed places of worship' is 'not a Hindu issue. Or a religious issue. [...] It is a civilisational issue.' Citing numbers 'as high as 40,000,' he demands that Hindu temples be 'resurrected' on all of them.[500] Obviously, such views offer little space for a pathway to reconciliation. Equally obviously: they are based on a historical delusion. Consider Indonesia, where an effort has been underway since 2013 to construct a digital database cataloging all of the country's mosques. As of early 2021, more than a quarter million had been identified.[501] Before the arrival of Islam in Indonesia in the late middle ages, many of these would have been the sites of Hindu temples.

In a country where the Muslim population today rivals that of Indonesia, there are no doubt tens of thousands of local temples that at some point in history were converted into mosques when their patrons converted to Islam. The suggestion that they should all be turned back into temples, even in neighbourhoods and villages where there are no Hindus left to worship at them, is patently absurd. A more reasonable demand is that a small number of highly symbolic temples sites be restored: the three most often mentioned are in Ayodhya, Varanasi, and Mathura. This is a widely held view, and one that was even endorsed by the RSS in 2003 when the organisation resolved to:

> Call upon the Muslim leadership to seize the historic opportunity and give up their claim over the sites at Ayodhya, Mathura and Kashi [Varanasi] so as to pave way for creation of mutual goodwill and respect between Hindus and Muslims forever.[502]

Of course, Muslim Indians are under no injunction to make an offer of their consecrated sites, and Hindu Indians would be under no obligation to accept one. For now, temple disputes are being adjudicated in the courts—that is to say, by the state. Promisingly, some New India intellectuals have shown the maturity to understand that this is not the best way forward. Magazine editor Raghavan Jagannathan implies, but does not state outright, in his 2023 book *Dharmic Nation* that the Hindu community should settle for the reclamation of Ayodhya, Varanasi, and Mathura.[503] Television journalists Rahul Shivshankar and Siddhartha Talya argue in their 2023 *Modi & India* that 'while the state must certainly do most of the heavy lifting of creating an enabling environment, the people themselves must also do their bit to negotiate a lasting peace'; they urge civil society groups to work together to 'evolve a consensus' on the ownership of places of worship.[504] These are promising signs. But they come nowhere near the kind of valorisation of the Muslim experience in India that is likely a prerequisite for building a truly unified Indian nation.

A Hindu reckoning with history

History is written by historians, and for the first seven decades of the Indian republic, that truism was just as true for India as it is for the rest of the world. The reelection of Narendra Modi in 2019 with an enhanced majority, however, broke open the Establishment's monopoly on history. There had been many challenges to the conventional telling of Indian, and particularly Hindu, history by amateur historians before 2019. However, these were widely regarded as outsider narratives, not only by the general public, but by insiders themselves. Sometimes, these unconventional historians gained national fame with books that were widely discussed; Sita Ram Goel drove public debate with his 1990 book *Hindu Temples*, and Arun Shourie is well-known not only for his 1998 *Eminent Historians* but also for his critical appraisal of the Dalit leader B R Ambedkar, *Worshipping False Gods* (2012).[505] Another important intellectual who might nonetheless be characterised as an 'outsider' historian was the Trinidadian novelist V S Naipaul (1932-2018), whose Indian travelogues also served as popular revisionist histories.

Authors linked to the RSS in particular have produced many volumes that are often of high historiographical calibre, although their findings are rarely referenced in mainstream histories. Many of their books focus on the RSS itself. For example, the technology consultant and RSS researcher Ratan Sharda has written several books on the history of the RSS, most importantly *The Sangh & Swaraj* (2021) an insightful history of the role played by the RSS in India's independence struggle.[506] Another important RSS intellectual is Ram Madhav, whose 2021 book *The Hindutva Paradigm* is an indispensable guide to the thinking of Deendayal Upadhyaya (1916-1968), the RSS *pracharak* whose programme of 'integral humanism' is still the official philosophy of the BJP.[507] Madhav is also the author of an important revisionist history of India's independence struggle, *Partitioned Freedom* (2022).[508] It is a sign of the growing influence of such authors that the INC parliamentarian and intellectual Shashi Tharoor devoted the bulk of his 2021 *The Struggle for India's Soul* to refuting their ideas.[509]

Books authored by RSS-linked intellectuals have sometimes achieved popular success in India, but they could never really challenge Establishment narratives. The intellectual legitimacy of India's Establishment was derived not only from the official support of successive INC governments, but also from international connections. Until very recently, when Western academic associations, newspapers, or literary reviews looked for interpretations of India, they invariably turned to members of the Establishment. This has now begun to change. Diaspora intellectuals like the computer scientist Rajiv Malhotra have played key roles in delegitimizing the Indian Establishment's authority over Western understandings of India. Malhotra's 2011 book *Breaking India* coauthored with Aravindan Neelakandan showed how international donors were funding Islamist, Marxist, and Dravidian separatist intellectual movements inside India.[510] His magisterial 2022 follow-up volume, *Snakes in the Ganga: Breaking India 2.0,* coauthored with Vijaya Viswanathan exhaustively documents how Indian money is laundered through American universities to legitimise

Establishment intellectual movements back in India.[511]

All of these ideological warriors are, however, of a different generation from the New India authors who are now actively seeking to rewrite their country's history to suit the ambitions of a twenty-first century emerging geopolitical superpower. If there is a ringleader of this new generation of Indian intellectuals, it is the popular historian Vikram Sampath. A serious historian of music with an Australian doctorate, Sampath became a nationally prominent intellectual with the 2019 publication of the first volume of his two-volume biography of V D Savarkar.[512] The biography brought Savarkar back to the centre of debates over India's identity as a Hindu nation. The publication of the second volume in 2022 cemented Savarkar's reputation as a major figure of India's independence struggle and Sampath's reputation as a major interpreter of India's Hindu nationhood.[513] Later in 2022, Sampath went on to publish a popular history of mostly Hindu Indian heroes, and in 2024 he published an excoriating biography of Tipu Sultan, an eighteenth century Muslim king who fought the expanding East India Company.[514]

Sampath waded into India's temple controversies in 2024 with the publication of *Waiting for Shiva*, a kind of sourcebook documenting Hindu claims that a Shiva temple lies under the Gyanvapi Mosque in Varanasi.[515] Before this book, Sampath seemed keen to maintain a reputation as a dispassionate historian correcting the historical record without fear or favour, but *Waiting for Shiva* is a clearly partisan—though nonetheless scholarly—entry in New India's culture wars. The journalist Abhijit Majumder approvingly writes of the young historian in his 2024 book *India's New Right* that Sampath is 'acutely targeted by the Left cabal's criticism,' and indeed Sampath has become a magnet for national and international intellectual opprobrium.[516] In a sign that New

India is now the dominant India, even the international criticism doesn't seem to have blunted Sampath's domestic reputation. Nor do other New India icons like the novelist Amith Tripathi or the economist Sanjeev Sanyal (both authors of popular history books) seem to have suffered from being labelled as apostles of 'India's new right'.

Other New India writers have avoided the culture wars to focus instead on economic and political reform. The most prominent of these is the structural chemist Gautam R Desiraju, who, unlike the other New India authors profiled here, is a senior and highly acclaimed academic—though not a credentialed social scientist. Desiraju advocates the reinvention of modern India as a Hindu-centric civilisational state, arguing that:

> In Sanskrit, the political state is known as the *rajya* which straddles the underlying civilisation or nation termed the *rashtra*. The boundaries of these two entities may or may not overlap exactly. However, in a civilisational state, the principles of governance of the political state are expected to be derived from the cultural practices of the civilisation.[517]

This is, in essence, the 'civilisational nation' argument, with the wrinkle that the Indian nation is here elevated to the status of a 'civilisation.' Had Desiraju left the matter there, it would be just one more terminologically confused entry in the civilisational state literature. Desiraju, however, makes good his claim to apply the 'principles of governance' of Hindu civilisation, as he understands them, to the reform of the Indian state.

Inspired by Mahatma Gandhi's independence-era advocacy of a local and diverse village-based democracy, Desiraju proposes a radical decentralisation of governance in India. Believing that Indians 'should revel' in the diversity of their country, he argues that 'once diversity is enabled effectively by further *division* into smaller states, civilisational blooming will follow naturally.'[518] By this, he seems to mean that the solution to India's communal, caste, and linguistic gridlock is to break India's large states, which suffer from an enforced uniformity into smaller states that can embrace more organic, locally-rooted identities. Leaving aside the political practicality of redividing India into as many as seventy to eighty new states, Desiraju's openness to 'demarcating regions where different religious denominations might be in the majority' would not so much end social exclusion in a national India as create a multiplicity of inclusive spaces in a federal India.[519]

Muslims might indeed thrive in an almost exclusively Muslim state of Kashmir. The only problem is that they would thrive as Muslim Kashmiris, and not necessarily as Muslim Indians.

The business of India

No serious intellectual, whether of the Establishment or the New India persuasion, doubts that Muslims played a major role in India's history—and consequently, in the development of its 'great' civilisation. At the same time, no one who honestly engages with modern India will deny that the main strand of its civilisation is Hindu. India's great Hindu civilisation, just as Varma claims, 'commenced at the dawn of time and ... in spite of the historical vicissitudes it went through later, survives even today.'[520] The Hindu gods Krishna and Shiva are not, like Athena and Poseidon, relegated to ruined temple museums that tourists must pay to visit; the *Mahabharata* and the *Ramayana* are not, like the *Iliad* and the *Odyssey*, read as the ancient literature of a mostly forgotten culture. The *Bhagavad Gita* is a sacred guide to faith like the *Bible* and the *Quran*, not a secular work of philosophy like Plato's *Republic*. But India's constitution, and—more importantly—its state institutions, do not rest on the authority of the *Bhagavad Gita*, or on any other work of Hindu faith. Modern India is not a Hindu state.

Yet the secular Indian state does rest on the foundation of a nation that is fundamentally Hindu in culture and outlook. Hindu civil society in India is characterised by what sociologists call 'organic solidarity': the functional integration of individuals into the collective social life of the community. The term was introduced in the founding work of the discipline, Émile Durkheim's (1893) *The Division of Labor in Society*. As the title suggests, this book focused primarily on explaining how social solidarity emerged from participation in the modern economy, but his theoretical argument was much broader. For Durkheim, the increasing division of labour undermined the old 'mechanical solidarity' of traditional societies, replacing it with an 'organic solidarity' based on mutual interdependence. This was a bottom-up process; it could not, he argued, be imposed from above.

After World War Two, many postcolonial countries were born that lacked any real organic solidarity, inheriting little more than randomly drawn borders and legacy state institutions. In the absence of a shared sense of belonging, they were set up for failure. In those countries where the state assumed complete control of the economy, societies remained stunted, with dire consequences when those states failed. Durkheim had indeed called the idea that the state could unify society 'a veritable sociological monstrosity.' Writing two decades before the emergence of the Soviet Union, he explained in an extended 1902 preface to *The Division of Labor* that:

> ...collective activity is always too complex to be able to be expressed through the single and unique organ of the State.

> Moreover, the State is too remote from individuals; its relations with them too external and intermittent to penetrate deeply into individual consciences and socialize them within.

Durkheim looked instead to the nation as the primary arena for the development of modern society, though he insisted that:

> A nation can be maintained only if, between the State and the individual, there is intercalated a whole series of secondary groups near enough to the individuals to attract them strongly in their sphere of action and drag them, in this way, into the general torrent of social life.[521]

Occupations were among these 'secondary groups,' but they were not the only such groups. In India, which even today is not such a thoroughly commercialised society as was 1890s France, the role of integrating society could not have been left to participation in businesses, professional associations, and trade unions. It was performed instead by Hindu civil society organisations. The fact that these organisations would construct a nation using broadly Hindu concepts, symbols, and songs was probably unavoidable. With the separation of the majority of colonial India's Muslim population into the independent state of Pakistan, it became inevitable.

Gautam Desiraju has observed that 'the business of India is religion,' and most of India's independence leaders were wise enough to realise that.[522] Even Nehru, the hero of Indian secularism, wrote that without the 'foundation of *dharma* there is no true happiness and society cannot hold together.'[523] But Muslim Indians are never going to be drawn into a rhetoric of national unity centred on the language of *dharma*. Nor are Christian Indians, or even many secular Hindus and Sikhs. Talk of a Hindu 'civilisational state' replacing the modern secular state is even less likely to inspire a sense of inclusion. Only a more humane and capacious understanding of India's Hindu civilisational inheritance can move the country forward toward greater social solidarity in a truly inclusive democracy. This need not involve anything novel; Swami Vivekananda preached just such an understanding before India even achieved independence. In an 1897 lecture on The Future of India", he observed that:

> Here have been the Aryan, the Dravidian, the Tartar, the Turk, the Mogul, the European–all the nations of the world, as it were, pouring their blood into this land. Of languages the most wonderful conglomeration is here; of manners and customs there is more difference between two Indian races than between the European and the Eastern races. The one common ground that we have is our sacred tradition, our religion. That is the only common ground, and upon that we shall have to build.[524]

The religion he spoke of was the Hindu religion. He was not, as some would make out, a unitarian. Like Hazrat Inayat Khan before him, Swami Vivekananda preached the universality of religious experience, not the equivalence of all religions. He was very conscious that he was neither a Muslim nor a Christian, but a Hindu, and he thought it crucially important for the future of India that Hindus of all stripes develop an awareness of themselves as practitioners of a single Hindu faith. This advocacy of Hindu unity was the easy part of his ministry; it was readily accepted, and it contributed greatly to the formation of a unified Hindu nation in India. The challenging part of his ministry was his plea for Hindus to also accept their Muslim neighbours as fellow Indians: not only to tolerate the Muslim in their midst, but 'to do what is much more difficult, to sympathise ... and feel *with him* in his aspirations and seeking after God.'

This is the *dharma* of inclusion that Hindu Indians must embrace if Muslim Indians are ever to be fully integrated into the Indian nation. The history of Islam in India must be accepted as part of Indian history, and even of Hindu history. Interestingly, Hindu fundamentalist resentment of the thousand years of Muslim rule in India seems to be a relatively recent phenomenon. Works from the independence era openly acknowledge the violence of the Muslim conquests, but do not seem to exhibit the same kind of anger over them. Even the Hindutva ideologue V D Savarkar recognised 'the valour of Babar [Babur], Humayun, or Akbar' in constructing his history of Indian opposition to British rule.[525] It may be that the rise of new passions over historical wrongs is a natural reaction to five decades of historical repression. Alternatively, rising Islamophobia may simply be the result of divisive electoral strategies in a highly competitive democracy. Either way, Indian nationhood will remain incomplete until Hindu Indians can find an honourable place for their Muslim neighbours in their shared national story.

The New Establishment

The pressing need for Hindu-Muslim reconciliation is nowhere so self-evident as in Yogi Adityanath's home state of Uttar Pradesh. Roughly 20 per cent of UP's population is Muslim; its 40 million Muslims would make it the tenth largest Muslim country in the world. Uttar Pradesh has the largest Muslim population of any Indian state or union territory, and is the fourth highest in terms of the percentage of its population that is Muslim. The world-famous Taj Mahal, the 1631 mausoleum built by the Mughal emperor Shah Jahan to honour his wife Mumtaz Mahal, is in the western part of the state. Nearby is Fatehpur Sikri, Akbar's abandoned first capital and now a major heritage site. On the other side of the state in eastern UP is the medieval city of Jaunpur, the capital city of the pre-Mughal Jaunpur Sultanate. It is an undiscovered potential tourist destination boasting a plethora of fifteenth century forts, mosques, and tombs, with the bonus of a massive 10-arch stone bridge built by Mughal emperor Akbar. With proper care and development, it could become an Indian Rialto.

In the middle of UP are the cities of Lucknow and Kanpur,

its capital and largest city, respectively. It was here that, in 1857, Muslims and Hindus took a joint stand against the foreign rule of the British East India Company. Savarkar styled this conflict *The Indian War of Independence of 1857* in his 1909 book on the event. Published anonymously by 'an Indian nationalist,' it was banned by the British as being seditious—for describing events that had occurred half a century earlier. Savarkar, who would later come to be seen as a stridently anti-Muslim communalist, used the book to praise Hindu-Muslim unity in the fight against the British. He didn't like the idea of Muslims as rulers, but speaking through the imagined thoughts of a Hindu leader, he reasoned that since 'Hindu sovereignty had defeated the rulership of the Mahomedans and had come to its own all over India' by the time of the rebellion, it had become acceptable for Hindus to cooperate with Muslims. Savarkar explained that:

> It was no national shame to join hands with Mahomedans now, but it would, on the contrary, be an act of generosity. So, now, the original distinction between the Hindus and the Mahomedans was laid to eternal rest. Their present relation was one not of rulers and ruled, foreigner and native, but simply that of brothers with the one difference between them of religion alone. For, they were both children of the soil of Hindustan. Their names were different, but they were all children of the same Mother; India therefore being the common mother of these two, they were brothers by blood.[526]

So keen was Savarkar to use the events of 1857 to promote the idea of Hindu-Muslim unity against the British that he even closed his book with a quotation that he attributed to the last of the Mughals, the poet-emperor Bahadur Shah Zafar (1775-1862). According to Savarkar, 'there is a tradition' that the emperor gave up his throne with the couplet:

> As long as there remains the least trace of love of faith in the hearts of our heroes, so long the sword of Hindusthan shall be sharp, and one day shall flash even at the gates of London.[527]

If there was ever a place where India's Muslim heritage could be celebrated and popularised, it is Uttar Pradesh. Yet no one would accuse UP's chief minister Yogi Adityanath of valorising Muslim history. He won't even take the easy win of the Taj Mahal. In a *faux pas* that made global news, three months after becoming chief minister in 2017 he boasted that although 'foreign dignitaries visiting the country used to be gifted replicas of the Taj Mahal and other minarets which did not reflect Indian culture,' they were now given copies of the *Bhagavad Gita*.[528] In the international moral panic over the idea of a Hindu cleric leading a secular government, this soundbite was quickly clipped and widely recycled. As last as 2021, the *New York Times* was still reporting that Adityanath 'has said it does not 'reflect Indian culture.'[529] Never mind that by that time Adityanath, himself, had presented a portrait of India's Taj Mahal to the visiting American president Donald Trump, who was himself the one-time developer of a Taj-themed casino resort.[530]

The Taj Mahal blunder has become a standard trope of Western reporting on Adityanath, not least because it encapsulates in a neat and tidy package what seems to be the Yogi's position on Islamic culture in India: that it must be tolerated, but it need not be validated. Over the course of his time in office, however, Adityanath has shown signs of evolution and growth. A few months after Adityanath's 2017 Taj gaffe, a relatively obscure BJP politician said of the monument's builder Shah Jahan that it was 'quite sad and unfortunate that such tyrants are still part of our history,' calling for 'stories of the blot that Babur, Akbar and Aurangzeb stand for' to be removed from history books.[531] Once again, the international media had a field day. They neglected to mention that Adityanath's state-level BJP administration immediately disavowed the remarks.[532] Adityanath himself offered the rather evasive concession that the Taj 'was built from the blood and sweat of Indian labourers and that of the sons of Bharat Mata [Mother India].'[533] That wasn't exactly an open-armed embrace of India's Mughal heritage, but it was something.

Such incidents are the Indian equivalent of the outrageous remarks of a state legislator in the United States being represented in the international media as the official policy of one of the country's two major political parties. International newspapers don't do this for the United States in part because their readers are reasonably well-versed in the basics of American politics. But it is likely that racism—or at least its close cousin, neocolonialism—also plays a role. For example, when a local British or Australian politician says something provocative, it is unlikely to be presented in major American newspapers as indicative of the institutional character of a major political party. The general ignorance about Indian politics in the West opens space for journalists, especially those of Indian origin, with 'skin in the game', to present highly biased accounts that play on racist stereotypes and neocolonial generalisations. By focussing more on local electoral calculations than on their international reputations, Yogi Adityanath and his BJP colleagues don't help their case. That said, they might rightly respond that their duty is not to educate the international community about the reality of life in India, but to serve the actual people of India.

The natural party of government

The organisational antecedent to today's BJP, the Jana Sangh ('People's Party'), was founded in 1951 by maverick politician Syama Prasad Mookerjee (1901-1953) to offer a 'well-organised opposition' to the INC.[534] It was in effect sponsored by the RSS, which provided the organisational manpower to staff it, but it was not as closely affiliated with the organisation as the BJP would be after the re-founding of the party in 1980.[535] The Jana Sangh aspired to be a national political party, but it met with little success. In the five Lok Sabha parliamentary elections it contested, it never won more than 35 seats. With RSS support, it became the organisational core of the short-lived coalition that unseated Indira Gandhi in the 1977 elections, but politically it remained in the background. When the coalition collapsed in 1980, the RSS sponsored the foundation of the modern BJP, which won only 2 seats at its first outing in 1984. The BJP rose to lead coalition governments in 1996 (for sixteen days) and from 1998-2004, but until the election of 2014 it never commanded a parliamentary majority.

For the first sixty-three years of their existence, the BJP and its predecessor were outsiders parties. The RSS, which supported them had been formally banned twice by INC governments (1948 and 1975-1977) and temporarily proscribed for a third time in 1992-1993. In addition, for many decades, government employees were banned from joining the RSS. The founder of the Jana Sangh, S P Mookerjee, died mysteriously in 1953 after being imprisoned for violating an order from Nehru's INC government not to travel to Kashmir. The chief organiser and ideologue of the Jana Sangh, Deendayal Upadhyaya (1916-1968), was mysteriously murdered in 1968 in a crime that was never solved. When the BJP won its first outright majority in

2014, influential opinion journals began associating the RSS with 'fascism'.[536] When the BJP unexpectedly won with an increased majority in 2019, the *New York Times* and the *Washington Post* followed suit.[537] The German *Deutsche Welle* went further, citing 'experts' (actually two activist journalists) to claim that the RSS was a 'Hindu extremist group [that] glorifies Adolf Hitler.'[538]

In light of such a history, it is certainly understandable that the RSS and the BJP would develop something of a persecution complex. But the RSS and the BJP are no longer outsiders. Narendra Modi, the 'backward caste' son of a railway station teaseller, is the Prime Minister of India. Moreover, in a country that is riven with caste distinctions, he enjoys a 70 per cent approval rating.[539] Contradicting international stereotypes about India, 'upper' caste Hindus are considered his core supporters. The power elite vie for Modi's favour. Whether they realise it or not, the RSS, the BJP, and Narendra Modi have now become India's new Establishment.

That is not a mantle they have willingly worn. There is much more electoral advantage—and much greater rhetorical freedom—to be had in remaining outsiders. The historical legend of being a beleaguered party persecuted at every turn by an elite, disdainful, English-speaking Establishment makes for a much more attractive self-understanding than the present-day reality of being a rich, successful party supported by billionaires that is broadly accepted by the country's major media organisations. Thus the RSS goes to great lengths to keep alive the memory of its historical persecution at the hands of the INC and the intellectual Establishment, while the BJP refuses to acknowledge its status as the country's dominant political power, preferring instead to maintain the myth that the INC is the natural party of government in India. The RSS and the

BJP don't want to destroy or, worse, displace the Establishment, because the myth of opposition to the Establishment is at the core of their identity.

Conveniently, the BJP seems to use its self-image as an outsider party to absolve itself of responsibility for ensuring the full integration of the Indian nation. In a prior generation, the 'composite culture' thesis may have been a flawed effort at nation-building, but it reflected the Nehruvian INC's understanding of itself as an establishment party bearing responsibility for ensuring a healthy future for the country it led. Clearly, the Nehruvian INC did not succeed in this task, and the post-Indira INC seems to have given up trying. The INC had half a century to forge a unified multifaith nation in India, but although it took its responsibility seriously, it quite obviously failed to achieve its goals. A naïve acceptance of the Nehru-Gandhi clan's rhetoric as representing reality is largely responsible for the widespread adulation of the INC among Western academics. But had the Nehruvian project actually succeeded, India would not now be facing the problem of Muslim social exclusion that is so often pinned on the RSS and the BJP.

The BJP is fond of pointing out the failures of the INC and its policy of what the BJP routinely calls 'minority appeasement,' but it has never offered a viable alternative. It has instead demanded, in effect if not in so many words, that Muslim Indians adjust to life as a minority in a predominantly Hindu nation. For example, when the BJP is confronted over the fact that it runs so few Muslim candidates (in the 2022 UP state assembly elections, the BJP ran none at all), the party's answer is that it selects candidates 'on the basis of winnability.'[540] Accepting at face value the BJP's perception of itself as a scrappy electoral underdog, its position is entirely rational. But in light of the reality that the BJP is an electorally dominant party facing a fractured opposition, its reluctance to run Muslim candidates is shortsighted at best, and exclusionary at worst.

The point is not that Muslim Indians need Muslim BJP candidates to vote for—or more likely, not to vote for. The point is that the BJP should want to be perceived as a party that values Muslim Indians and will not tolerate intolerance within its own ranks. Whether it likes it or not, the BJP has now become the natural party of government in India. It may not always run the government, but it is likely to be the dominant party in India for decades to come. Thus, only the BJP is in a position to take responsibility for fostering the full integration of Muslim Indians into the national mainstream. If it accepts the challenge, it will, over time, attract many new voters. If it refuses the call, it will be left to govern over a diminished democracy. The BJP tends to perceive suggestions that it should work toward social inclusion as demands that it should pander to Muslims, and seen from that perspective, its refusal can be made out to be principled. A more productive approach might be to ask the BJP: would it rather portray itself as the party of Hindus, or as the party of Indians?

The responsibility for inclusion

As Narendra Modi's popularity and prestige climbed toward a historical peak in 2023, he personally fronted efforts to attract Muslim voters, and in particular, Muslim women. Modi spoke repeatedly on issues like civil divorce and secure streets, asking Muslim women to support BJP candidates in state and national elections in order to ensure their rights and safety.[541] He also hoped to exploit class differences within the Muslim community, with the BJP making a play for the votes of so-called Pasmanda ('left behind') Muslims. These are Muslims who are generally of 'lower' caste backgrounds and widely believed to be descended from Hindu converts to Islam instead of from Arab immigrants or Turkic invaders.[542] In both cases, the reasoning may have been that although the BJP was generally viewed as an anti-Muslim party, the Prime Minister's personal popularity might be sufficient to convince some Muslims to support the party's candidates.

These efforts focused on appealing to Muslims on the basis of gender and class, and not on appealing to Muslims as Muslims. Underlying the BJP's world-view is a set of implicit understandings about the meaning of Indian nationhood that are centered on the Hindu religion. These understandings are rooted in pre-Partition India and have been sculpted by decades spent in the political wilderness. As India has modernised, the BJP's understanding of Indian nationhood has evolved, and as the party adjusts to the responsibilities of power, it is possible that its relationship with religion will evolve, too. The prime mover in any such modernisation of the party will not come from its cadres, who seem to tend toward Hindu religious partisanship, but from the leadership, and in particular, from the RSS. Commentators who possess only a surface understanding of the RSS may revolt at the suggestion that it might push the BJP toward a rapprochement with Islam, but the RSS is first and foremost a nationalist organisation. It is much better understood as a nationalist organisation with a Hindu orientation than as a Hindu organisation with a nationalist orientation.

The RSS does not directly control the BJP or any of the organisations in the 'Sangh Parivar' family, but it does exert meaningful influence, and at time of any crisis, it serves as a steadying compass. The inherent Hinduness of the RSS makes it very difficult for the organisation to accommodate non-Hindu members, or even non-Hindu Sangh Parivar affiliates. Thus, the leading American scholars of the RSS, Walter Andersen and Shridhar D Damle, are pessimistic about the prospects for Muslim inclusion within the organisation.[543] This does not, however, necessarily mean that the RSS cannot come to support greater Muslim inclusion in Indian society. The problem is that Andersen and Damle view the issue of Muslim inclusion purely in terms of official engagement in Hindu-Muslim dialogue, not in terms of possible RSS accommodation to Muslim patriotism in India. The RSS will always oppose individuals and organisations that seek to reinforce a separate identity for Muslims in India, but it is not clear that the RSS would oppose a Muslim mirror image of itself.

One could very well imagine the RSS leadership someday applauding the formation of a Muslim organisation that glorified the roles played by Muslim heroes in the country's history, if the RSS leadership thought that it would enhance the patriotism of Muslim Indians. It would probably be unrealistic to expect the RSS to sponsor such an organisation, but it should not be taken for granted that the RSS leadership would oppose the creation of a kind of mirror-image 'Muslim RSS'. In fact, the RSS played a role in the creation of just such an organization, the Muslim Rashtriya Manch or Muslim National Forum, in the wake of the 2002 Gujarat riots. But this organisation never flourished into a mass movement, perhaps because of its association with the RSS, but more likely because of its relatively insipid rhetoric of national unity and support for RSS initiatives.[544] To put things in context, the RSS *Sarsanghchalak* Mohan Bhagwat, who often publicly pushes for Hindu conciliation with Muslim Indians on contentious issues, justifies Hindu assertiveness with the explanation that:

> Hindu society has been at war for over 1000 years. This fight has been going on against foreign aggressions, foreign influence and foreign conspiracies. [...] And it is because of all these that the Hindu society has awakened. It is but natural for those at war to be aggressive.[545]

The leaders of the Muslim Rashtriya Manch give no such stirring speeches to highlight the historical struggles of Muslim Indians. They certainly do not exhort their audiences to 'awaken' and go to 'war' to ensure the future of their community. They don't even seem to exhort their Muslim audiences to work for the greater glory of India—the sort of rhetoric that would be par for the course at an RSS gathering. It is hard to escape the conclusion that the Muslim Rashtriya Manch is little more than an astroturfed front organisation, not a genuine mass membership movement.

The closest Muslim Indian analog to the RSS is the Jamaat-e-Islami Hind, but the latter is more focused on raising Muslim consciousness in India than on inculcating any sense of Indian national pride among its members and followers. The president of the Jamaat-e-Islami Hind since 2019, Syed Sadatullah Husaini, often speaks out against Islamophobia and in support of the Palestinian cause, positioning his organisation as the voice of Muslim Indian respectability. He and his organisation do not seem to be interested in developing what would inevitably be a contentious retelling of Muslim history in India.

That challenge has instead been taken up by young independent authors like Syed Ubaidur Rahman and Shehla Rashid. Rahman has published several books on the prominent roles played by Muslims in the development of Indian history, most notably his 2023 *Forgotten Muslim Empires of South*

India.[546] Rahman's 2021 *Biographical Encyclopedia of Indian Freedom Fighters* even more explicitly serves as a kind of 'hero book' for patriotic young Muslims seeking to connect with their national heritage.[547] Along similar lines, the much more media-savvy author Shehla Rashid has published a 2024 collection of interviews with highly accomplished Muslim Indians that is actually titled *Role Models*. Her intention is 'to humanise the discourse about Muslims by presenting inspiring life stories,' and she is certainly correct to observe that 'highlighting the work of notable Muslims in contemporary India was a long-overdue task.'[548] It is, however, a task that can more effectively be performed by well-institutionalised civil society organisations like the RSS, and by responsible political parties like the BJP.

The modernisation of India's political parties

The BJP has led the government of India since 2014 and the government of Uttar Pradesh, India's largest state, since 2017. Although it has never won a majority of the popular vote either nationally or in the state, victories on that scale are rare in India's fractured multiparty democracy. Even the INC at the height of its dominance in the second half of the twentieth century did not win outright popular vote majorities. Today, the BJP is sufficiently dominant that it is able to set the agenda for Indian politics, both nationally and in Uttar Pradesh. The 2022 Uttar Pradesh election left it with a reduced majority in the state, but still holding more than twice as many seats as its nearest competitor. Similarly, in the 2024 national elections, the BJP won twice as many parliamentary seats as the INC. Despite its reduced dominance, the BJP remains the party to beat. That is all the more so because among all of India's political parties, the BJP alone is organised on a modern bureaucratic basis.

All societies have politics, but bureaucratically organised political parties are the distinctive form of political organisations in modern representative democracies. The German sociologist Max Weber (1864-1920) contrasted modern political parties with 'administration by notables ... [which] is, for instance, typical of political parties that have not been bureaucratized.'[549] In the premodern world, politics were contested along religious, tribal, or dynastic lines, with feudal loyalties taking precedence over formal bureaucratic obligations. In the modern world, politics continues to be concerned with the 'pursuit of interests' by groups and individuals, but 'interests oriented ideologically,' not around personal loyalties.[550] Weber's political sociology was never fully developed, but the nub of Weber's analysis—that modern politics are conducted by bureaucratically organised political parties, not clientelist organisations based on caste or family ties—forms the basic foundation of the field of political sociology.[551]

Translated to the Indian context, the Weberian approach implies that the many Indian political parties that are held together primarily by family, caste, or religious loyalties are, at a fundamental level, not truly 'modern'. This implication may be fiercely resisted by opponents of the BJP, but the description 'modern' is an analytical distinction, not a compliment. Nonetheless, Weberian theory does imply that parties that are characterised by premodern forms of social organisation are likely to fall by the wayside as India continues to modernise. For example, the BJP's chief opponent in Uttar Pradesh in 2024 was the Samajwadi Party, a caste-based party that also seeks to strategically represent Muslims who oppose the BJP.[552] Such identitarian alliances may succeed for a time, but they are unlikely to flourish in an ever-modernising social environment. At the national level, the INC faces similar challenges. It has been said that 'the trouble' with the INC 'is that Congress has never succeeded in evolving into a modern political party'—an observation attributed to none other than Indira Gandhi herself.[553]

In 2020, nearly four decades after Indira Gandhi's death, a group of 23 senior party figures wrote to the current INC party matriarch, Sonia Gandhi, to appeal for reforms that would have included professional party leadership and internal party democracy.[554] It was credibly reported that 'over 200' INC insiders supported the proposed reforms.[555] Nonetheless, the reform effort was quashed. One of the reformers, the then sixty-six-year-old member of parliament and former senior United Nations official Shashi Tharoor ran for the party presidency in 2022 but was decisively defeated by an 80-year-old Gandhi family 'loyalist.'[556] In the run-up to the 2024 national elections, a succession of would-be parliamentary candidates made the pilgrimage to the Gandhi family home seeking 'tickets'; the party and the press made no secret of the fact that Sonia, Rahul, and the latest family scion Priyanka (Rahul Gandhi's younger sister Priyanka Gandhi Vadra) were personally picking the INC's candidates for the 2024 national elections.

Few people outside India are aware that today's INC political party is not in any meaningful sense the heir to colonial India's big-tent INC national liberation movement. On the very eve of his assassination in 1948, Mahatma Gandhi was busy drafting a new constitution for the INC that would 'disband the existing Congress organisation' in order to ensure that it was 'kept out of unhealthy competition with political parties.'[557] That plan ended with his death, but many INC politicians did leave to start competing parties, including Syama Prasad Mookerjee, who founded the Jana Sangh. Then in 1969, Indira Gandhi was ejected from the INC. She started a competing INC, which ultimately overtook the original and in 1971 obtained recognition as its legal successor party.[558] In 1978, Mrs Gandhi resigned from the INC to protest its lack of support for her after her post-Emergency election defeat. The new 'INC' she founded once again flourished and came to be recognised as the legal successor party in 1981.[559]

The current INC is entirely the creation of Indira Gandhi. In the first two decades after independence, her father Jawaharlal Nehru transformed the INC from a national liberation movement into the archetype for what would become the Third World strongman party. When he died in harness in 1964, the party wavered, since he had not unambiguously set up his daughter to assume the reins of power. It took Indira Gandhi two years to fight her way to the Prime Ministership, literally over the dead body of her main rival, and then a further decade for her to transform the INC through two party splits into what would become the archetype of the South Asian family party. The INC remains a family fiefdom even today. It is not, in any sense, a modern political party. The political scientist Ashutosh Varshney goes further, characterising dynastic political parties like the INC as 'inherently anti-modern.'[560]

The 2020 reform effort was only made possible by a succession of serious political defeats that saw the INC's parliamentary representation reduced from 206 seats in 2009 to just forty-four seats in 2014 and fifty-two seats in 2019. Like a medieval monarch doling out dukedoms, a family that controls a political party is only able to command the loyalty of ambitious local grandees by demonstrating its ability to distribute political patronage. By failing to deliver Lok Sabha seats, the Gandhi family was not only weakening its control over the INC, but undermining the very rationale for the continued existence of the party. Many locally prominent politicians simply left the INC to join regional challengers or even the BJP, presumably in the hope of improving their electoral prospects. According to data from the non-partisan Association for Democratic Reforms, 35.4 per cent of all Indian national and state parliamentarians who switched parties between 2014 and 2021 were people leaving the INC, compared to 6.6 per cent who were leaving the BJP.[561] But with the party's bounce back to ninety-nine seats in the 2024 parliamentary elections under the very public campaign leadership of Rahul Gandhi, all momentum toward internal party reform came to an abrupt end.

Politics, ideology, and effective opposition

Rahul Gandhi's perceived success in the 2024 elections set back the potential reform of the INC by a decade or more. Of the ninety-nine INC members of parliament elected in 2024, only 24 were sitting incumbents.[562] The implication is that roughly three-quarters of the INC's parliamentarians owe their seats to the Gandhi family. Similar calculations apply to seats in the upper house, perhaps even more so, and to seats in state legislatures. Thus, although the INC clearly lost the 2024 election,, winning just 99 seats to the BJP's 240, the Gandhi family decisively won the battle for control of the INC. Even if the party suffers serious reversals in the next elections (expected in 2029), the family will be able to spin the narrative that the loss was only a random fluke—the same narrative that kept the Gandhis in control after the wipeout loss of 2014. It will likely take two consecutive reversals for the INC to once again be ripe for reform. On that timeline, the INC is likely to remain a family party at least until the 2030s.

This poses a serious problem for Indian democracy, because no other party is in a position to offer a coherent ideological alternative to the BJP. In a careful quantitative study of Indian political party ideologies in the 2014 elections, political scientists Pradeep K Chhibber and Rahul Verma found that the BJP presented a clear ideological programme centered on support for society and for the individual, or as they put it, opposition to the idea that 'the Indian state should be ontologically prior to society and should remake social norms' and opposition to 'special recognition for marginalised social groups through reservations, or quotas.'[563] The INC, by contrast, exhibited no clear position on either scale. With the exception of a few vestigial communist parties, India's hundreds of small, regional parties offer no grand narratives whatsoever. As a result, the key challenge facing Indian nationhood—ensuring full social inclusion of Muslim Indians—remains unaddressed.

The BJP has only been able to abjure responsibility for Muslim inclusion because no other party since the passing of Nehruvian idealism in the late 1960s has clearly articulated a vision of Indian national identity that explicitly incorporates Muslim Indians into the country's national story. Other parties have instead appealed for the votes of Muslim Indians on the basis of favours given to the Muslim religious establishment or by stoking fears of the BJP. Nor have they appealed to non-Muslim voters on the basis of an inspiring national story to rival the BJP's celebration of thousands of years of Hindu history in India stretching back to the mythological past. By opposing the BJP mainly on the basis of local and particularistic issues, India's ideologically inchoate opposition has in effect ceded the definition of India's national identity to the BJP.

International and academic critics of the BJP have focused on demonising the party for presenting an exclusionary vision of India's national identity, instead of asking why no other party is presenting a more inclusive vision. Their facile explanation for the success of the BJP's narrative is almost always 'majoritarianism'. Majoritarianism is a highly contested concept that lacks a consensus definition, but at its heart is the idea that a majority community in a democracy organises politically as a community and uses its political power to enact laws that give it advantages relative to other communities. The economist Kausik Gangopadhyay compiled a global database of the use of the terms 'majoritarian' and 'majoritarianism' for the three years 2020-2022, and found that in 80.0 per cent of all instances, the majority community referenced was the Hindu community of India.[564] This compares to 1.8 per cent for the Muslims of Pakistan and 0.8 per cent for the Buddhists of Myanmar, two communities that have almost entirely evicted adherents of minority religions from their countries. Clearly, the label is not being applied dispassionately to India.

The widespread characterisation of India as a Hindu majoritarian country documented by Gangopadhyay is out of all proportion to the scattered evidence of majoritarianism that can be adduced to make the case. Statistically, the accusation of majoritarianism is also a non-starter: the supposedly majoritarian BJP has never even reached 50 per cent of the Hindu vote in a national election. Nonetheless, there is a kernel of truth in the association of the BJP with an imagined Hindu majoritarianism, and that kernel is to be found in the BJP's Hindu-centric construction of Indianness. Though the BJP does not, as the international media routinely claims, subscribe to Savarkar's exclusionary formulation of Hindutva ideology, it does advocate a robust cultural nationalism that is unambiguously Hindu in inspiration and orientation.

Returning to Chhibber and Verma, the BJP doesn't just happen to oppose the very specific proposition that 'the Indian state should be ontologically prior to society and should remake social norms,' and its opposition to 'special recognition for marginalised social groups through reservations, or quotas' is not inherently anti-minority. As a careful reading of Chhibber and Verma would confirm, the BJP's resistance to using the state to impose social norms is actually anti-majoritarian, and most of the marginalised groups that receive the special reservations opposed by the BJP are Hindu. The BJP's ideology doesn't prioritise Hindu Indians over all other Indians. It prioritises a unified vision of Hinduness that is national, modern, and reformist above multiple other visions of Hinduness that are local, organic, and traditional. The BJP's perceived aversion to Muslimness is not so much organic as instrumental: nothing unites the Hindu community so much as distinguishing Hindus from Muslims, instead of distinguishing multiple Hindu communities from each other.

As the INC ideologue Shashi Tharoor explained in his 2018 book *Why I Am a Hindu*, the Hindu faith is characterised by a 'manifest diversity' which is reflected in its being practised 'differently by people in different parts of the country.'[565] Like many liberals, Tharoor averts his eyes from the ugly side of the diversity that he embraces in the abstract. He glosses over the persistence of a myriad of unreconstructed Hindu orders that have long opposed the modernisation and homogenisation of Hindu society. A prime example of this diversity is the Gorakhnath Math headed by Yogi Adityanath. The Yogi's ancient religious order is representative of hundreds (if not thousands) of expressions of Hinduness that are local, varied, traditional—and thoroughly illiberal. In a profoundly religious country like India, the most likely successful ideological opposition to the BJP would come not from a progressive alliance of globalist liberals, but from an identitarian alliance of localist reactionaries. The BJP might be very wise to keep the Yogi on their side.

The emerging fault lines of Indian politics

The 2024 elections saw the INC cobble together an unstable coalition of disparate state-level parties that could not agree on any shared principles other than opposition to the BJP. Looking forward to 2029, one possible future is that the state parties could dump the INC and unify behind a coherent ideological programme of identitarian localism. The only thing stopping them may be the lack of any natural nucleus, other than the INC, around which such a 'mafia style' coalition of local bosses could coalesce. If any one of India's dozens of local political dons were to win a crushing victory over the BJP in his or her home state, or even more impressively, in a neighbouring state, it could catalyse a reorganisation of the Indian party system into one in which the BJP faces off against an alliance of the regions, with the INC reduced to the status of a perennial also-ran. A development like this would reconfigure India's democracy into a more sociologically mature—even if less politically progressive—competition between two groups with clearly delineated ideologies of Indianness.

Such an outcome would incense the international political science establishment, but it might better reflect the emerging political fault lines of twenty-first century India. The key fault line of twentieth century India—the secular-Hindu, Englishstan-Hindustan, India-Bharat division—has largely played itself out.

Even the INC that once stood for a secular, English-speaking India no longer stands by these principles. The centerpieces of Rahul Gandhi's 2024 election campaign were a three-month *Bharat Jodo Yatra* followed by a three-month *Bharat Jodo Nyay Yatra*. In both marches, notice the use of 'Bharat' instead of 'India' in the branding. In the course of these events, he visited dozens of temples, sat for publicity photos with priests, and gave fiery speeches with ostentatious *tilaks* painted on his forehead. There is nothing untoward in any of this. It simply demonstrates that conspicuous secularism is no longer the cornerstone of the INC's sense of its own identity.

For its part, the BJP insists that it stands for 'genuine secularism' in contrast to the INC's 'pseudo secularism.'[566] Whatever form of secularism India has—and notwithstanding the many shrill warnings to the contrary, the secularism of the Indian state sits well within the boundaries exhibited by Western democracies—the secularism of the Indian state is no longer a major election issue in India. The branding of the BJP as a 'communal' Hindu party is no longer sufficient to deny it votes; when international critics condemn it as communal, the BJP leverages their interference to stoke nationalist sympathy and actually win votes. Even the country's most senior communist party leader, the Kerala chief minister Pinarayi Vijayan, now openly campaigns for the support of local temples in his home state, despite sitting on the 'politburo' of a party that literally has 'Marxist' in its name.[567] The old secular-Hindu faultline that once defined Indian politics has not disappeared, but it has lost much of its old relevance, and seems unlikely to make a comeback.

The alternative local-national fault line has always existed in India—especially in the form of the north-south linguistic divide—but it has always been more relevant for state than for national politics. It is tempting to assume that as India continues to modernise, the particularistic issues on which India's sixty or so state-level political parties fight elections will become less important, and that many of these clientelist and patronage-based political parties will either merge into the national parties, or disintegrate. But although modernisation will not favour parties that are organised around family, caste, or linguistic loyalties, this does not necessarily mean that the distinctively local issues on which they tend to fight elections will disappear. In recent years, many developed democracies have seen a resurgence in the importance of local identities. In the West, this resurgence has generally been framed in opposition to globalisation, but it may be that in India, increased localism will be framed as opposition to greater national integration.

This is not to suggest that local identities in India are in any sense anti-nationalist. It is possible, however, that the issues that matter most to many Indians are local, not national, and that many Indians would prioritise local goals like better air quality over national priorities like industrial development. There is a general post-election consensus that the BJP failed to maintain its absolute parliamentary majority in the 2024 elections because it centred its campaign around the national popularity of Narendra Modi instead of focusing on local constituency issues. There is even some ad hoc evidence of a religious dimension to this split. For example, Modi made a very public spectacle of his role in the consecration of the Ram Mandir in Ayodhya, characterising the temple opening as a national milestone for a new India. Yet when the people of Ayodhya went to the polls just four months later, they turned against the BJP incumbent with a five-point swing that cost him his seat.

It has long been fashionable in Western political science to discount the role of ideology in party formation, but classically, it was believed that democracy flourished when ideologically motivated political parties offered voters clearly defined alternative visions for the futures of their countries. Edmund Burke (1729-1798) argued as early as 1770 that the 'generous contention for power, on such manly and honourable maxims' as might be put forward by 'a body of men united ... upon some particular principle in which they are all agreed' is the foundation of good government.[568] It might be added that what Burke called 'manly and honourable maxims'—in more modern terms, unambiguous political programmes—are the key to establishing a party identity in the minds of voters. The one-third of the Indian electorate who form the bedrock voter base of the BJP have no doubt that they are supporting an unabashedly nationalistic ideology with an integrative Hindu tinge. If no other Indian party has such a solid voter base, it may be because no other Indian party offers such a clear ideological message.

Whatever its critics may think of it, the BJP is solidly united around fundamental principles that remain consistent from election to election. Most of the parties that oppose it, however, oppose the BJP on particularistic local issues, not on grand national narratives. When they seek Muslim Indian votes, they often don't offer any agenda at all, other than the need to defeat the BJP. If India's regional parties can turn their fractured opposition into a systematic ideological alternative based on localism and diversity, they would be well on their way to forming an effective national opposition. In the absence of such a grand narrative, they will remain scattered guerillas sniping at the BJP from their local fortresses without ever gaining power at the centre.

The calculus of inclusion

India is often described as having a 'dominant party' political system in which one party naturally prevails, but in reality, Indian election results are quite chaotic. For example, the BJP won 282 seats in parliament with just 31.0 per cent of the national vote in 2014 and 303 seats on 37.4 per cent of the vote in 2019, but it was knocked back to 240 seats in 2024 despite holding on to 36.6 per cent of the vote. In such a complex system, it would not take much of a shift to catapult a new party or party coalition to prominence. Advances in communications technology have dramatically reduced the costs of coordination, and it may be only a matter of time before a political genius emerges who can network together India's disparate local parties into a coherent national opposition. What effect the existence of such a coalition might have on the BJP is, of course, impossible to forecast. But one optimistic scenario is that it might push the BJP to work harder for Muslim votes—and to better integrate Muslim Indians into its version of India's national story.

In the historical secular-Hindu alignment of Indian politics, an obvious tactic for the BJP as an insurgent challenger was to squeeze the INC at its most vulnerable pressure point: its support for the Muslim community. In 2006, the technocratic INC Prime Minister Manmohan Singh (1932-2024) made an epic political error when he remarked in passing in a speech on infrastructure development that:

> We will have to devise innovative plans to ensure that minorities, particularly the Muslim minority, are empowered to share equitably in the fruits of development. They must have the first claim on resources.[569]

Notwithstanding an immediate clarification, the damage was done, and the BJP has relentlessly quoted (and often misquoted) this passage ever since. Singh's verbal slip has allowed the BJP to portray the INC as a specifically pro-Muslim party, thus portraying them as an implicitly anti-Hindu party. To be fair, the INC routinely portrays the BJP as an anti-Muslim party; that's politics. But as the BJP increasingly faces off against regional rivals, many of them closely connected to local Hindu communities, the BJP's tried-and-tested rhetoric of 'Muslim appeasement' will likely prove less effective.

In the wake of the BJP's 2024 national election reversals in Uttar Pradesh, the BJP chief minister Yogi Adityanath accused the SP of 'crossing all limits' to appease Muslim Indians.[570] The charge simply didn't stick. That is likely because the Samajwadi (Socialist) Party, though nominally secular, is in reality a caste-based party run by a Hindu family dynasty.[571] Despite relying on Muslims for roughly half of its votes, it ran only 4 Muslim candidates for the sixty-two parliamentary seats it contested in 2024, reportedly 'in a bid to shrug off its image as a party of Muslims and Yadavs.'[572] The party did indeed run five members from the Yadav caste, all from party leader Akhilesh Yadav's own family.[573] In good secular form, Yadav turned down the invitation to attend Narendra Modi's opening of the Ram Mandir in Ayodhya.[574] Instead, he led a Hindu prayer service actually inside his party headquarters to consecrate a stone that will form the centre of worship at a massive Shiva temple in his home district of Etawah.[575]

The competition between the BJP and the SP in Uttar Pradesh is emblematic of the new fault line that has opened up in Indian politics. It has little to do with the old ideological competition between secular and Hindu constructions of

Indian nationhood. It represents instead a choice between two competing visions of a Hindu India: one national and integrative, the other local and diverse. Arguably, a place for Muslim inclusion could be found in either of these. The BJP's national vision could be expanded to subsume India's Muslim heritage within a larger, more capacious national history—much as Savarkar sought to incorporate Muslim resistance to British rule into the story of Indian patriotism. Alternatively, India's regional parties could come to celebrate their local Muslim communities on the same basis that they now celebrate Hindu communities—thus valorising Muslim cultural achievements instead of merely promising to shield Muslims from the BJP.

Right now, both scenarios may seem equally far-fetched, but India's politics are highly competitive. With very few Muslim votes in its bank, the BJP has the most to gain. Its old strategy of prying Hindus away from the INC by leveraging instrumental Islamophobia is yielding diminishing returns. To continue growing, it must win at least some Muslim Indians over to its side. The party will never compromise with the Muslim religious establishment on issues like Sharia education, charity administration, or family law, but there are many anticlerical Muslims who actually favour the BJP's stance on these issues. They might be tempted to support the party electorally, but not until the BJP changes its historically anti-Muslim rhetoric. The BJP will never win a majority of the Muslim vote, but it doesn't need many Muslim votes to completely transform its electoral chances. As the party learnt in 2024, the margin between an absolute majority and a coalition government can be as thin as 0.8 per cent.

The core ideology of the BJP is not Islamophobia, or even Hindutva. It is hyper-nationalism. The BJP's most natural form of Muslim outreach would be to start adding historically prominent Muslim Indians to its growing pantheon of patriotic heroes. It has already appropriated the memories of both Mahatma Gandhi and the Dalit icon B R Ambedkar, despite having previously vilified both. No BJP leader will ever dedicate a statue to Aurangzeb, but in 2023, the Modi government featured Akbar in its G-20 Summit publicity materials, praising the Mughal emperor's 'democratic thinking' for being 'way ahead of its time'.[576] In recent years, the BJP's parent organisation, the RSS, has been careful to avoid potentially inflammatory anti-Muslim rhetoric. Judging from its awkward but seemingly genuine efforts at Muslim outreach, it may be that the RSS has come to see Hindu-Muslim reconciliation as being an important part of the organisation's *rashtra dharma* ('national duty'). In the wake of its 2024 election reversals, the somewhat more worldly BJP just might find the wisdom to follow suit.

India as *vishwa guru*

India's political parties may be divided by religion, but all of them agree that India is, and ought to be, a secular state. That was true even before Indira Gandhi inserted the word 'secular' into the Constitution in 1976-1977. The secular nature of the future Indian state had been hotly debated by India's Constituent Assembly; an amendment to characterise India as a 'secular' republic was put forward, but defeated. The chief drafter of the Constitution, B R Ambedkar, opposed the amendment on the grounds that the inclusion of the word was 'purely superfluous'; others pointed out that a legally secular state could not make special provisions for the protection of minority religions.[577] Although many members of the assembly thought that God deserved a place in the Constitution, nearly everyone agreed that the state should be secular, even those who advocated a

Hindu tinge. The only problem was that no one could quite agree what the word 'secular' meant.[578]

In India, the English text of the Constitution is the authoritative text, and the debate over what exactly the word 'secular' means in the Indian context has never gone away. For India's old INC Establishment, secular means *dharma nirpeksh* or indifferent to *dharma*. But for the new BJP Establishment, it means *panth nirpeksh* or indifferent to sect.[579] The dispute is fundamentally semantic, but it is also revealing. The BJP side argues that there can be no such thing as a state that is indifferent to *dharma*. The INC side responds that, in this context, *dharma* simply means 'religion' and the BJP side rightly replies that Muslims and Christians would never accept that their religions are 'dharmic.' The debate illustrates that even India's avowed secularists are in mind and spirit Hindu secularists: when they imagine a state that is indifferent to religion, they reflexively imagine one that is indifferent to the Hindu religion. The idea of Muslim secularism probably never crosses their minds.

The intellectual trap of defining secularism with respect to one's own religion is not a uniquely Indian phenomenon. But as the staunchly secular intellectual Shashi Tharoor writes, for many Hindus 'the distinction between 'religious' and 'secular' is an artificial one: there is no such compartmentalisation in Hinduism'. Echoing arguments that were already current a century ago, he asks:

> When you conduct your life by performing your duties ethically, are you 'secular' or (since you are fulfilling your *dharma* while adhering to a moral code) a 'good Hindu'?[580]

Tharoor wants to see his fellow Hindu Indians 'return to the tolerant, holistic, just, pluralist *dharma* articulated so effectively by Swami Vivekananda, which embraces both worldly and spiritual duty,' but it is not clear that they ever abandoned it. Tharoor's main political targets, the BJP and the RSS, publicly perform a deep commitment to toleration and religious pluralism, despite the fact that many of their members passionately dislike both Christianity and Islam. Tharoor's *bête noire*, the UP chief minister Yogi Adityanath, shows respect for Islam even as he disparages Muslim Indians and neglects their heritage sites. The key to reconciling such contradictions is to understand the sacred character of the Hindu commitment to *dharma*. A sacred commitment to duty is not needed to convince people to do things that they find easy, pleasant, or attractive. It is required to persuade people to take actions that they find arduous, distasteful, or repugnant—but correct.

An immediate challenge facing India's nation-builders throughout the colonial period and through to independence in 1947 was to prevent people killing each other in the name of religion. To foster tolerance, many of the leading figures of India's national liberation movement emphasised *dharma* or duty. During the violence of Partition, Gandhi fasted to remind Hindus and Sikhs of their duty 'not to touch a single Muslim' in retribution.[581] Speaking at the outset of the Constituent Assembly debates, Sarvepalli Radhakrishnan even demanded that *dharma* be made the basis of India's republican Constitution:

> Much has been said about the sovereignty of the people. We have held that the ultimate sovereignty rests with the moral law, with the conscience of humanity. People as well as kings are subordinate to that. Dharma, righteousness, is the king of kings. It is the ruler of both the people and the rulers themselves.[582]

Radhakrishnan's formulation is deeply conservative, but nothing in it is inconsistent with Western norms of democratic governance. It is not in any way opposed to democracy. In fact, it is strongly reminiscent of John Adams' famous dictum that a republic meant a '*government of laws, and not of men.*'[583] [italics in the original] Like Adams' government of laws, Radhakrishnan's government of *dharma* expresses a sentiment that is antecedent to democracy: not a sufficient condition for democracy, but a necessary one.

The sociologist Émile Durkheim wrote at the turn of the twentieth century that the increasing division of labour had created 'among men an entire system of rights and duties which link them together in a durable way.' Sounding quite Indian, Durkheim introspected that 'the duties of the individual towards himself are, in reality, duties towards society.'[584] Or in Hindu terms: one's *sva* [own] *dharma* is none other than *dharma* itself. In Western societies, the social solidarity or sense of duty toward society that arose during the transition to modernity is taken for granted when theorising democracy. But in India, and in the rest of the colonised world, that transition came late and was much less thorough. The impressive social solidarity of today's India did not arise from a modernising division of labour that undermined the old religious basis of society. It arose rather from the modernisation of religion itself, and it took its rhetoric from the religion that Hindus knew best: the religion that many Hindus call *Sanatana Dharma* or Eternal Dharma, and that Westerners call 'Hinduism.'

Narendra Modi likes to talk about India becoming a *vishwa guru* or world teacher. He tends to use the term in relation to uncontroversial initiatives like agricultural cooperation and the global spread of yoga. But if there is one thing that India really could teach the world, it is how to run a democracy in a poor, non-Western country where liberal individualism has no historical or philosophical roots. Western-style democracy has proven a tough sell in the developing world, especially in the deeply religious countries of Africa, Asia, and the Middle East. India's model of a democracy of duties—of a *dharma* democracy—might prove more palatable. Although the word *dharma* may not travel, the ideal of duty exists in every traditional culture. India might serve as a working model for how it can be leveraged to support the global spread of a more stable and more viable form of democracy.

The discovery of Bharat

The survival and, arguably, the flourishing of Indian democracy demonstrate that the Western path to democratic resilience is not the only one, and perhaps not even the most effective one for the highly traditional societies of the postcolonial world. The American experience looms large in the Western democracy literature, but the soaring rhetoric on which American democracy was founded is not necessarily applicable to poor, postcolonial countries struggling to form democratic nations in weak and fractured states. India's nation-builders worked under exactly such conditions, and the democracy they produced, though as flawed as any other, has stood the test of time. The Indian independence literature is largely autochthonous, having grown out of India's own fertile intellectual soil, and it is almost wholly unknown in the West. Yet its classics are engagingly argued, easily accessible, and nearly all written in English. They should be more widely read.

By far, the best-known work of India's independence era is Jawaharlal Nehru's 1946 book *The Discovery of India*. It is an insightful analysis of nationhood written by a practically minded politician. Nehru's diagnoses of the maladies of colonialism will raise no objections, but his admiration for the Soviet Union and aspirations that India should follow a Soviet model of industrialisation have aged poorly. On the opposite side of the ledger is Mahatma Gandhi's 1909 masterwork *Hind Swaraj* or *Indian Home Rule*. Whereas Nehru endorsed a Stalinist vision of forced industrialisation, Gandhi embraced a Tolstoyan idyll of peasant communalism. In *Hind Swaraj*, Gandhi made a political argument for *ahimsa* (non-violence), translating it from a religious principle into a policy agenda. His seemingly genuine belief that it was better to give one's life than to harm another in self-defence may have helped tamp down the violence of Partition. Arguably, it also cost many innocent lives.

Nehru and Gandhi represent opposing intellectual poles of the old India that was India. Other authors, no less prominent in their day, are perhaps more relevant to the New India that is Bharat. The most controversial of these is V D Savarkar, whose *Hindutva* (1923) has been the source of much debate. The more universally respected Sri Aurobindo Ghose is mainly known as a religious writer, but his 'Asiatic Democracy' essay of 1908 should be read by anyone who is interested in the foundations of democracy in the non-Western world. Beyond these two, every Indian is familiar with a trio who are affectionately remembered under the mnemonic 'Lal-Bal-Pal': Lala Lajpat Rai, Bal Gangadhar Tilak, and Bipin Chandra Pal. In their day, they were known as the 'extremists' of the INC who turned the movement from gentlemanly accommodation with the British toward advocacy of Indian freedom. Their works form the core of a solid library of careful thinking about democratic nation-formation in the non-Western world.

The 'Lion of Punjab' Lala Lapjat Rai (1865-1928) was an early advocate of Indian independence who in 1907 attempted to push the INC away from accommodation with the British. His best-known works are *The Story of My Deportation* (1908; an account of his exile to Burma for revolutionary activities) and *Young India* (1916; a history of Indian nationalism to that date). Americans in particular might be interested to read his 1916 travelogue *The United States of America: A Hindu's Impressions and a Study*, in which he lionises the African-American civil rights leaders Booker T Washington and W E B Du Bois. Less often read but much more important for the study of nationhood, however, is his 1919 book *The Political Future of India*. It offers a practical analysis of the challenges of living under foreign rule and the policies needed to support the formation of an independent nation-state.

The Maharastrian revolutionary Bal Gangadhar Tilak (1856-1920) was also exiled to Burma in 1907 for his participation in anti-colonial agitations and imprisoned there for six years. His most famous work is his 1903 book arguing that ancient Sanskrit speakers had migrated to India from the polar regions, *The Arctic Home in the Vedas*. Much more relevant for nation-formation, however, are his 1905 speech on language sovereignty, 'A Standard Character for Indian Languages,' and his 1908 speech on the centralisation of power, 'The Decentralisation Commission.' Equally enduring is his 1908 speech 'National Education,' which offers an incisive analysis of four issues: the role of religion in education, the use of English or local medium instruction, the importance of vocational education, and education in civics. All three speeches can be found in *Bal Gangadhar Tilak: His Writings and Speeches* (1918), a volume that is prefaced by an appreciation of Tilak by none other than Sri Aurobindo Ghose.

The Bengali journalist Bipin Chandra Pal (1858-1932) was the one professional writer of the Lal-Bal-Pal trio. His 1911 collection of essays *The Soul of India* was dedicated to the Hindu god Krishna. Anyone looking for the intellectual antecedents of the Indian civilisational nation can find them there, in the essays 'Dharma – The Basis of Our Civilisation' and 'The Character of Indian Unity.' Pal's 1916 collection *Nationality and Empire* is an outgrowth of the final essays of his previous book, in which he had argued that empires could only be justified as stepping stones toward world government. In the chapter on 'National Independence or Imperial Federation,' which was originally published in 1914, he wrote that full independence would mean the partition of India along religious lines. He predicted this sixteen years before the Muslim League called for a separate state.

Finally, to understand the formation of Indian nationhood, the *Bhagavad Gita* must be read. Its influence is inestimable; many of India's independence leaders actually published commentaries on the *Gita*, and all used it as a common reference point. The *Bhagavad Gita* is a 700-verse meditation on *dharma* that is the most accessible of all the ancient Hindu scriptures. It is a dialogue between the warrior Arjuna and the god Krishna, who explains to Arjuna that incarnating one's true being in this transitory life is the very essence of *dharma*. In the most widely cited passage of the *Bhagavad Gita*, Krishna advises that:

> One's own *dharma*, however badly done, is a higher good than another's *dharma*, however well done.

This exact sentiment is expressed on three different occasions in the *Gita*.[585] It represents the core teaching of the core text of popular Hindu spirituality. India's independence leaders made this passage the basis for responsible citizenship by successfully associating the warrior's *sva dharma* (own duty) with the citizen's *rashtra dharma* (national duty). This was the great accomplishment of India's nation-builders, and is the foundation of Indian democracy. Leaders as ideologically diverse as Mahatma Gandhi, Indira Gandhi, and Narendra Modi all placed supreme importance on this doctrine of duty. For them—and, if we listen carefully, for us—the discovery of Bharat is nothing other than the discovery of *dharma*.

References

1. Sri Aurobindo Ghose, 1908, 'Asiatic Democracy,' *Bande Mataram*, 16 March (pages 929-932 in *The Complete Works of Sri Aurobindo*, Volumes 6 and 7, 2002, Sri Aurobindo Ashram Trust, page 932).
2. Multiple authors, 2024, *Democracy Winning and Losing at the Ballot*, Varieties of Democracy Institute, page 17.
3. Ashoka Mody, 2023, *India Is Broken: A People Betrayed, Independence to Today*, Stanford University Press, pages 233, 18, and 19.
4. Christophe Jaffrelot, 2021, *Modi's India: Hindu Nationalism and the Rise of Ethnic Democracy*, translated by Cynthia Schoch, Princeton University Press, pages 349 and 405.
5. Debasish Roy Chowdhury and John Keane, 2021, *To Kill a Democracy: India's Passage to Despotism*, Oxford University Press, pages 198-216 and 264.
6. Maya Tudor, 2023, 'Why India's Democracy Is Dying,' *Journal of Democracy* 34(3):121-132, page 122.
7. Rahul Verma, 2023, 'The Exaggerated Death of Indian Democracy,' *Journal of Democracy* 34(3):153-161, pages 153 and 159.
8. Shekhar Gupta, 2024, 'Those Who Said Democracy Was Dead, Sit Down. Game's on in Indian Political League after a Frozen Decade,' *The Print*, 4 June.

9. Rajdeep Sardesai, 2024, *2024: The Election That Surprised India*, HarperCollins, pages xvii and 470.
10. Rahul Gandhi, 2024, 'Rahul Gandhi in the U.S. Targets Modi Government's Handling of China but Agrees with Its Approach on Pakistan,' *The Hindu*, 11 September.
11. Sarvepalli Radhakrishnan, 1927, *The Hindu View of Life*, Unwin Books, page 56.
12. Giuseppe Mazzini, 1890 [1861], *The Life and Writings of Joseph Mazzini*, Volume 1, Smith, Elder, & Company, pages 289 and 288.
13. M.K. Gandhi, 1938 [1909], *Hind Swaraj, or Indian Home Rule*, Revised New Edition, Navajivan Press, page 101.
14. Sri Aurobindo Ghose, 1908, 'Asiatic Democracy,' *Bande Mataram*, 16 March (pages 929-932 in *The Complete Works of Sri Aurobindo*, Volumes 6 and 7, 2002, Sri Aurobindo Ashram Trust, page 930).
15. Bal Gangadhar Tilak, 1919 [1918], *Bal Gangadhar Tilak: His Writings and Speeches*, Ganesh & Co., page 324.
16. R.K. Laxman, 1977, Cartoon, *Times of India*, 22 March.
17. Gyan Prakash, 2019, *Emergency Chronicles: Indira Gandhi and Democracy's Turning Point*, Princeton University Press, pages 279-299.
18. Alan Arian and Samuel H. Barnes, 1974, 'The Dominant Party System: A Neglected Model of Democratic Stability,' *Journal of Politics* 36(3): 592-614.
19. Matthijs Bogaards, 2005, 'Dominant Parties and Democratic Defects,' *Georgetown Journal of International Affairs* 6(2): 29-35.
20. Alberto Penadés and Sergio Velasco, 2022, 'Plebiscites: A Tool for Dictatorship,' *European Political Science Review* 14(1): 74-93.

21. Ted Robert Gurr, 1974, 'Persistence and Change in Political Systems, 1800-1971,' *American Political Science Review* 68(4): 1482-1504.

22. Monty G. Marshall and Ted Robert Gurr, 2020, *Polity5: Political Regime Characteristics and Transitions, 1800-2018*, Center for Systemic Peace.

23. Multiple authors, 2017, *Democracy at Dusk?*, Varieties of Democracy Institute, page 8.

24. Multiple authors, 2021, *Autocratization Turns Viral*, Varieties of Democracy Institute, pages 9 and 20.

25. Multiple authors, 2024, *Democracy Winning and Losing at the Ballot*, Varieties of Democracy Institute, page 29.

26. Unsigned, 2024, *Age of Conflict*, Economist Intelligence Unit.

27. Unsigned, 2023, *European Union Election Observation Mission Maldives: Preliminary Statement*, European Union, pages 2, 4, and 8.

28. Unsigned, 2022, *Maldives 2022 Human Rights Report*, US Department of State, page 10.

29. Multiple authors, 2024, *V-Dem Methodology V14*, Varieties of Democracy Institute, pages 18-19 and 21-23.

30. Aurel Croissant and Lars Pelke, 2022, 'Measuring Policy Performance, Democracy, and Governance Capacities: A Conceptual and Methodological Assessment of the Sustainable Governance Indicators (SGI),' *European Policy Analysis* 8(2): 136-159, page 142.

31. Betwa Sharma, 2023, 'India's Demotion to Electoral Autocracy Is Fair, Repeated Dismissal of International Surveys Unhelpful, Global Ranking Expert Explains,' *Article 14*, 9 January; Staffan Lindberg and Natalia Natsika, 2023, 'What Democratic Backsliding Means for India: A Q&A with V-Dem's Director and Program Manager,' The Carter Center, 10 February.

32. Multiple authors, 2024, *Democracy Winning and Losing at the Ballot*, Varieties of Democracy Institute, page 25.
33. Unsigned, undated, 'India,' Freedom House, accessed 20 April 2024.
34. Unsigned, 2023, *Rule of Law Index 2023*, World Justice Project.
35. Unsigned, undated, 'India,' Reporters Without Borders, accessed 20 April 2024.
36. Samirah Majumdar and Sarah Crawford, 2024, *Globally, Government Restrictions on Religion Reached Peak Levels in 2021, While Social Hostilities Went Down*, Pew Research Center.
37. Unsigned, 2024, *Countries at Risk for Mass Killing 2023-24*, United States Holocaust Memorial Museum, page 12.
38. Ian Vásquez, Fred McMahon, Ryan Murphy, and Guillermina Sutter Schneider, 2023, *The Human Freedom Index 2023*, Cato Institute and Fraser Institute.
39. Katrin Kinzelbach, Staffan I. Lindberg, Lars Pelke, and Janika Spannagel, 2023, *Academic Freedom Index Update 2023*, FAU Erlangen-Nürnberg and V-Dem Institute.
40. Hans-Joachim Lauth and Oliver Schlenkrich, 2020, *Conception of the Democracy Matrix*, Chair of Comparative Politics and German Government, University of Würzburg.
41. Unsigned, 2024, *Freedom in the World 2024 Methodology Questions*, Freedom House, page 2.
42. Vanessa A. Boese, 2019, 'How (not) to Measure Democracy,' *International Area Studies Review* 22(2): 95-127.
43. Multiple authors, 2024, *V-Dem Methodology V14*, Varieties of Democracy Institute, pages 13-14.
44. Unsigned, 2024, 'Global Team,' Varieties of Democracy Institute, accessed 20 April 2024.
45. Anna Lührmann, Marcus Tannenberg, and Staffan I. Lindberg,

2018, 'Regimes of the World (RoW): Opening New Avenues for the Comparative Study of Political Regimes,' Politics and Governance 6(1): 60-77.

46. Jan Teorell, Michael Coppedge, Staffan Lindberg, and Svend-Erik Skaaning, 2019, 'Measuring Polyarchy across the Globe, 1900–2017,' *Studies in Comparative International Development* 54(1): 71-95.
47. Robert A. Dahl and Charles E. Lindblom, 2017 [1953], *Politics, Economics, and Welfare*, Routledge, page 23.
48. Ibid., page 41.
49. Robert A. Dahl, 2006 [1956], *A Preface to Democratic Theory*, University of Chicago Press, page 84.
50. Robert A. Dahl, 1971, *Polyarchy: Participation and Opposition*, Yale University Press, page 3.
51. Robert A. Dahl, 1989, *Democracy and Its Critics*, Yale University Press, page 233.
52. Unsigned, 2024, *Age of Conflict*, Economist Intelligence Unit, page 64.
53. Multiple authors, 2024, *V-Dem Methodology V14*, Varieties of Democracy Institute, page 5.
54. Multiple authors, 2024, *V-Dem Codebook V14*, Varieties of Democracy Institute, page 51.
55. Robert A. Dahl, 1971, *Polyarchy: Participation and Opposition*, Yale University Press, pages 4-9.
56. Multiple authors, 2024, *V-Dem Codebook V14*, Varieties of Democracy Institute, page 52.
57. Pradeep K. Chhibber and Rahul Verma, 2018, *Ideology and Identity: The Changing Party Systems of India*, Oxford University Press, page 130.
58. Unsigned, undated, 'India,' Freedom House, accessed 20 April 2024.

59. Amit Ahuja and Susan Ostermann, 2021, 'The Election Commission of India: Guardian of Democracy,' pp. 37-62 in *Guardians of Public Value: How Public Organisations Become and Remain Institutions*, edited by Arjen Boin, Lauren A. Fahy, and Paul 't Hart, Palgrave Macmillan, pages 38 and 53.
60. Unsigned, 2019, 'Military Veterans, Academics & Ex-Civil Servants Slam EC over 'Least Fair' Lok Sabha Polls,' *The Print*, 3 July.
61. Alistair McMillan, 2010, 'The Election Commission,' pp. 98-116 in *The Oxford Companion to Politics in India*, edited by Niraja Gopal Jayal and Pratap Bhanu Mehta, Oxford University Press, page 109.
62. Alistair McMillan, 2012, 'The Election Commission of India and the Regulation and Administration of Electoral Politics,' *Election Law Journal* 11(2): 187-201, page 189.
63. Multiple authors, 2015, 'Faculty Statement on Narendra Modi Visit to Silicon Valley,' *Academe Blog*, 27 August.
64. Multiple authors, 2019, 'Dismay at Gates Foundation Prize for Narendra Modi,' *The Guardian*, 24 September.
65. Unsigned, 2023, 'More Than 500 Indian Scientists, Academics Slam Govt for Blocking BBC Documentary on Modi,' *The Wire*, 3 February.
66. Helen Packer, 2024, "Crisis' as Indian States Battle BJP for Control of Universities,' *Times Higher Education*, 1 April
67. Divya Trivedi, 2016, 'Personnel Matters,' *Frontline*, 3 February.
68. Ashlin Mathew, 2020, 'The Inside Story of Why Delhi University VC Yogesh K Tyagi Was Suspended,' *National Herald*, 29 October.
69. Deeptiman Tiwary, 2024, 'Since 2014, 25 Opposition Leaders Facing Corruption Probe Crossed Over to BJP, 23 of Them Got Reprieve,' *Indian Express*, 4 April.

70. Multiple authors, 2024, *V-Dem Codebook V14*, Varieties of Democracy Institute, page 202.
71. Multiple authors, 2024, *Democracy Winning and Losing at the Ballot*, Varieties of Democracy Institute, page 13.
72. Christopher Hernandez-Roy and Michael McKenna, 2023, 'Brazil's Misaligned Censorship Policy Risks Cutting Off Free Speech to Spite Disinformation,' Center for Strategic and International Studies, 25 May; Murillo Camarotto, 2024, 'Under Attack from So Many Quarters, Press Freedom in Brazil Is Now Threatened by Some Judges Too,' Reuters Institute for the Study of Journalism, 9 April.
73. Karishma Mehrotra and Joseph Menn, 2023, 'How India Tamed Twitter and Set a Global Standard for Online Censorship,' *Washington Post*, 8 November; unsigned, 2023, '16 Indian Journalists Have Been Charged Under UAPA, 7 Are Currently Behind Bars,' *The Wire*, 6 October.
74. The Constitution (First Amendment) Act, 1951.
75. Unsigned, 1951, 'Freedom of the Press,' *Times of India*, 21 May.
76. Unsigned, 1951, 'Freedom of the Press,' *Times of India*, 23 June.
77. Unsigned, 1951, 'Talking Too Much,' *Washington Post*, 28 June.
78. Unsigned, 1951, 'India's Press Law,' *New York Times*, 8 October.
79. Unsigned, 1954, 'Journalists Treated Like 'Criminal Tribes,' *Times of India*, 11 March.
80. Multiple authors, 2024, *V-Dem Codebook V14*, Varieties of Democracy Institute, pages 207, 210, and 188-189.
81. Ibid., page 210.
82. Hayam Qayyoum, Muhammad Riaz Raza, and Ayesha Sadaf, 2023, 'Analyzing the Impact of Censorship on Journalistic Practices: The Case of Pakistan,' *Pakistan Journal of Social Research* 5(2): 584-593.

83. Multiple authors, 2024, *V-Dem Codebook V14*, Varieties of Democracy Institute, page 210.
84. Ibid., page 209.
85. Ibid., page 208.
86. Ibid., page 209.
87. Siddhartha Deb, 2019, 'Killing Press Freedom in India,' pages 281-205 in *Press Freedom in Contemporary Asia*, edited by Tina Burrett and Jeffrey Kingston, Routledge.
88. Unsigned, undated, 'India,' Reporters Without Borders, accessed 20 April 2024.
89. Unsigned, undated, 'Explore All CPJ Data,' Committee to Protect Journalists, accessed 20 April 2024.
90. Multiple authors, 2024, *V-Dem Codebook V14*, Varieties of Democracy Institute, page 189.
91. Caroline Davies and Harriet Sherwood, 2024, 'UK Professor Suffered Discrimination Due to Anti-Zionist Beliefs, Tribunal Rules,' *The Guardian*, 6 February; Richard Adams, 2019, 'Cambridge College Sacks Researcher over Links with Far Right,' *The Guardian*, 2 May; Haroon Siddique, 2024, 'Open University Academic Wins Tribunal Case over Gender-Critical Views,' *The Guardian*, 23 January; James Reynolds, 2023, 'Law Lecturer Sacked after 'Objecting to Curriculum that Indoctrinated Students in Gender Identity Theory' at Open University,' *Daily Mail*, 19 August; unsigned, 2020, 'Southampton Lecturer Sacked over Racial Stereotype Comments,' *BBC News*, 22 July; Michael Koziol, 2022, 'University Unlawfully Sacked Lecturer over Nazi Swastika Incident, Court Finds,' *Sydney Morning Herald*, 28 October.
92. Unsigned, 2023, 'Support Grows for Ashoka University Economics Professor Who Resigned; 3 More Departments Issue Statements,' *Indian Express*, 18 August.

93. Unsigned, 2023, 'Ashoka University Political Science Department Extends Solidarity to Ex-Professors,' *Hindustan Times*, 17 August.

94. Anju Agnihotri Chaba and Bashaarat Masood, 2019, 'Kashmiri Professor at LPU Says Morphed Photo of FB Post Forced Him to Resign,' *Indian Express*, 20 February; Kamaldeep Singh Brar, 2022, 'Punjab: Lovely Professional University Sacks Faculty Member for 'Insulting' Lord Ram,' *Indian Express*, 24 April.

95. RG Sudharson, 2021, 'The Real Cause of a Summary Dismissal from an Academic Institution amidst the Pandemic,' GroundXero, 2 June.

96. Niraja Gopal Jayal, 2023, 'Academic Freedom in India,' pages 64-91 in *University Autonomy Decline Causes, Responses, and Implications for Academic Freedom*, edited by Kirsten Roberts Lyer, Ilyas Saliba, and Janika Spannagel, Routledge, page 64.

97. Pola Lem, 2022, 'Scholars 'Reprimanded by Universities' for Criticising Indian Government,' *Times Higher Education*, 20 July.

98. Sonia Sarkar, 2023, 'Row at India's Premier Private University Sparks Debate on Academic Freedom,' *Al Jazeera*, 28 August.

99. James Kierstead, 2024, 'Unpopular Opinions: Academic Freedom in New Zealand,' New Zealand Initiative, pages 20-31.

100. Laura Silver and Janell Fetterolf, 2024, 'Who Likes Authoritarianism, and How Do They Want to Change Their Government?' Pew Research Center, 28 February.

101. Richard Wike, Janell Fetterolf, Maria Smerkovich, Sarah Austin, Sneha Gubbala, and Jordan Lippert, 2024, 'Representative Democracy Remains a Popular Ideal, but People Around the World Are Critical of How It's Working,' Pew Research Center, 28 February, pages 102-106.

102. Unsigned, 2021, 'Writing Survey Questions,' Pew Research Center, 26 May.

103. Laura Silver and Janell Fetterolf, 2024, 'Who Likes Authoritarianism, and How Do They Want to Change Their Government?' Pew Research Center, 28 February.

104. Multiple authors, 2021, *Autocratization Turns Viral*, Varieties of Democracy Institute, page 14.

105. Ibid., page 9.

106. Salvatore Babones, 2024, "A Keralian Is Worth 1.8 Rajasthanis': Delimitation Is the Final Barrier to Real Democracy in India,' Firstpost, 29 March.

107. Andrew T. Little and Anne Meng, 2024, 'Measuring Democratic Backsliding,' *PS: Political Science & Politics* 57(2): 149-161, page 149.

108. Unsigned, 2010, 'Liberal Democracy,' *Oxford English Dictionary*, Third Edition, Oxford University Press.

109. Unsigned, 2018, *The Age Gap in Religion around the World*, Pew Research Center, page 58.

110. Carl O'Brien, 2020, 'Catholic Symbols in State Schools to Be Phased Out,' *Irish Times*, 12 October.

111. Pradeep K. Chhibber, 2014, *Religious Practice and Democracy in India*, Cambridge University Press, page 22.

112. Census 2011, undated, 'Uttar Pradesh Population 2011-2021,' *Census Population 2021 Data*, accessed 28 January 2021.

113. Reserve Bank of India, 2023, 'Table 25: Per Capita Net State Domestic Product (Current Prices),' *Handbook of Statistics on Indian States*, 15 November.

114. Stephanie Kramer, 2021, *Religious Composition of India*, Pew Research Center, pages 22 and 36; unsigned, 2015, 'Government Implementing Various Measures for Welfare of SCS,' Indian Ministry of Social Justice & Empowerment, 10 March.

115. Stephanie Kramer, 2021, *Religious Composition of India*, Pew Research Center, page 25; Amit Kapoor and Michael Green, 2022, *Social Progress Index: States and Districts of India*, Center for Inclusive Growth, page 302.
116. Uday Mahurkar, 2017, 'How They Won,' *India Today*, 18 March.
117. Shantanu Gupta, 2017, *The Monk Who Became Chief Minister*, Bloomsbury, page 161.
118. Unsigned, 2017, 'What is Yogi Adityanath's Hindu Yuva Vahini?' *Indian Express*, 17 May.
119. Sharat Pradhan, 2017, 'Yogi Adityanath's Own People Are Dragging His Reputation Down in UP,' *Daily O*, 1 May.
120. Unsigned, 2007, 'Yogi to Go with Hindu Mahasabha,' *Indian Express*, 27 March.
121. Shashank Chaturvedi, David N. Gellner, and Sanjay Kumar Pandey, 2019, 'Politics in Gorakhpur since the 1920s: The Making of a Safe 'Hindu' Constituency,' *Contemporary South Asia* 27(1): 40-57.
122. Shantanu Gupta, 2017, *The Monk Who Became Chief Minister*, Bloomsbury, pages 33-34.
123. Rahul Verma and Shashwat Dhar, 2018, 'The Muslims Voting for the BJP Are Richer, More Educated and Conservative,' *The Print*, 21 September.
124. Hilal Ahmed, 2019, 'BJP Is Emerging as Second-Most Preferred Political Choice for Muslim Voters in India,' *The Print*, 24 April.
125. Rahul Verma and Shashwat Dhar, 2018, 'The Muslims Voting for the BJP Are Richer, More Educated and Conservative,' *The Print*, 21 September.
126. Feyaad Allie, 2024, 'Mapping Muslim Voting Behavior in India,' Carnegie Endowment for International Peace, 9 February.

127. Salvatore Babones, 2021, 'For Modi, Courting the Arab World Begins With India's Muslims,' *Foreign Policy*, 19 January.
128. Damayanti Datta, 2017, 'Oye Romeo!' *India Today*, 31 March.
129. Unsigned, 2017, 'Adityanath Starts Term by Unleashing 'Anti-Romeo Squads' on UP Streets,' *The Wire*, 22 March.
130. Nita Bhalla, 2017, 'India's 'Anti-Romeo Squads' Accused of Harassing Couples, Shaming Young Men,' *Reuters*, 5 April.
131. Piyush Rai, 2018, 'Hindu Yuva Vahini Men Thrash Muslim Youths, Assault Journalist,' *Times of India*, 31 January.
132. Unsigned, 2017, ' UP's Anti-Romeo Squad Shave the Head of Man Held for Allegedly Molesting a Woman,' *Firstpost*, 1 April.
133. Unsigned, 2018, 'Yogi Adityanath's Anti-Romeo Squad to Be Strengthened: Here's Set of Guidelines Issued by UP Police,' *Financial Express*, 14 July.
134. Unsigned, 2019, 'Re-Activate Anti-Romeo Squads: UP Chief Minister Yogi Adityanath,' *Times of India*, 11 June.
135. Varghese K. George, 2019, 'U.P.'s Law and Order Has Become a Model for the Country: CM Adityanath,' *The Hindu*, 19 March.
136. Tanseem Haider, 2020, 'Hathras Horror: Police, Victim's Family Give Contradictory Accounts,' *India Today*, 30 September.
137. Geeta Pandey, 2020, 'Hathras Case: A Fatal Assault, a Cremation and No Goodbye,' *BBC News*, 7 October.
138. Unsigned, 2020, 'Hathras Case a Small Issue, Woman Was Not Gang-Raped, Says UP minister,' *The Print*, 2 October.
139. Unsigned, 2020, 'Hathras Woman Was Not Raped, Forensic Report Shows No Sperm, Claims UP Police,' *The Print*, 1 October.
140. Alok Pandey, 2020, "Deep Conspiracy In Hathras': UP Police Files 19 Cases Across State,' *NDTV*, 5 October.
141. Unsigned, 2020, 'Yogi Adityanath Suspends Hathras SP, Wants Narco-Analysis Tests to Be Conducted,' *Hindustan Times*, 2 October.

142. Unsigned, 2020, 'UP CM Yogi Adityanath Recommends CBI Probe in Hathras Gang-Rape Case,' *Hindustan Times*, 3 October.
143. Unsigned, 2020, 'CBI Says Hathras Teen Was Gangraped; Question Marks over UP Police Claim,' *Indian Express*, 19 December.
144. Milan Sharma, 2023, "Got the Justice a Dalit Deserves': Hathras Victim's Family after 3 Accused Walk Free,' *India Today*, 4 March.
145. Sanya Dhingra, 2020, 'Who Are Thakurs of UP and Why Are They Powerful? Answers Are Key To Understanding Hathras, *The Print*, 9 October.
146. Krishnanand Tripathi, 2019, 'BJP Counts on Support of Influential Thakur Community in Hindi Heartland,' *Financial Express*, 22 March.
147. Nikhil Rampal, 2019, 'How BJP Wrested Dalit Seats in UP… with Help from Turncoats,' *India Today*, 30 July.
148. Brinda Karat, 2000, 'Adityanath's Caste Code on Full Display in Hathras,' *NDTV*, 1 October.
149. Prashant Srivastava, 2020, 'Yogi Govt Approves 'Love Jihad' Ordinance with 3-10 Years of Jail Term, Rs 50,000 Penalty,' *The Print*, 24 November.
150. Arundhati Katju, 2020, 'The Hindu Nationalist Myth of Love Jihad,' *Foreign Affairs*, 23 December.
151. Soutik Biswas, 2020, 'Love Jihad: The Indian Law Threatening Interfaith Love,' *BBC News*, 8 December.
152. Manju Sara Rajan, 2009, 'The Catholic Fatwa against Love Jihad,' *Open*, 22 October.
153. Revathi Krishnan, 2020, 'Uttar Pradesh Police Makes First Arrest under New 'Love Jihad' Law,' *The Print*, 2 December.
154. Revathi Krishnan, 2020, 'Hindu Families Seek 'Justice', Muslims Bereft – UP 'Love Jihad' Law Has Bareilly in Frenzy,' *The Print*, 5 December.

155. Unsigned, 2023, 'Conversions: 855 Arrests in UP since 2020,' *Times of India*, 13 May.
156. Prashnu Mishra, 2020, 'Conspicuous by Absence: Term 'Love Jihad' Not Mentioned in UP Govt's Proposed Law Against Forced Religious Conversion,' *News18*, 20 November.
157. Neha Sahgal, Jonathan Evans, Ariana Monique Salazar, Kelsey Jo Starr, and Manolo Corichi, 2021, *Religion in India: Tolerance and Segregation*, Pew Research Center, 'Topline Questionnaire' supplemental file, pages 19 and 100.
158. Anushree Jairath, 2020, 'How Special Marriage Act Is Condemning Interfaith Couples to UP-Style Anti-Conversion Laws,' *The Print*, 29 December.
159. Aneesha Mathur, 2020, 'Anti-Conversion Laws in India: How States Deal with Religious Conversion,' *India Today*, 23 December.
160. Mohan Rao, 2011, 'Love Jihad and Demographic Fears,' *Indian Journal of Gender Studies* 18(3): 425-430.
161. Sebastian Schwecke, 2011, *New Cultural Identitarian Political Movements in Developing Societies: The Bharatiya Janata Party*, Routledge, page 59.
162. M. Mohibul Haque and Abdullah Khan, 2023, 'Mapping Islamophobia: The Indian Media Environment,' *Islamophobia Studies Journal* 8(1): 83-99, page 90.
163. Véronique Bouillier, 2020, 'Yogi Adityanath's Background and Rise to Power,' *South Asia Multidisciplinary Academic Journal* 24/25, unpaginated.
164. Shantanu Gupta, 2017, *The Monk Who Became Chief Minister*, Bloomsbury, pages 99-100.
165. Kaushik Deka, 2024, 'Best CMs: Reigning Supreme,' *India Today*, 19 February.
166. Gulam Jeelani and Abdul Jadid, 2017, 'Yogi Adityanath's Band of Rebels Want to Teach BJP a Lesson in Eastern UP,'

Hindustan Times, 11 February.

167. Rohini Singh, 2017, 'Why Narendra Modi and Amit Shah picked Yogi Adityanath as Uttar Pradesh CM,' *Economic Times*, 20 March.
168. Radhika Ramaseshan, 2017, '3 Reasons that Endeared Yogi Adityanath to Shah-Modi,' *Rediff*, 8 April.
169. Gautam Siddharth, 2017, 'Gorakhnath Math, That Is Hub of Politics, Has Non-Brahmin Priests,' *Economic Times*, 19 March.
170. Rajdeep Sardesai, 2024, *2024: The Election That Surprised India*, HarperCollins, page 365.
171. Uday Mahurkar, 2016, 'The Other Modis,' *India Today*, 29 December.
172. Abhishek Mishra, 2022, 'Yogi Adityanath Declares Assets Worth Rs 1.54 Crore; Owns Revolver, Rifle, Samsung Phone,' *India Today*, 4 February.
173. Joel Kurian, 2020, 'Yogi Adityanath's Sister Shashi's Simple Lifestyle In Village Leaves Celebs, Netizens Awed,' *Republic World*, 7 April.
174. Dhirendra K Jha, 2017, 'RSS Said to Have Asked Adityanath to Disband Hindu Yuva Vahini,' *Scroll*, 16 May.
175. Shivam Vij, 2019, 'With Yogi as CM, His Hindu Yuva Vahini Has All but Disappeared from Gorakhpur,' *The Print*, 14 May.
176. Unsigned, 2018, 'Hindu Mahasabha Accuses Yogi Adityanath of Dividing Hindus, Wants EC to Ban Him from Addressing Polls Rallies in Rajasthan,' *Janata Kai Reporter*, 30 November.
177. Namita Bajpai, 2022, ' Yogi's Hindu Yuva Vahini Dissolved, to Be Revamped Soon to Assist BJP in 2024 LS Polls,' *New Indian Express*, 5 August.
178. Duncan McDonnell and Luis Cabrera, 2019, 'The Right-Wing Populism of India's Bharatiya Janata Party (and Why Comparativists Should Care),' *Democratization*, 26(3) 484-501, page 495.

179. Uday Mahurkar, 2017, 'The Yogi of Fear and Hope,' *India Today*, 27 March.
180. Unsigned, 2019, 'UP Police Constable Recruitment Exam Fraud: 24 People Arrested,' *Times of India*, 28 January.
181. Kumar Anshuman, 2018, 'A Million Students in UP Have Dropped Out of Board Exams Because They Couldn't Cheat,' *The Print*, 15 February.
182. Unsigned, 2020, '50% Attendance and 9:30 am in Time Must for Gov't Offices: UP CM Yogi Adityanath,' *Times of India*, 29 August.
183. Neha Lalchandani, 2020, 'In UP Cities, Yogi Adityanath Government to Deliver Food at Doorsteps,' *Times of India*, 25 March.
184. Preeti Panwar, 2017, 'Will Call You Anytime, Be Present in Office Always: Yogi Adityanath Warns Babus,' *One India*, 28 April.
185. K. Krishna Murthy, 1996, 'Dharma – Its Etymology,' *The Tibet Journal* 21(1): 84-87, page 85.
186. Laurie L. Patton, 2008, *The Bhagavad Gita*, Penguin Books, page 24 (verse 2:31).
187. Garrett W Brown, Iain McLean, and Alistair McMillan, 2018, 'Hindu Nationalism,' *Concise Oxford Dictionary of Politics and International Relations*, Fourth Edition, Oxford University Press.
188. Christophe Jaffrelot, 2014, 'The Other Saffron,' *Indian Express*, 6 October.
189. Angana P. Chatterji, 2019, 'Remaking the Hindu/Nation: Terror and Impunity in Uttar Pradesh,' pp. 397-418 in *Majoritarian State: How Hindu Nationalism Is Changing India*, edited by Angana P. Chatterji, Thomas Blom Hansen, and Christophe Jaffrelot, Hurst & Company, page 397.
190. Raman Kirpal, 2013, 'Muzaffarnagar Riots: How BJP, SP and BSP Fanned the Flames,' *Firstpost*, 16 September.

191. Unsigned, 2013, 'Conditions at Relief Camps Appalling: NHRC,' *Indian Express*, 22 October.

192. Soumik Mukherjee, 2013, 'How the SP Has Shockingly Failed Its Muzaffarnagar Refugees,' *Firstpost*, 20 December.

193. Harsh Mander, 2016, 'Muzaffarnagar, Three Years Later,' *Indian Express*, 7 September.

194. Kaushik Deka, 2024, 'Best CMs: Reigning Supreme,' *India Today*, 19 February.

195. Hilal Ahmed, 2019, 'Muslim Votes Matter: Here's How They Voted for BJP after 2014,' *The Print*, 10 April.

196. Debalina Dey, 2020, 'Arundhati Roy Joins Shashi Tharoor, Kangana Ranaut in List of 'Casteless' Upper-Caste Indians,' The Print, 6 September.

197. Jawaharlal Nehru, 1947, Constituent Assembly Debates, 14 August.

198. Muhammad Ali Jinnah, 2000 [1947], *Jinnah Papers, Volume 5 – Pakistan: Pangs of Birth*, Oxford University Press, page 1.

199. Sarvepalli Radhakrishnan, 1947, Constituent Assembly Debates, 14 August.

200. Unsigned, 2024, 'Lord Ram's Homecoming, PM Modi Leads Rituals in Ayodhya, Celebrations across India,' *India Today*, 22 January.

201. Sravasti Dasgupta, 2024, 'PM Modi in Ram Temple Pran Prathishtha: End of Secularism as 'Distance' between State and Religion?' *The Wire*, 21 January.

202. Unsigned, 2024, "Clearly an RSS-BJP Event': Congress Says Won't Attend Ram Mandir Inauguration, *Indian Express*, 10 January.

203. Vir Sanghvi, 2024, 'Is Ram a Symbol of a United India or of Hindu Victory? The Answer Will Shape New India,' *The Print*, 25 January.

204. Unsigned, 1929, 'The U.P. Tour,' *Young India* 11(38): 305-307, page 305.
205. Unsigned, 2020, 'Ram Mandir Bhumi Pujan: Full Text of PM Narendra Modi's Speech in Ayodhya,' *Indian Express*, 5 August.
206. Unsigned, 2024, "Ram is Not a Dispute, Ram Is a Solution' - Full Text of PM Modi's Speech at Ayodhya Consecration,' *The Print*, 23 January.
207. Unsigned, 2010, 'Merkel Urges Germans: Stand Up for Christian Values,' *Reuters*, 16 November.
208. Soeren Kern, 2010, 'Islam 'Does Not Belong' to Germany,' Gatestone Institute, 9 March.
209. G.T. Nanavati and Akshay H. Mehta, 2008, *Report by the Commission of Inquiry*, Part 2, Government of Gujarat, page 8.
210. G.T. Nanavati and Akshay H. Mehta, 2008, *Report by the Commission of Inquiry*, Part 1, Government of Gujarat, page 158.
211. Darpan Singh, 2002, 'Gujarat Riots Clean Chit to PM: Two Decades of Legal Battle and What's Next,' *India Today*, 24 June.
212. Unsigned, 1946, "Either Divided or Destroyed India': Frontier Leader's View,' *Times of India*, 30 July.
213. Unsigned, 1946, 'Direct Action for Pakistan: Moslems Withdraw Their Agreement: Fears of Congress,' *Manchester Guardian*, 30 July.
214. Unsigned, 1946, 'Congress at Centre to Be Resisted: League Secretary's Avowal,' *Times of India*, 6 August.
215. Unsigned, 1946, "Either Divided or Destroyed India': Frontier Leader's View,' *Times of India*, 30 July.
216. Unsigned, 1946, "No Violence on August 16: Mr. Jinnah's Appeal to Muslims,' *Times of India*, 15 August.

217. Anita Inder Singh, 1989, *The Origins of the Partition of India, 1936-1947*, Oxford University Press, pages 181-182.
218. George E. Jones, 1946, 'Premier Is Blamed in Calcutta Riots,' *New York Times*, 22 August.
219. Bidyut Chakrabarty, 2004, *The Partition of Bengal and Assam, 1932-1947: Contour of Freedom*, Routledge Curzon, pages 99-101.
220. Claude Markovits, 2007, 'The Calcutta Riots of 1946,' *Violence de Masse et Résistance - Réseau de Recherche*, 5 November.
221. Bidyut Chakrabarty, 2004, *The Partition of Bengal and Assam, 1932-1947: Contour of Freedom*, Routledge Curzon, pages 126-127.
222. Muhammad Jinnah, 1945, 'Extract from a Speech Delivered by Muhammad Jinnah,' *The National Archives* (UK), 6 December.
223. A.G. Noorani, 1980 [1946], 'Review: Prelude to Partition,' *Economic and Political Weekly* 15(50): 2090-2094, page 2093.
224. Crispin Bates, 2011, 'The Hidden Story of Partition and Its Legacies,' *BBC News*, 3 March.
225. S.P. Singh, 1998, 'Indian Nationalism and Burma,' *Proceedings of the Indian History Congress* 59: 891-900, page 893.
226. M.S. Golwalkar, 1966 [1960], *Bunch of Thoughts*, Sharda Press, pages 80-84.
227. Manu Goswami, 2004, *Producing India: From Colonial Economy to National Space*,' Chicago: University of Chicago Press, page 191.
228. Francis Robinson, 2001, 'The British Empire and the Muslim World,' pages 398-420 in *The Oxford History of the British Empire*, Volume 4, edited by Judith M. Brown, Oxford University Press.
229. J.A. Baines, 1893, *Census of India, 1891: General Report*, Eyre and Spottswood, page 171; W.W.M. Yeatts, 1943, 'The Indian Census of 1941,' *Journal of the Royal Society of Arts* 91(4634): 182-194, page 185.

230. Unsigned, undated, 'Independence and Partition, 1947,' UK National Army Museum, accessed 13 January 2024.
231. Unsigned, 1930 [1929], 'Documents concerning the Origin and Purpose of the Indian Statutory Commission,' *International Conciliation* 13 (258): 129-187, page 130.
232. Unsigned, undated, 'Nehru Report (Motilal Nehru,1928),' *Constitution of India*, accessed 27 March, 2021.
233. Unsigned, undated, 'Fourteen Points Proposed by M.A. Jinnah on Behalf of the Muslim League (1929),' *Routledge History of India*, accessed 17 March 2021.
234. Muhammad Iqbal, 1930, 'Presidential Address to the 25th Session of the All-India Muslim League,' 29 December. Muhammad Ali Jinnah, 1940, 'Presidential address by Muhammad Ali Jinnah to the Muslim League,' 22 March.
235. Asoka Mehta and Achyut Patwardhan, 1942, *The Communal Triangle in India*, Allahabad: Kitabistan, pages 52-79.
236. V.P. Menon, 1957, *The Transfer of Power in India*, Princeton University Press, page 438.
237. Rajendra Prasad, 1940, *Pakistan*, Allied Publishers, page 8.
238. B.R. Ambedkar, 1945, *Pakistan or Partition of India*, Second Edition, Thacker and Company, page 102; see also page 358.
239. Jawaharlal Nehru, 1982 [1946], *The Discovery of India*, Oxford University Press, page 528.
240. Rajendra Prasad, 1947, *India Divided*, Third Edition, Kitabs, page 367.
241. B.R. Ambedkar, 1945, *Pakistan or Partition of India*, Second Edition, Thacker and Company, page 178.
242. Ibid., page 365.
243. Braj Kishore Singh, 1990, *The Indian National Congress & the Partition of India, 1937-47*, Capital Publishing House, pages 91-94.

244. Rajendra Prasad, 1947, *India Divided*, Third Edition, Kitabs, page 337.
245. M.K. Gandhi, 1984 [1948], 'Draft Constitution of Congress,' pages 526-258 in *The Collected Works of Mahatma Gandhi*, Volume 90, Government of India, page 526-527.
246. Unsigned, 1948, '3 Cities in India Swept by Rioting,' *New York Times*, 1 February; Unsigned, 1948, 'India-Wide Arrests of R.S.S. and Sabha Men,' *Times of India*, 8 February.
247. Jawaharlal Nehru, 1982 [1946], *The Discovery of India*, Oxford University Press, page 396.
248. Ibid., page 190.
249. F. K. Khan Durrani, 1988 [1944], *The Meaning of Pakistan*, Islamic Book Service, pages 78 and 109.
250. Prabhu Bapu, 2013, *Hindu Mahasabha in Colonial North India, 1915-1930: Constructing Nation and History*, Routledge, page 77.
251. B.R. Ambedkar, 1945, *Pakistan or Partition of India*, Second Edition, Thacker and Company, page 131.
252. V.D. Savarkar, 1969 [1923], *Hindutva: Who Is a Hindu?*, Fifth Edition, S.S. Savarkar, page 134.
253. Ibid., pages 83-84.
254. Vikram Visana, 2020, 'Savarkar before Hindutva: Sovereignty, Republicanism, and Populism in India, c.1900-1920,' *Modern Intellectual History* (preprint): 1-24, page 24.
255. Janaki Bakhle, 2010, 'Savarkar (1883–1966), Sedition and Surveillance: The Rule of Law in a Colonial Situation', *Social History*, 35(1): 51-75, page 52.
256. Jennifer Jackson Preece, 1998, *National Minorities and the European Nation-States System*, Oxford University Press, page 75.
257. Arun Anand, 2020, 'Why 1921 Malabar Moplah Rebellion Wasn't a Peasant Uprising but an 'Anti-Hindu Genocide',' *The Print*, 20 August.

258. B.R. Nanda, 2002, *Gandhi: Pan-Islamism, Imperialism and Nationalism in India*, Oxford University Press, pages 312 and 319.
259. Robert L. Hardgrave, Jr., 1977, 'The Mappilla Rebellion, 1921: Peasant Revolt in Malabar,' *Modern Asian Studies* 11(1): 57-99, pages 83 and 99.
260. F.K. Khan Durrani, 1929, *The Future of Islam in India: A Warning and a Call*, Muslim India, pages 89, 94, 25.
261. John Stuart Mill, 1861, *Considerations on Representative Government*, Parker, Son, and Bourne, page 287.
262. Woodrow Wilson, 1907 [1898], *The State: Elements of Historical and Practical Politics*, Revised Edition, D.C. Heath & Co., page 306.
263. James Bryce, 1922, *International Relations: Eight Lectures Delivered in the United States in August, 1921*, Macmillan, page 116.
264. Rajendra Prasad, 1947, *India Divided*, Third Edition, Kitabs, pages 8 and 10 (emphasis in original).
265. Ibid., page 14.
266. John R. McLane, 1977, *Indian Nationalism and the Early Congress*, Princeton University Press, page 21.
267. Thomas Macaulay, 1920 [1835], 'Minute on Education,' pages 107-117 in *Selections from Educational Records, Part I (1781-1839)*, edited by H. Sharp, Superintendent Government Printing, India, page 116.
268. Tavleen Singh, 2024, 'I Met Nobody in Rural India Who Saw Modi as Corrupt and Autocratic,' *Indian Express*, 25 April.
269. Jawaharlal Nehru, 1947 Constituent Assembly Debates, 14 August.
270. Benedict Anderson, 1983, *Imagined Communities: Reflections on the Origin and Spread of Nationalism*, Verso, page 16.
271. Louis Mountbatten, 1982 [1971-1973], *Mountbatten and the Partition of India*, Volume 1, edited by Larry Collins and Dominique Lapierre, Vikas Publishing, page 70.

272. Jeffrey Prager, 1986, *Building Democracy in Ireland: Political Order and Cultural Integration in a Newly Independent Nation*, Cambridge University Press, page 5.

273. Jeffrey Prager, 1981, 'Moral Integration and Political Inclusion: A Comparison of Durkheim's and Weber's Theories of Democracy,' *Social Forces* 59(4): 918-950, page 946.

274. Jeffrey Prager, 1986, *Building Democracy in Ireland: Political Order and Cultural Integration in a Newly Independent Nation*, Cambridge University Press, page 4.

275. Rabindranath Tagore, 1917, *Nationalism*, Book Club of California, page 117.

276. Ibid., pages 15, 118, and 139.

277. Ibid., page 127.

278. Ibid., pages 131 and 133.

279. Ibid., pages 95-99 and 144-147.

280. Ibid., pages 19-20.

281. Émile Durkheim, 1958 [1890-1912], *Professional Ethics and Civic Morals*, translated by Cornelia Brookfield, Free Press, page 98.

282. Woodrow Wilson, 1918, Address to Congress, 11 February.

283. Seymour Martin Lipset, 1959, 'Some Social Requisites of Democracy: Economic Development and Political Legitimacy,' *American Political Science Review* 53(1): 69-105, page 86.

284. Barrington Moore, Jr., 1966, *Social Origins of Dictatorship and Democracy: Lord and Peasant in the Making of the Modern World*, Beacon Press, page 418.

285. Seymour Martin Lipset, 1960, *Political Man: The Social Bases of Politics*, Doubleday, page 50.

286. Unsigned, 2023, *Education at a Glance 2023*, OECD Publishing, page 50.

287. Adam Przeworski, Michael E. Alvarez, Jose Antonio Cheibub, Fernando Limongi, 2000, *Democracy and Development: Political Institutions and Well-Being in the World, 1950-1990*, Cambridge University Press, page 87.
288. Joseph Henrich, 2020, *The WEIRDest People in the World: How the West Became Psychologically Peculiar and Particularly Prosperous*, Farrar, Straus and Giroux.
289. Jacques Nevard, 1964, 'Shastri Worries India: State of Prime Minister's Health Is a Cause for Concern in Face of the Nation's Many Problems,' *New York Times*, 25 July.
290. Soutik Biswas, 2009, 'Was Mr Shastri Murdered?' *BBC News*, 27 August.
291. Putnam Welles Hangen, 1963, *After Nehru, Who?* Harcourt, Brace, pages 277 and 279.
292. Ravi Visvesvaraya Sharada Prasad, 2020, 'Nehru Wanted Jayaprakash Narayan as His Political Successor, not Indira Gandhi,' *The Print*, 27 May.
293. Jawaharlal Nehru, 1947, Constituent Assembly Debates, 14 August.
294. Unsigned, 1969, 'P.M. Hits Back as Party Chief Gives Her Grave Warning,' *Times of India*, 4 November.
295. Ramachandra Guha, 2007, *India after Gandhi: The History of the World's Largest Democracy*, HarperCollins, page 448.
296. Amrith Lal, 2015, '40 Years on, Those 21 Months of Emergency,' *Express*, 20 July.
297. Aaron S. Klieman, 1981, 'Indira's India: Democracy and Crisis Government,' *Political Science Quarterly* 96(2): 241-259, pages 245-251.
298. Sarvepalli Radhakrishnan, 1947, Constituent Assembly Debates, 14 August.
299. Granville Austin, 1999, *Working a Democratic Constitution: A*

History of the Indian Experience, Oxford University Press, page 394.

300. Ravi Visvesvaraya Sharada Prasad, 2021, 'The Inside Story of Why Indira Gandhi Called the 1977 Elections,' *Hindustan Times*, 19 March.
301. Purav Thakur, 2023, 'Row Over 'Secular' and 'Socialist': How and Why Were the Words Added to the Preamble?' *India Today*, 20 September.
302. Shashi Skekhar, 2023, *Collective Spirit, Concrete Action: Mann Ki Baat and Its Influence on India*, Rupa Publications India, page 182; G. N. Sarma, 1980, 'Gandhi's Concept of Duty,' *Indian Journal of Political Science* 41(2): 214-231.
303. Narendra Modi, 1999, 'Why India and the World Need Gandhi,' *New York Times*, 2 October.
304. Samuel Moyn, 2016, 'Rights vs. Duties: Reclaiming Civic Balance,' *Boston Review*, 16 May.
305. Unsigned, 2012, 'Charter of Fundamental Rights of the European Union,' *Official Journal of the European Union*, 26 October.
306. Vineeth Krishna, 2019, 'Modi's New Love: Fundamental Duties Indira Gandhi Inserted in Constitution During Emergency,' *The Print*, 26 November; Mohandas K. Gandhi, 1938, *Hind Swaraj or Indian Home Rule*, Revised New Edition. Navajivan Press, page 107.
307. Unsigned, 2022, 'CJI: Fundamental Duties Not Merely Pedantic or Technical, Key to Social Transformation,' *The Statesman*, 15 August.
308. Bindu Puri, 2015, 'The Rights of Man: A Gandhian Intervention,' pages 231-255 in *Human Rights: India and the West*, edited by Ashwani Peetush and Jay Drydyk, Oxford University Press, page 248.
309. Sri Aurobindo Ghose, 1908, 'Asiatic Democracy,' *Bande Mataram*, 16 March (pages 929-932 in *The Complete Works of*

Sri Aurobindo, Volumes 6 and 7, 2002, Sri Aurobindo Ashram Trust, page 932).

310. Sri Aurobindo Ghose, 1909, 'Opinion & Comments,' *Karmayogin*, 3 July (pages 84-91 in *The Complete Works of Sri Aurobindo*, Volume 8, 1997, Sri Aurobindo Ashram Trust, page 85).

311. Rajendra Prasad, 1949, Constituent Assembly Debates, 26 November.

312. Neha Sahgal, Jonathan Evans, Ariana Monique Salazar, Kelsey Jo Starr, and Manolo Corichi, 2021, *Religion in India: Tolerance and Segregation*, Pew Research Center, 'Topline Questionnaire' supplemental file,' page 85.

313. World Values Survey, Waves 2-6, 'Aims of Respondent: First Choice'; note that in Wave 5 (2006/2007), the top-ranked first choice was 'fighting rising prices,' followed by 'maintaining order in the nation.'

314. Christian Welzel, 2021, 'Democratic Horizons: What Value Change Reveals about the Future of Democracy,' *Democratization* 28(5): 992-1016, page 1012.

315. Aaron S. Klieman, 1981, 'Indira's India: Democracy and Crisis Government,' *Political Science Quarterly* 96(2): 241-259.

316. Apurba Kundu, 1998, *Militarism in India: The Army and Civil Society in Consensus*, Taurus Academic Studies, pages 158-164.

317. Jaskirat Singh Bawa, 2015, 'What Was the Army Doing During the Emergency?' *The Quint*, 25 June.

318. Rakesh Ankit, 2013, 'Great Britain and Kashmir, 1947-49,' *India Review* 12(1): 20-40, page 33.

319. Bishnu Raj Upreti, 2021, 'Nepal: The Role of the Military in Politics, 1990-2020,' *Oxford Research Encyclopedia of Politics*, unpaginated.

320. Zoltan Barany, 2012, *The Soldier and the Changing State: Building Democratic Armies in Africa, Asia, Europe, and the*

Americas, Princeton University Press, page 220.

321. Aqil Shah, 2017, 'The Dog that Did Not Bark: The Army and the Emergency in India,' *Commonwealth & Comparative Politics* 55(4): 489-508, page 503.
322. Gerald James Larson, 1995, *India's Agony over Religion*, State University of New York Press, pages 133-134.
323. Charles Herman Heimsath, 1964, *Indian Nationalism and Hindu Social Reform*, Princeton University Press, pages 315-316.
324. Winston Churchill, 1931, 'Speech at the Constitutional Club, London,' 26 March.
325. Rolland Ray Lutz, 1976, "Father' Jahn and his Teacher-Revolutionaries from the German Student Movement,' *Journal of Modern History* 48(2/supplement): 1-34, page 9.
326. Walter K. Andersen and Shridhar D. Damle, 1987, *The Brotherhood in Saffron: The Rashtriya Swayamsevak Sangh and Hindu Revivalism*, Penguin Books, page 31.
327. Rakesh Sinha, 2015, *Builders of Modern India: Dr. Keshav Baliram Hedgewar*, Government of India, quoting Hedgewar without citation on pages 85 and 84.
328. Walter Andersen, 1972, 'The Rashtriya Swayamsevak Sangh: I: Early Concerns,' *Economic and Political Weekly* 7(11): 589-597, page 589.
329. Unsigned, Undated, 'Rashtriya Swayamsevak Sangh / RSS,' Library of Congress Item N0002938, accessed 13 January 2024.
330. M.S. Golwalkar, 1966 [1960], *Bunch of Thoughts*, Sharda Press, page xxvi.
331. Ibid., pages 101-103.
332. Unsigned, 2023, 'All Indians Are Hindus and Hindu Represents All Indians: RSS Chief Mohan Bhagwat,' *India Today*, 1 September.

333. William Borders, 1975, 'India Orders Ban on Major Groups in the Opposition,' *New York Times*, 5 July.
334. Unsigned, 1975, 'RSS, Marg, Jamaat among 26 Banned,' *Times of India*, 5 July.
335. J.C. Shah, 1978, *Shah Commission of Inquiry: Third and Final Report*, Government of India, pages 78-79, 118, and 107.
336. Walter K. Andersen and Shridhar D. Damle, 1987, *The Brotherhood in Saffron: The Rashtriya Swayamsevak Sangh and Hindu Revivalism*, Penguin Books, page 223.
337. A.G. Noorani, 2018, 'RSS & Emergency,' *Frontline*, 18 July.
338. Unsigned, 2015, 'RSS: The Mission,' Rashtriya Swayamsevak Sangh, 13 March.
339. K.R. Malkani, 1980, *The RSS Story*, Impex India, page 58 (quoting K.M. Munshi).
340. Robert D. Putnam, Robert Leonardi, and Raffaella Y. Nanetti, 1994, *Making Democracy Work: Civic Traditions in Modern Italy*, Princeton University Press, pages 181-185.
341. Ibid., pages 173 and 175.
342. Gordon White, 1994, 'Civil Society, Democratization and Development (I): Clearing the Analytical Ground,' *Democratization* 1(3): 375-390, pages 382-384.
343. Anna Lührmann, Marcus Tannenberg, and Staffan I. Lindberg, 2018, 'Regimes of the World (RoW): Opening New Avenues for the Comparative Study of Political Regimes,' *Politics and Governance* 6(1): 60–77, pages 63-67.
344. Constitution of the United States, Article I, Section 2.
345. Milan Vaishnav, 2019, ' Religious Nationalism and India's Future,' Carnegie Endowment for International Peace, 4 April.
346. Ruth Parsons, 1946, 'The Indian Electorate,' *Far Eastern Survey* 15(3): 44-47, page 44.

347. Braja Paikaray, 2015, 'Indian Constituent Assembly–the Historical Backdrop,' *Odisha Review* 71(6): 60-61, page 60.
348. Saquib Salim, 2023, 'Muslims in Constituent Assembly Opposed Reservation, Minority Tag,' *Awaz – The Voice*, 25 January.
349. Shefali Jha, 2002, 'Secularism in the Constituent Assembly Debates, 1946-1950,' *Economic and Political Weekly* 37(30): 3175-3180, page 3179.
350. Unsigned, 2019, 'Vellore Woman A Sneha Parthibaraja Wins 9-Year-Long Battle for a 'No Caste, No Religion' Identity,' Firstpost, 14 February.
351. Volker Tiirk, 2023, 'Letter by the High Commissioner to the Foreign Minister,' United Nations Office of the High Commissioner for Human Rights, 17 July, page 2.
352. Multiple authors, 2024, 'India: UN Experts Urge Corrective Action to Protect Human Rights and End Attacks against Minorities in Lead Up to Elections,' United Nations Office of the High Commissioner for Human Rights, 7 March.
353. Unsigned, 2023, *World Report 2023*, Human Rights Watch, page 291.
354. Unsigned, 2024, *The State of the World's Human Rights*, Amnesty International, page 194.
355. Michelle Bachelete, 2021, 'Letter by the High Commissioner to the Foreign Minister,' United Nations Office of the High Commissioner for Human Rights, 17 May, pages 3-8.
356. Unsigned, 2023, *World Report 2023*, Human Rights Watch, page 661.
357. Unsigned, 2024, *The State of the World's Human Rights*, Amnesty International, page 393.
358. Unsigned, 2009, *Global Restrictions on Religion*, Pew Research Center, page 5.
359. Ibid., page 1.

360. Pew *Global Restrictions on Religion* reports, various years.
361. Unsigned, 2009, *Global Restrictions on Religion*, Pew Research Center, pages 45-48.
362. Chad M. Bauman, undated, 'The Complexity of Anti-Christian Violence in India,' Cornell University Press, accessed 5 January 2022.
363. Stephanie Kramer, 2021, *Religious Composition of India*, Pew Research Center, pages 7 and 36.
364. Samirah Majumdar and Sarah Crawford, 2024, *Globally, Government Restrictions on Religion Reached Peak Levels in 2021, While Social Hostilities Went Down*, Pew Research Center, pages 45-46.
365. Laurie Goodstein, 1998, 'A Rising Movement Cites Persecution Facing Christians,' *New York Times*, 9 November.
366. Pat M. Holt, 1998, 'Good Cause, Bad Legislation,' *Christian Science Monitor*, 2 December.
367. Unsigned, 2021, '2020 Report on International Religious Freedom: India,' U.S. Department of State, 12 May.
368. Aziz Haniffa, 2009, 'Another Indian-American Appointed to Obama's Legal Team,' *Rediff News*, 30 January.
369. Unsigned, 2022, '2021 Report on International Religious Freedom: India,' U.S. Department of State, 2 June.
370. Unsigned, 2023, '2022 Report on International Religious Freedom: India,' U.S. Department of State, 15 May.
371. Neha Sahgal, Jonathan Evans, Ariana Monique Salazar, Kelsey Jo Starr, and Manolo Corichi, 2021, *Religion in India: Tolerance and Segregation*, Pew Research Center, page 6.
372. Neha Sahgal, Jonathan Evans, Ariana Monique Salazar, Kelsey Jo Starr, and Manolo Corichi, 2021, *Religion in India: Tolerance and Segregation*, Pew Research Center, 'Topline Questionnaire' supplemental file, page 15.

373. Ibid., pages 6-7.

374. Ibid., page 21.

375. Andrew Daniller, 2021, 'Majorities of Americans See at Least Some Discrimination against Black, Hispanic and Asian People in the U.S.,' Pew Research Center, 18 March.

376. Neha Sahgal, Jonathan Evans, Ariana Monique Salazar, Kelsey Jo Starr, and Manolo Corichi, 2021, *Religion in India: Tolerance and Segregation*, Pew Research Center, 'Topline Questionnaire' supplemental file, pages 3-5.

377. Ibid., page 11.

378. Ibid., page 83.

379. Mohd Sanjeer Alam, 2010, 'Social Exclusion of Muslims in India and Deficient Debates about Affirmative Action: Suggestions for a New Approach,' *South Asia Research* 30(1): 43-65, page 57.

380. Rajesh Shuka, 2024, *The Declining Income Gap between Hindu and Muslim Families in India*, PRICE, pages 2-3.

381. Unsigned, 2022, *National Family Health Survey (NFHS-5)*, Ministry of Health and Family Welfare, page 44.

382. Ibid., pages 62-63; Shujaat Ali Quadri and P. Faziluddin, 2023, *Indianness of Indian Muslim*, BlueRose Publishers, page 108; Atul Thakar, 2020, 'Literacy Rate for Muslims Worse than SC/STs,' *Times of India*, 13 August; author analysis of 2019 data from the *World Development Indicators Databank*, World Bank.

383. Maidul Islam, 2019, *Indian Muslim(s) after Liberalization*, Oxford University Press, pages 65-66.

384. Rizwana Shamshad, 2017, *Bangladeshi Migrants in India: Foreigners, Refugees, or Infiltrators?*, Oxford University Press, page 5.

385. Unsigned, 2024, 'CAA: India's New Citizenship Law Explained,' *BBC News*, 12 March; Mukul Kesavan, 2019, 'The Greatest Threat to Indian Democracy Today,' *The Telegraph Online*, 28 July.
386. Unsigned, 2024, 'India: Citizenship Amendment Act Is a Blow to Indian Constitutional Values and International Standards,' Amnesty International, 14 March.
387. Unsigned, 2019, 'India: Citizenship Bill Discriminates against Muslims,' Human Rights Watch, 11 December.
388. Unsigned, 2020, 'Factsheet on The Citizenship (Amendment) Act in India,' United States Commission on International Religious Freedom, February.
389. Kanishka Singh, 2024, 'US, UN Express Concern about India's Religion-Based Citizenship Law,' *Reuters*, 14 March.
390. Aditi Bhandari and Anand Katakam, 2020, 'India's Citizenship Protests,' *Reuters*, 30 March.
391. Smriti Kak Ramachandran, 2024, 'CAA Rules Notified: BJP Fulfils Another Promise Made in 2019 Poll Manifesto,' *Hindustan Times*, 12 March.
392. Milan Vaishnav, 2018, 'What Is the Secret to the Success of India's Bharatiya Janata Party (BJP)?' Carnegie Endowment for International Peace, 11 October.
393. Unsigned, 2024, 'Report 2023: Hate Speech Events in India,' India Hate Lab, 25 February.
394. Faisal Malik, 2023, 'Telangana MLA T Raja Singh Has a Long List of Hate Speeches in Maharashtra,' *Hindustan Times*, 31 March.
395. Neha Sahgal, Jonathan Evans, Ariana Monique Salazar, Kelsey Jo Starr, and Manolo Corichi, 2021, *Religion in India: Tolerance and Segregation*, Pew Research Center, 'Topline Questionnaire' supplemental file, page 90.

396. Zainab Farhat, 2024, 'Spatial Segregation and Muslims in India: A Review,' *Journal of Muslim Minority Affairs*, online first.

397. Trina Vithayathil and Gayatri Singh, 2012, 'Spaces of Discrimination: Residential Segregation in Indian Cities,' *Economic and Political Weekly* 47(37): 60-66, pages 61, 64, and 65.

398. Anjali Adukia, Sam Asher, Paul Novosad, and Brandon Tan, 2019, 'Residential Segregation in Urban India,' University of California Center for Effective Global Action, pages 7 and 13.

399. Sam Asher, Kritarth Jha, Paul Novosad, Anjali Adukia, Brandon Tan, 2024, 'Residential Segregation and Unequal Access to Local Public Services in India: Evidence from 1.5m Neighborhoods,' Pearson Institute Discussion Paper 2024-14, pages 3-4 and 53.

400. Aditi Raja, 2024, 'Muslim Woman Allotted Flat under CM Scheme in Vadodara, Residents Protest,' *Indian Express*, 15 June.

401. Neha Sahgal, Jonathan Evans, Ariana Monique Salazar, Kelsey Jo Starr, and Manolo Corichi, 2021, *Religion in India: Tolerance and Segregation*, Pew Research Center, 'Topline Questionnaire' supplemental file, page 78.

402. Rishika Dugyala, 2021, 'Asian Americans Are the Least Likely to Hold Elected Office,' *Politico*, 4 May; Allison Abbe, 2022, 'Diversity as a Strategic Asset: How Asian-Americans Strengthen the Force,' *The War Room*, 12 May.

403. Maidul Islam, 2019, *Indian Muslim(s) after Liberalization*, Oxford University Press, page 105.

404. Sanjeev Kumar H.M., 2013, 'Constructing the Nation's Enemy: Hindutva, Popular Culture and the Muslim 'Other' in Bollywood Cinema,' *Third World Quarterly* 34(3): 458-469, page 459.

405. Saubhadra Chatterji , 2023, 'Congress UCC Meet: Party Rejects Uniformity in All Laws,' *Hindustan Times*, 16 July.
406. Vikas Pathak, 2024, 'Amid UCC Saga, PM Modi Pitch for 'Secular Civil Code' a Bid to Put Oppn on the Back Foot,' *Indian Express*, 16 August.
407. Shemin Joy, 2023, "Dog-Whistle Politics': Opposition Parties Slam PM Modi's UCC Remarks in Madhya Pradesh,' *Deccan Herald*, 27 June.
408. Adnan Farooqui, 2020, 'Political Representation of a Minority: Muslim Representation in Contemporary India,' *India Review* 19(2): 153-175, pages 154-156.
409. Anjishnu Das, 2024, 'Muslim Representation in New Lok Sabha: 24 MPs, None from BJP-Led NDA,' *Indian Express*, 8 June; Nitika Francis and Vignesh Radhakrishnan, 2014, 'Eighteenth Lok Sabha Has Lowest Share of Muslim MPs in Six Decades,' *The Hindu*, 18 June.
410. Christophe Jaffrelot and Hilal Ahmed, 2024, 'Indian Muslims: (Self-) Perceptions and Voting Trends in 2024,' *Studies in Indian Politics* 12(2): 289-302, page 298.
411. Unsigned, 2024, 'Indian Muslim CM List: 6 States that Had Muslim Chief Ministers,' *Top Indian List*, 8 February.
412. Shekhar Gupta, 2022, "Othered' Muslim in Modi-BJP Era: 3 Essentials before Mounting a Political Challenge to Correct It,' *The Print*, 16 July.
413. Nootan Sharma, 2024, 'Over 70% Jump in Muslim Civil Services Recruits. Four of Them Make It to Top 100,' *The Print*, 17 April.
414. Unsigned, 2024, "Systematic injustice': Only 16 Muslim Judges in India's Supreme Court over 75 Years,' *Muslim Mirror*, 24 October.
415. Prashant Bharadwaj, Asim I. Khwaja, and Atif Mian, 2014,

'Population Exchange and Its Impact on Literacy, Occupation and Gender – Evidence from the Partition of India,' *International Migration* 53(4): 90-106, pages 94 and 96.

416. Steven I. Wilkinson, 2015, *Army and Nation: The Military and Indian Democracy since Independence*, Harvard University Press, page 88-89.

417. Ralph Braibanti, 1963, 'Public Bureaucracy and Judiciary in Pakistan,' pages 360-440 in *Bureaucracy and Political Development*, edited by Joseph LaPalombara, Princeton University Press, pages 366, 365.

418. Sanya Dhingra, 2020, '50% IAS, IFS Recruits Are Children of Govt Servants. But This Is a Story of Their Merit,' *The Print*, 11 August.

419. Ana Laura Ferrari, 2020, 'India's Polarized Society and the Role of Religion,' Varieties of Democracy Institute, 25 November.

420. Ashish Malhotra, 2019, 'Allegations of Mass Voter Exclusion Cast Shadow on India Election,' *Al Jazeera*, 30 April.

421. Abusaleh Shariff and Khalid Saifullah, 2018, 'Electoral Exclusion of Muslims Continues to Plague Indian Democracy,' *Economic and Political Weekly (Engage)* 53(20): 2-20, page 2.

422. Ibid., page 6.

423. Mobashra Tazamal, 2022, *Is a Genocide of Muslims Underway in India?*, Georgetown University Bridge Initiative, page 3.

424. Amitabh Kundu, Khalid Khan, Varghese K., S. Madheswaran, Karthick V., and Anushree K.N., 2022, *India Discrimination Report 2022*, Oxfam India, page 28.

425. Unsigned, 2024, 'National Election Study Pre-Poll Questionnaire,' Centre for the Study of Developing Societies, page 5.

426. Christophe Jaffrelot and Hilal Ahmed, 2024, 'Indian Muslims: (Self-) Perceptions and Voting Trends in 2024,' *Studies in Indian Politics* 12(2): 289-302, pages 293 and 292.

427. Ibid., page 293.
428. Ananya Chakravarti, Purnima Dhavan, Manan Ahmed, Supriya Gandhi, Dheepa Sundaram, Audrey Truschke, and Simran Jeet Singh. 2021, 'Hindutva's Threat to Academic Freedom,' *Religion News Service*, 7 July.
429. Neha Sahgal, Jonathan Evans, Ariana Monique Salazar, Kelsey Jo Starr, and Manolo Corichi, 2021, *Religion in India: Tolerance and Segregation*, Pew Research Center, 'Topline Questionnaire' supplemental file, page 86.
430. Unsigned, 2019, 'It Will Reduce India to Hindutva Version of Pakistan: Shashi Tharoor on CAB,' *Outlook*, 8 December.
431. Ramesh Thakur, 2023, "They Called Us Illegal. How Is It Possible?',' Toda Peace Institute Policy Brief 102, page 4.
432. Maidul Islam, 2019, *Indian Muslim(s) after Liberalization*, Oxford University Press, pages 80 and 83.
433. K. Rahman Khan, 2021, *Indian Muslims: The Way Forward*, Notion Press, pages 48, 52, and 137.
434. Romain Rollard, 1930, *Prophets of the New India*, translated by E.F. Malcolm-Smith, Cassell and Company, page 497.
435. Rajshree Dutta, 2017, 'Socio-Political Thoughts of Swami Vivekananda and the Constitutional Interpretation of India,' *The Indian Journal of Political Science* 78(2): 193-200, page 193.
436. Brijesh Kalappa, 2017, 'The Only Thing PM Modi & Swami Vivekananda Share Is Their First Name,' *The Print*, 15 September.
437. Shashi Tharoor, 2018, *Why I Am a Hindu*, Scribe Publications, page 13; Narendra Modi, 2015, *Jyotipunj*, Prabhat Prakashan, pages 29-34.
438. Unsigned, 2005, 'Rabindranath Tagore on Swami Vivekananda,' *VivekaVani*, 17 January.

439. Swami Vivekananda, 1940 [1893], 'Response to Welcome,' pages 3-4 in *The Complete Works Of Swami Vivekananda*, Mayavati Memorial Edition, Volume 1, Advaita Ashrama, page 3.
440. Ibid., page 4.
441. Laurie L. Patton, 2008, *The Bhagavad Gita*, Penguin Books, pages 52 and 51 (verses 4:11 and 4:7).
442. Swami Vivekananda, 1907 [1893], 'The Hindoo Religion,' pages 481-484 in *The Complete Works of Swami Vivekananda*, Mayavati Memorial Edition, Volume 1, Advaita Ashrama, page 483.
443. Karl R. Popper, 1994 [1945], *The Open Society and Its Enemies*, Princeton University Press, pages 443 and 581.
444. Ibid., page 581.
445. Swami Vivekananda, 1956 [undated], 'Lessons on Bhakti-Yoga,' pages 137-145 in *The Complete Works of Swami Vivekananda*, Sixth Edition, Volume 6, Advaita Ashrama, page 137-138.
446. Swami Vivekananda, 1907 [1897], 'First Public Lecture in the East,' pages 103-115 in *The Complete Works of Swami Vivekananda*, Mayavati Memorial Edition, Volume 3, Advaita Ashrama, page 114.
447. Swami Vivekananda, 1907 [1900], 'The Way to the Realisation of a Universal Religion,' pages 359-374 in *The Complete Works of Swami Vivekananda*, Mayavati Memorial Edition, Volume 2, Advaita Ashrama, pages 373-374.
448. Patrick Olivelle, 2024, *Ashoka: Portrait of a Philosopher King*, Yale University Press, page 240-241.
449. Romila Thapar (with Arthur Llewellyn Basham), 2012 (1997), *Aśoka and the Decline of the Mauryas*, Third Edition, Oxford University Press, page 382.
450. Patrick Olivelle, 2024, *Ashoka: Portrait of a Philosopher King*, Yale University Press, pages 294-295.

451. Hazrat Inayat Khan, 1960 [1922], 'The Way of Illumination,' pages 9-60 in *The Sufi Message of Hazrat Inayat Khan*, Volume 1, Barrie and Rockliff, page 34.
452. Ibid., pages 16 and 17.
453. Dietrich Reetz, 2007, 'The Deoband Universe: What Makes a Transcultural and Transnational Educational Movement of Islam?' *Comparative Studies of South Asia, Africa and the Middle East* 27(1): 139-159, pages 140 and 144.
454. Barbara D. Metcalf, 1982, *Islamic Revival in British India: Deoband, 1860-1900*, Princeton University Press, page 153.
455. Kausar Ali and Huang Minxing, 2021, 'Muslims Preaching Movements in British-India: An Appraisal of the Tablighi Jamaat and Its Competitors,' *Liberal Arts & Social Sciences International Journal* 5(1): 356-371, page 362.
456. Ayesha Jalal, 1985, *The Sole Spokesman: Jinnah, the Muslim League and the Demand for Pakistan*, Cambridge University Press, pages 53-54 and 3.
457. Muhammad Ali Shaikh, 2022, 'History: The Quaid-i-Azam's Last Will,' *Dawn*, 11 September.
458. Jeffrey Prager, 1986, *Building Democracy in Ireland: Political Order and Cultural Integration in a Newly Independent Nation*, Cambridge University Press, page 4.
459. Google Books Ngram search, July 2024 database.
460. Pavan Varma, 2010, *Becoming Indian: The Unfinished Revolution of Culture and Identity*, Penguin, page 17.
461. Rajdeep Sardesai, 2013, 'Kejriwal and Modi – Bringing Politics Back to the Common Man,' *Hindustan Times*, 23 November.
462. Unsigned, 2019, 'PM Narendra Modi Interview,' *Indian Express*, 12 May.
463. Somya Lakhani, 2019, 'Khan Market's Humble Beginnings: Meant for Refugees, 'Doomed to Fail',' *Indian Express*, 17 May.

464. Santhi Kavuri-Bauer, 2011, *Monumental Matters: The Power, Subjectivity, and Space of India's Mughal Architecture*, Duke University Press, pages 148.

465. Javeed Alam, 1999, 'The Composite Culture and Its Historiography,' *South Asia: Journal of South Asian Studies* 22(supplement): 29-37, page 30.

466. Ramachandra Guha, 2007, *India after Gandhi: The History of the World's Largest Democracy*, HarperCollins, pages 1-2.

467. John Stuart Mill, 1861, *Considerations on Representative Government*, Parker, Son, and Bourne, page 287.

468. Annemarie Schimmel, 2004 [2000], *The Empire of the Great Mughals: History, Art and Culture*, translated by Corinne Attwood, Reaktion Books, page 113.

469. Wendy Doniger, 2010, *The Hindus: An Alternative History*, Oxford University Press, pages 15, 531, and 527.

470. Farhat Hasan, 2019, 'Nationalist Representations of the Mughal State: The Views of Tilak and Gandhi,' *Studies in People's History* 6(1): 52-62, page 61.

471. Jawaharlal Nehru, 1981 [1946], *The Discovery of India*, Oxford University Press, pages 75-76 and 142.

472. Vincent Arthur Smith, 1917, *Akbar the Great Mogul: 1542-1605*, Oxford University Press, pages 221 and 213.

473. Rizvi, Saiyid Athar Abbas, 1993 [1987], *The Wonder That Was India*, Volume 2, Rupa & Co., page xviii.

474. Ibid., page 138.

475. Audrey Truschke, 2017, *Aurangzeb The Life and Legacy of India's Most Controversial King*, Stanford University Press, page 86.

476. Romila Thapar, Muzaffar Alam, Sarvepalli Gopal, and 'Others,' 1986, 'Letters: Communal Twist,' *Times of India*, 28 October.

477. Arun Shourie, 2004 [1998], *Eminent Historians: Their Technology, Their Line, Their Fraud*, Rupa & Co., page 136.
478. Pavan K. Varma, 2021, *The Great Hindu Civilisation: Achievement, Neglect, Bias and the Way Forward*, Westland, pages 190, 202, and 205.
479. Pavan K. Varma, 2002, 'Learning to Belong,' *Seminar* 515: 31-33, page 31.
480. Pavan K. Varma, 2021, *The Great Hindu Civilisation: Achievement, Neglect, Bias and the Way Forward*, Westland, pages 328-349.
481. Ibid., pages 349-352.
482. Ibid., page 362.
483. Diana L. Eck, 2012, *India: A Sacred Geography, Harmony Books*, page 6.
484. J. Sai Deepak, 2021, *India That Is Bharat: Coloniality, Civilisation, Constitution*, Bloomsbury, pages 161-164.
485. Ibid., page 212.
486. Ibid., page 217.
487. Ibid., page 217.
488. Ibid., pages 185 and 179.
489. Anandaroop Sen, 2023, 'J Sai Deepak's *India that is Bharat: Coloniality, Civilisation, Constitution*,' *Social Dynamics* 49(2): 376-385, pages 379-380.
490. Martin Jacques, 2009, *When China Rules the World: Rise of the Middle Kingdom and the End of the Western World*, Penguin, page 196.
491. Martin Jacques, 2012, *When China Rules the World: Rise of the Middle Kingdom and the End of the Western World*, Second Edition, Penguin, page 245.
492. M.S. Prabhakara, 2011, 'The Nation State and Its Territory,' *The Hindu*, 8 June.

493. Romila Thapar, 2001, 'Remembering Ravinder Kumar,' *Social Scientist* 29(5/6): 83-86, page 85.

494. Gerald James Larson, 1995, *India's Agony Over Religion*, State University of New York Press, pages 36-37, 145-145, 162-163, 200-201, etc.

495. Ravinder Kumar, 2002 [1989] 'India: A 'Nation-State' or 'Civilisation-State'?' *South Asia: Journal of South Asian Studies* 25(2): 13-32, pages 31 and 32.

496. Unsigned, 2010, 'State [III.26.a.],' *Oxford English Dictionary*, Third Edition, Oxford University Press.

497. Ajoy Sinha Karpuram, 2024, '10 Pending Suits in Mosque-Temple Disputes, from Sambhal to Mathura,' *Indian Express*, 13 December.

498. Unsigned, 2018, 'AIMPLB Sacks Cleric for Suggesting Shifting Babri Mosque Site,' *Times of India*, 12 February.

499. Anand Ranganathan, 2023, Hindus in Hindu Rashtra: Eight-Class Citizens and Victims of State-Sanctioned Apartheid, BlueOne Ink, pages 102 and 103; reiterated in television interviews for *News18* (26 November 2024) and *India Today* (25 December 2024).

500. Natalia Santi and Emma Connors, 2021, 'Indonesia's 'Mosque Hunters' Help Fight Radicalism,' *Australian Financial Review*, 7 May.

501. Unsigned, 2003, 'A.B.K.M. 2003: Ayodhya, Mathura and Kashi,' Rashtriya Swayamsevak Sangh, accessed 1 February 2025.

502. Raghavan Jagannathan, 2023, *Dharmic Nation: Freeing Bharat, Remaking India*, Rupa, pages 159-167.

503. Rahul Shivshankar, 2023, *Modi & India: 2024 and the Battle for Bharat*, Penguin, pages 229 and 230-231.

504. Arun Shourie, 2012, *Worshipping False Gods: Ambedkar and the Facts That Have Been Erased*, HarperCollins.

505. Ratan Sharda, 2019, *The Sangh & Swaraj: Role of RSS in Freedom Struggle*, Prabhat Prakashan.
506. Ram Madhav, 2021, *The Hindutva Paradigm: Integral Humanism and Quest for a Non-Western Worldview*, Westland.
507. Ram Madhav, 2022, *Partitioned Freedom: Unraveling the Tale of India's Independence*, Prabhat Prakashan.
508. Shashi Tharoor, 2021, *The Struggle for India's Soul: Nationalism and the Fate of Democracy*, Hurst.
509. Rajiv Malhotra and Aravindan Neelakandan , 2011, *Breaking India: Western Interventions in Dravidian and Dalit Faultlines*, Amaryllis.
510. Rajiv Malhotra and Vijaya Viswanathan, 2022, *Snakes in the Ganga: Breaking India 2.0*, BluOne Ink.
511. Vikram Sampath, 2019, *Savarkar: Echoes from a Forgotten Past, 1883-1924*, Penguin.
512. Vikram Sampath, 2022, *Savarkar: A Contested Legacy, 1924-1966*, Penguin.
513. Vikram Sampath, 2022, *Bravehearts of Bharat: Vignettes from Indian History*, Penguin; Vikram Sampath, 2024, *Tipu Sultan: The Saga of Mysore's Interregnum (1760–1799)*, Penguin.
514. Vikram Sampath, 2024, *Waiting for Shiva: Unearthing the Truth of Kashi's Gyan Vapi*, BlueOne Ink.
515. Abhijit Majumder, *India's New Right: Powering the Current Wave of Nationalism and Civilisational Revival*, BlueOne Ink, page 111.
516. Gautam R. Desiraju, 2022, *Bhārat: India 2.0*, Vitasta, pages 227-228.
517. Ibid., page 271.
518. Ibid., pages 283-284.
519. Pavan K. Varma, 2021, *The Great Hindu Civilisation: Achievement, Neglect, Bias and the Way Forward*, Westland, page 3.

520. Émile Durkheim, 1964 [1893/1902], *The Division of Labor in Society*, translated by George Simpson, The Free Press, page 28.
521. Gautam R. Desiraju, 2022, *Bhārat: India 2.0*, Vitasta, page 229.
522. Jawaharlal Nehru, 1981 [1946], *The Discovery of India*, Oxford University Press, page 107.
523. Swami Vivekananda, 1907 [1897], 'The Future of India,' pages 285-304 in *The Complete Works of Swami Vivekananda*, Mayavati Memorial Edition, Volume 3, Advaita Ashrama, pages 287-288.
524. V.D. Savarkar, 1909, *The Indian War of Independence of 1857*, publisher unknown, page 280.
525. Ibid., pages 62-63.
526. Ibid., page 444.
527. Sanjeev Kumar Verma, 2017, 'Yogi Pits Taj against Gita – 'Minarets Don't Reflect Indian Culture'.' *The Telegraph India*, 15 June.
528. Emily Schmall and Karan Deep Singh, 2021, 'Don't Sacrifice Your Life to Visit the Taj Mahal': India Reopens but Fear Pervades,' *New York Times*, 6 July.
529. Unsigned, 2020, 'Yogi Adityanath Presents Large Portrait of Taj Mahal to Donald Trump,' NDTV, 24 February.
530. Unsigned, 2017, 'Another Stab at Taj Mahal's Heritage,' *The Hindu*, 16 October.
531. Unsigned, 2017, "Members Can Hold Any View': BJP Distances Itself from Som's Taj Mahal Remarks,' *Hindustan Times*, 16 October.
532. Omar Rashid, 2017, 'Taj Mahal Built with Blood, Sweat of Indians: Adityanath,' *The Hindu*, 17 October.
533. Tathagata Roy, 2020, *The Life and Times of Dr. Syama Prasad Mookerjee: A Complete Biography*, Prabhat, page 293.
534. Walter K. Andersen and Shridhar D. Damle, 2019 [1987], *The Brotherhood in Saffron: The Rashtriya Swayamsevak Sangh*

and Hindu Revivalism, Penguin, pages 110 and 158-159.

535. Barbara Crossette, 2014, 'Why Narendra Modi's Election Threatens Democracy in India,' *The Nation*, 23 May; William Dalrymple, 2014, 'Narendra Modi: Man of the Masses,' *The New Statesman*, 12 May.

536. Jeffrey Gettleman, 2019, 'The Rise of Modi: India's Rightward Turn,' *New York Times* podcast, 21 May; Rana Ayyub, 2019, 'India's Protests Could Be a Tipping Point against Authoritarianism,' *Washington Post*, 18 December.

537. Shamil Shams, 2010, 'Germany Envoy Visits Extremist Hindu Group,' *Deutsche Welle*, 21 July.

538. Unsigned, 2024, 'PM Modi's Approval Rating (AR) Remains Steady at 70% in November 2024,' Ipsos, 1 December.

539. Unsigned, 2022, 'Amit Shah on Why BJP Has Not Fielded Muslim Candidate in Assembly Elections,' *Deccan Herald*, 2 March.

540. YP Rajesh, 2023, 'How Modi's BJP Seeks Muslim Vote in India's 2024 Election,' *Reuters*, 10 November.

541. Unsigned, 2022, 'Explained: Who Are the Pasmanda Muslims, the Group that BJP Is Trying to Woo?,' *Times of India*, 9 July.

542. Walter Andersen and Shridhar D. Damle, 2019, *Messengers of Hindu Nationalism: How the RSS Reshaped India*, Hurst, pages 101-106.

543. Felix Pal, 2020, 'Why Muslims Join the Muslim Wing of the RSS,' *Contemporary South Asia* 28(3): 275-287.

544. Unsigned, 2023, 'Hindu Society Has Been at War for Over 1000 Years,' *Organiser*, 10 January.

545. Syed Ubaidur Rahman, 2023, *Forgotten Muslim Empires of South India: Bahmani Empire, Madurai, Bijapur, Ahmadnagar, Golconda & Mysore Sultanates*, Global Media Publications.

546. Syed Ubaidur Rahman, 2021, *Biographical Encyclopedia of*

Indian Muslim Freedom Fighters, Global Media Publications.

547. Shehla Rashid, 2024, *Role Models: Inspiring Stories of Indian Muslim Achievers*, Penguin, page xxii.
548. Max Weber, 2019 [1921], *Economy and Society: A New Translation*, translated by Keith Tribe, Harvard University Press, page 436.
549. Ibid., page 429.
550. Reinhard Bendix and Seymour Martin Lipset, 1957, 'Political Sociology: An Essay with Special Reference to the Development of Research in the United States of America and Western Europe,' *Current Sociology* 6(2): 79-99.
551. Adrija Roychowdhury, 2024, 'Samajwadi Party and the Caste-Based Social Justice It Promised,' *Indian Express*, 8 June.
552. Ved Mehta, 1970, *Portrait of India*, Penguin Books, page 545.
553. Manoj C.G., 2020, '23 Senior Congress Leaders Stand Up, Write to Sonia Gandhi Calling for Sweeping Changes,' *Indian Express*, 24 August.
554. D.K. Singh, 2020, 'Why Gandhi Family Loyalists in Congress Are Turning against Rahul,' *The Print*, 23 August.
555. Unsigned, 2022, 'Mallikarjun Kharge: A Gandhi Family Loyalist Becomes Congress President,' *Frontline*, 19 October.
556. M.K. Gandhi, 1984 [1948], 'Draft Constitution of Congress,' pages 526-258 in *The Collected Works of Mahatma Gandhi*, Volume 90, Government of India, page 527.
557. Shyamlal Yadav, 2024, 'The Story of Party Symbols in Indian Elections, and How Congress Got the Hand, BJP the Lotus,' *Indian Express*, 15 April.
558. Unsigned, 2025, 'Indian National Congress,' *Encyclopaedia Britannica*, 6 February.
559. Ashutosh Varshney, 2014, *Battles Half Won: India's Improbable Democracy*, Penguin, page 26.

560. Unsigned, 2021, 'Analysis of Re-Contesting Candidates and MPs/MLAs Who Changed Parties in the Lok Sabha and Assembly Elections,' Association for Democratic Reforms, 9 September.
561. Unsigned, 2024, 'Election Results 2024: 37% of BJP's Sitting MPs Who Recontested, Lost Polls,' *The Hindu*, 5 June.
562. Pradeep K. Chhibber, Rahul Verma, 2018, *Ideology and Identity: The Changing Party Systems of India*, Oxford University Press, pages 36-38.
563. Kausik Gangopadhyay, 2024, *The Majoritarian Myth: How Unscientific Social Theories Create Disharmony*, Garuda Prakashan, page 59.
564. Shashi Tharoor, 2018, *Why I Am a Hindu*, Hurst, page 136.
565. Milan Vaishnav, 2019, 'Religious Nationalism and India's Future,' pages 5-21 in *The BJP in Power: Indian Democracy and Religious Nationalism*, edited by Milan Vaishnav, Carnegie Endowment for International Peace, page 15.
566. Dileep V. Kumar, 2025, 'Rebranding the Red: CPI(M)'s Calculated Move to Consolidate Hindu Voters in Kerala,' *South First*, 5 January.
567. Edmund Burke, 1770, *Thoughts on the Cause of the Present Discontents*, J. Dodsley, pages 75 and 74.
568. Manmohan Singh, 2006, 'PM's Address at the Meeting of National Development Council 2006,' Government of India.
569. Unsigned, 2024, 'Samajwadi Party Crossed All Limits in the Name of Muslim Appeasement, Says CM Yogi Adityanath,' *Times of India*, 30 September.
570. Prabhy Chawla, 2024, 'Akhilesh Redefines and Reinvents Himself,' *New Indian Express*, 28 July.
571. Unsigned, 2024, 'The Game Changers: In UP, All Four of Samajwadi Party's (SP) Muslim Candidates Win,' *Times of India*, 5 June.

572. Biswajeet Banerjee, 2024, 'All in the Family: SP Fields Only 5 Yadav Candidates, All from 'Saifai Parivaar',' *MoneyControl*, 30 April.

573. Unsigned, 2024, 'Akhilesh Won't Attend Ram Mandir Inauguration, Will Visit Later with Family,' *Hindustan Times*, 13 January.

574. Unsigned, 2024, 'At SP Office, Puja of Stone Brought to Make Etawah Temple Shivling,' *Indian Express*, 15 February.

575. Unsigned, 2023, *Bharat: The Mother of Democracy*, Government of India, page 38.

576. B.R. Ambedkar, 1948, Constituent Assembly Debates, 15 November.

577. Rita Kothari, 2020, 'Secular, Secularism and Non-Translations,' *Economic & Political Weekly* 55(38): 40-46, page 41.

578. Krzysztof Iwanek, 2018, "Secularism' as Understood and Interpreted by Hindu Nationalists,' *Journal of Language and Politics* 17(4): 533-551, pages 539-542.

579. Shashi Tharoor, 2018, *Why I Am Hindu*, Hurst, pages 103-104.

580. M.K. Gandhi, 1984 [1948], 'Speech at Prayer Meeting,' pages 313-417 in *The Collected Works of Mahatma Gandhi*, Volume 90, Government of India, page 416.

581. Sarvepalli Radhakrishnan, 1947, Constituent Assembly Debates, 20 January.

582. John Adams, 1851 [1774], 'Novanglus,' pages 3-177 in *The Works of John Adams*, Volume 4, Little, Brown, page 106.

583. Émile Durkheim, 1964 [1893/1902], *The Division of Labor in Society*, Translated by George Simpson, The Free Press, pages 406 and 399.

584. Laurie L. Patton, 2008, *The Bhagavad Gita*, Penguin Books, pages 196-197 (verse 18:47).

585. *Bhagavad Gita* verses 2:31, 3:35, and 18:47.

Index

Symbols

2017 election 60
2019 elections 19, 31, 35, 166, 175, 176
2024 elections viii, 75, 173, 234, 238, 240

A

academic freedom 14, 29–33
Academic Freedom Index 8
acquiescence bias 34–35
Adams, John 248
Adityanath, Yogi 48, 50, 57–58, 60, 68, 75, 219, 221–222, 237, 243, 247
Afghanistan 158, 164–165
African-Americans 110, 148–149, 161–162, 168, 170, 179–180, 207
After Nehru, Who? 119, 278
ahimsa 250
Akbar 195–197, 218–219, 222, 245
akharas 133
Aligarh Muslim University 191
Al Jazeera 32, 175
All-India Muslim League 78
All India Women's Conference 103
Ambassador at Large for International Religious Freedom 159
Ambedkar, B.R. ix, 90–92, 96, 101, 104, 110, 210, 245
American Bar Association 8
Amethi 2
Amnesty International 152–153, 165
Ananda Marga 137

Anderson, Benedict 105
anti-Romeo campaign 51
anti-Romeo squads 52
Arya Samaj 130
Ashoka the Great 187
Asian-Americans 161, 169
Asiatic Democracy 250
Assam 166
Association for Democratic Reforms 234
Aurangzeb 197–198, 222, 245
Aurobindo vii, xi, 124–125, 250, 252
Austin, Granville 122
Australia xxii, xxiv, 30, 33, 41, 45, 112, 147
autocracy vii, 3, 5, 9, 11, 23, 35, 37, 147, 177, 179
Avaidyanath, Mahant 49
Awami League 108
Ayodhya 46, 48, 75, 78, 195, 207–209, 240, 243
Azerbaijan 158

B

Babri Masjid 75, 195
Babur's martial genius 207
Bahadur Shah Zafar 220
Bahujan Samaj Party 59
Bangladesh xiv, xv, xvi, 27, 86, 93–95, 106–108, 117, 129, 163–166
Barany, Zoltan 129
Belarus 16
Belgium 45, 71, 147–148
Bengal 79, 82, 95, 106, 138, 174
Bhagavad Gita xvii, 64, 131, 185, 190, 214–215, 221, 252
Bhagwat, Mohan 136, 228
Bharat 77, 101, 104, 136, 202, 238, 249–250, 253
Bharatiya Janata Party v, xvi, 2, 7, 43
Bharat Jodo Yatra 239
Bihar 36, 40, 80, 127
Biographical Encyclopedia of Indian Freedom Fighters 230
Bisht, Ajay Mohan 48
Bollywood 170, 287
Bombay 86, 174

bourgeoisie 114–115
Boxers 133
Brahmo Samaj 130
Brazil 22–25
Breaking India 211
breakup 98, 108
British Empire ix, 88, 112–113, 193
British India xiii, xiv, xv, xvi, 71–72, 80–82, 85–86, 89–90, 94–96, 106–107, 130, 139, 173, 191
Bryce, James 100
Buddhism 136
Burke, Edmund 241
Burma xiv, 84–85, 106, 251

C

Cabinet Mission 80–82, 92
Calcutta 79–80
Cambodia 30
Canada 8, 19, 30, 112
caste background 59–60
caste-based discrimination 110, 131
Cato Institute 8
censorship 20, 24–27, 122
Center for the Study of Organized Hate 167
Centre for the Study of Developing Societies 177
Ceylon 85
China xxiii, 16–17, 23, 29, 35, 37, 39, 101, 115, 125, 133, 148, 203–204
Christian Indians 160, 216
Christianity xvii, 45, 155, 247
Christian persecution movement 157
Christian Science Monitor 157
Citizenship Amendment Act v, 164
civilisational nation 205, 213, 252
civilization-state 204
civil-military relations 129
civil rights 7, 54, 97, 118, 144, 179, 251
civil society 7, 14, 22, 49, 113, 117, 137–146, 182, 192, 208, 210, 215–216, 230

Committee of Parliament on Official Language 103
Committee to Protect Journalists (CPJ) 29
Communist Party of India 118, 144
Communist Party of India (Marxist-Leninist) 137
composite culture thesis 198
comprador elite 102
compradors 101
Congress Party 149
Considerations on Representative Government 98
Constituent Assembly xii, 80–81, 103–104, 126, 149–150, 245, 247
Constitution 7, 24–25, 43, 76, 81, 90, 104, 118, 121–123, 148–150, 184, 191, 202, 245–247
Constitutional Conduct Group 19
Czechoslovakia 97, 133

D

Dalits 54
Datta, Narendranath 183
definition xiv, 12, 39, 88, 99, 134, 136, 179, 235, 236
Delhi ii, 52, 155, 164, 166, 174, 193–194, 197, 199, 201, 204
Delhi University 21
Democracy vii, viii, ix, x, xi, xvi, xviii, xxi, xxii, xxiii, 3–7, 9–14, 16–19, 22–24, 27, 32, 34–44, 46–47, 60, 62, 69, 71, 76, 82, 93, 108–110, 112–118, 120–122, 124, 126–127, 130, 138, 140–144, 147, 151, 156, 165, 172, 175, 177, 179, 213, 217–218, 226, 230, 232, 235–236, 238, 241, 248–250, 253
democracy rankings 6, 156
Denmark 11
Deobandi movement 190
Desiraju, Gautam R 213–214, 216
Deutsches Volksthum 132
Deutsche Welle 224
dharma x, xi, xii, xv, xvi, xvii, xxi, 63–64, 66, 124, 185, 187–189, 216, 218, 245–249, 252–253
Dharma–The Basis of Our Civilisation 252
Dharmic Nation 209
Direct Action Day 78–80, 82, 91–92
discrimination 54, 110, 131, 152, 155–156, 159–165, 167, 175, 177, 180, 206
disenfranchisement 165, 180

dominant party system 3
Dugin, Aleksandr 205
Durkheim, Émile 112, 215–216, 248
Durrani, F K Khan 98

E

Eck, Diana L 201
Economist Intelligence Unit (EIU) 5
education levels 140, 163
Egypt 144
Election Commission of India 18–19, 62, 176
Eminent Historians 198, 210
Englishstan 101, 238
Eritrea 16, 158
Etawah 243
Eternal Dharma 248
European x, xi, 4–6, 40, 45, 68, 77, 111–113, 123–125, 202, 204, 206–207, 217

F

family dynasties xviii
Fatehpur Sikri 219
father of the nation ix
film industry 170
First Amendment 24–25
First War of Indian Independence 47
Forgotten Muslim Empires of South India 229
Fourteen Points 87
France 89, 97, 132, 147, 216
Fraser Institute 8
free and fair elections vii, 19
Freedom House 8–9, 19
freedom of association 11, 14, 22–23, 37
freedom of expression 7, 11, 13–14, 23,–26, 29, 33, 37
Fundamental Duties 123, 125

G

G-20 Summit 245
Gandhi family ix, 2, 119, 232, 234

Gandhi, Indira viii, xviii, 1–3, 24, 36, 119, 121–124, 127–128, 143–144, 150, 223, 232–233, 245, 253
Gandhi, M K ix, xi, xii, 74, 76, 80, 92, 95, 101–102, 110, 113, 119–120, 122–124, 134, 137, 140, 183, 213, 232–234, 239, 245, 247, 250, 253
Gangopadhyay, Kausik 236
Germany xx, 45, 77, 112, 132–133, 147
Goa xiv, 85, 107
Godse, Nathuram 134
Golwalkar, M S 135
Gorakhnath Math 48–50, 60–61, 237
Gorakhpur 49–50, 61
Government Restrictions Index (GRI) 153
Gujarat 78, 104, 127, 168, 228
Gyanvapi Mosque 212

H

Hamas 8, 19, 30
harassment of journalists 28, 30
Hassan al-Banna 133
hate speech 31, 152, 167–168
Hathras incident 53–54
Hedgewar, Dr Keshav Baliram 133
Herder, Johann 125
Hindi Heartland 46
Hind Swaraj xi, 113, 250
Hindu Adoptions and Maintenance Act (1956) 171
Hindu civil society 49, 140, 142–146, 215–216
Hindu code bills 171
Hindu Mahasabha 49, 61–62, 64, 80, 94–96
Hindu Marriage Act (1955) 171
Hindu Minority and Guardianship Act (1956) 171
Hindu-Muslim unity 140, 220
Hindu nationalism 64, 66, 97, 109, 136, 201, 204
Hindu reform movements 130–131, 142, 185
Hindustan 101, 104, 220, 238
Hindu Temples: What Happened to Them? 199
Hindutva 97, 100, 104, 171, 211, 218, 236, 244, 250
Hindu Yuva Vahini (HYV) 49

Hitler, Adolf 97, 224
Ho Chi Minh xiii
Home Rule xi, 113, 250
hostage theory 92
Human Freedom Index 8
human rights xx, 1, 8, 20, 51, 65, 152–153, 159, 163–165, 180
Human Rights Watch 152, 165
Humayun 218
Hyderabad xiv, 95, 106

I

ideology xiv, xvi, xx, 97, 200, 234, 237, 241, 244
illegal immigrants 164–166
India After Gandhi 194
India: A Sacred Geography 201
Indian Home Rule xi, 113, 250
Indian National Congress (INC) xviii, 3, 43, 80
Indian state 55, 71, 74, 77, 98, 109, 130, 133, 151, 175, 191, 202–203, 213, 215, 219, 235, 237, 239, 245
India's Agony over Religion 204
India's New Right 212
India That Is Bharat 201
India Today 28, 58
instrumental 138–139, 144, 237, 244
integral humanism 211
interfaith marriage 55, 57
international connections 211
international religious freedom 157, 159
International Religious Freedom v, 156–159
International Religious Freedom Act (1998) 156, 158
international religious freedom reports 159
International Religious Freedom reports 157
Iqbal, Muhammad 87, 101
Iraq 6
Ireland 45, 112–113
Islam, Maidul 181–182
Islamophobia 167, 218, 229
Israel 114–115

J

Jacques, Martin 203
Jaffrelot, Christophe viii
Jahn, Friedrich 132–133, 281
Jainism 136
Jamaat-e-Islami Hind 137, 191
Jamiat Ulama-i-Hind (JUH) 139
Jammu and Kashmir 93, 173
janapadas 117
Jana Sangh 2, 57, 223, 233
Japan vii, 45, 111–112, 130–131
Jawaharlal Nehru University (JNU) 21
Jayal, Niraja Gopal 32
Jinnah, Muhammad Ali 72, 78, 150

K

Kalingas 189
Kanpur 219
Karnataka 175–176
Kashmir 93, 95, 106, 128, 173, 214, 223
Keane, John viii
Kenya 102
Kenyatta, Jomo 102
Kerala 36, 55, 98, 138, 144, 239
Khaliquzzaman, Chaudhry 103
Khan, Ahmed Raza 191
Khan, Dr Abdul Jabbar 102, 193
Khan, Hazrat Inayat 190, 217
Khan, Liaquat Ali 78, 101
Khan Market Gang 193, 200
Khan Sahib, Dr 193
Khan, Sir Sayyid Ahmad 191
Kolkata 183
Krishna (Lore Krishna) ix, 64, 101, 185, 190, 214, 252
Krishna Menon, V K ix, 101
Kumar, Ravinder 204

L

Lal-Bal-Pal 250, 252
Larson, Gerald James 130, 204
Lee, Kuan Yew 102
liberal democracy vii, xxi, 39, 40–42, 44, 62, 108, 147, 172, 177, 179
liberalism xvii
Library of Congress 134
Lindberg, Staffan 7
linguistic divide 103, 239
Lipset, Seymour Martin 114
Little, Andrew T 36
Locke, John 125
Lord Ram 48, 75–77, 195
Love Jihad 55
Lucknow 47, 49–50, 219
Lutyens' Delhi 193, 199, 201

M

Madras (now Chennai) 31–32, 106, 174
Mahabharata 214
Maharashtra 95, 106, 133, 144
Mahasabha 49, 61–62, 64, 80, 94–96
Mahesh Yogi, Maharishi 183
majoritarianism 149, 203, 236
Majumder, Abhijit 212
Malabar 98
Malaysia xiv, 102
Maldives xiv, 6, 7, 85, 164
Mao, Zedong xi
Marxist intellectuals 192
Mathura 46, 197, 208–209
Mauretania 158
Mayawati 59
Mazzini, Giuseppe xi, 133
McMillan, Alistair 19
Mehta, Hansal 103
Meng, Anne 36
Merkel, Angela 77

Mill, John Stuart 98, 106, 195, 201
minority treaties 97
Missing Voters 175
modernisation 47, 67, 69, 70, 116, 171, 227, 230, 237, 240, 248
modernity 63, 70, 124, 248
Modi & India 209
Modi, Narendra viii, xxi, 5–7, 9, 14, 18–23, 28–29, 32, 48, 50, 59, 61–62, 67, 69, 75–78, 104, 109, 123, 137, 167, 171, 184, 193, 199–200, 209–210, 224, 226, 240, 243, 245, 248, 253, 255
Mody, Ashoka viii
Mongolia 37
Moore, Barrington Jr 115
Mughal Empire 194, 197
multiculturalism xvii
Mumbai 86, 174
Muslim appeasement 243
Muslim-baiting 41
Muslim Brotherhood 137, 144
Muslim candidates 172, 225, 226, 243
Muslim civil society 208
Muslim Indians 109, 148, 151, 160–173, 177–182, 191–192, 194, 207–209, 214, 216, 218, 225–226, 228–230, 235, 242–245, 247
Muslim League 78–83, 87–89, 94–96, 100, 103, 139, 150, 189, 191, 252
Muslim nation 192
Muslim outreach 50, 244–245
Muslim Rashtriya Manch 228–229
Muslim reform movements 130, 190
Muslim representatives 150
Myanmar ix, 84–85, 95, 106, 115, 129, 236

N

Nagpur 133
name of India 202
Napoleon 3
Narayan, Jayaprakash 127, 278
National Capital Region 163, 166
National Education 251
national elite 103, 105

nationalism xiv, xv, 43, 44, 64, 66, 84, 88, 97, 104, 109–114, 125, 130–131, 133, 136, 149, 151, 201, 204, 237, 244, 251
Nationality and Empire 252
national liberation movement x, xi, xvi, xviii, 94–95, 118, 120, 133, 149, 232, 233, 247
national liberation movements x, xi, xvi, xviii, 94–95, 103, 118–120, 131, 133, 149, 232–233, 247
National Register of Citizens 166
National rejuvenation movements 132
national self-determination xiii, 97–99, 133
National War Memorial 104
nation-building xv, 42–43, 105, 107, 111, 136, 141, 149, 225
nationhood xii, xiii, xv, xvi, xx, 43, 44, 70–72, 74, 83, 91, 96–97, 111, 117–118, 125–126, 129, 131, 133, 135, 137–138, 140, 142, 146, 148, 149, 151, 188, 201, 206–207, 212, 218, 227, 235, 244, 250, 251, 252
nation-state xiii, xvi, 46, 70, 108, 112–113, 117, 125, 130, 182, 203–204, 251
Native Americans 110, 148, 206, 207
NBC News 119
Nehru-Gandhi family xviii
Nehru, Jawaharlal v, viii, ix, xviii, 3, 21, 72, 80, 86, 103, 118–119, 149, 171, 233, 249
Nehru Memorial Museum and Library 204
Nehru, Motilal 86, 119
Nehru Report 87
Nepal xiv, 85, 129
Netherlands 45
net worth 61
New India intellectuals 201, 209
New York Times 25, 79, 123, 137, 157, 221, 224
New Zealand 30, 33, 45, 112, 147
Nigeria 47, 154
Nishtar, Abdur Rab 79
Nkrumah, Kwame 102
non-violence 92, 250
North Korea 16, 17, 37
north-south linguistic divide 103, 239
North West Frontier Province 88
Nyerere, Julius 102

O

Oman 11
one-party dominant system 3
organic solidarity 215
Ottoman Empire 98
Oxfam 177

P

Pakistan ix, xiii, xiv, xv, xvi, xx, 22, 23, 26, 30, 71–72, 74, 78, 82–83, 86, 88–90, 92–95, 100, 102, 104, 106–108, 115, 117, 128–129, 131, 139, 149–150, 163–165, 170, 172, 174, 180–182, 191, 193–194, 196, 216, 236
Pal, Bipin Chandra 250, 252
partition xiii, xv, 78, 80–81, 82, 85, 88–93, 98, 173, 191
Partition iii, xiii, xv, xvi, 74, 82–83, 86–87, 89–93, 107, 128, 139, 149–150, 163, 171–172, 174, 181–182, 189, 191–193, 196, 227, 247, 250
Patel, "Sardar" Vallabhbhai 101
persecution 31, 153–154, 157, 162, 165, 176, 196, 224
Pew Research Center v, 8, 34, 153, 159
Poland 22, 89
political parties xix, 18, 41, 45, 83, 94–95, 115, 120, 145, 222, 230–233, 240–241, 245
political science vii, 99, 100, 115, 238, 241
polity 87, 194
Polity 3–5, 9
'Polity' dataset 3
polyarchy 12–13, 16, 37
Pondicherry xiv, 85, 107
Popper, Karl 186–187, 290
Prabhakara, M S 204
Prager, Jeffrey 107–108, 192
Prasad, Rajendra ix, 90–92, 100, 103, 126
preamble 122, 202
press freedom 8
Press Freedom Index 28
Press (Objectionable Matters) Act (1951) 25
princely states xiv, 85, 107, 133, 139
Proquest International Newsstream database 34

Przeworski, Adam 116, 277
Punjab 82, 88, 92, 95, 106, 174, 251
Putnam, Robert 141

Q

Qatar 15, 175

R

Radhakrishnan, Sarvepalli x, 72, 103, 121, 247
Rai, Lala Lajpat 250
Ramana, N V 124
Ramayana 131, 214
Ram Mandir 48–49, 63, 75–78, 240, 243
Ranganathan, Anand 208
rashtra dharma x, xv, xvii, xxi, 66, 245, 253
Rashtriya Swayamsevak Sangh (RSS) 133
Red Fort 194
refugees 65, 80, 166, 196
Regimes of the World 11
religious freedom 8, 20, 155–157, 159, 161
religious pluralism xvi, xvii, 158, 195, 247
religious tolerance 160, 187, 189–190, 197
religious toleration xvii
Reporters Without Borders (RSF) v, 8
residential segregation 80, 167, 168, 169
Rizvi, S A A 197
Role Models 230
Rolland, Romain 184
Rousseau, Jean-Jacques 125
Roy Chowdhury, Debasish viii
RSS intellectuals 136
RTI International 159
Russia 16, 37, 39

S

Sai Deepak, J 201
Samajwadi Party v, 59, 231
Sampath, Vikram 212
Sanatana Dharma 248

Sangh Parivar 135, 138–139, 142, 227, 228
Sanyal, Sanjeev 213
Sardesai, Rajdeep viii, 28, 60
Sarnath 46
Saudi Arabia 15, 17, 22
Savarkar ix, 96–98, 100–101, 104, 110, 171, 212, 218, 220, 236, 244, 250
Savarkar, V D ix, 110, 171, 212, 218, 250
Savarkar, Vinayak Damodar 96
Scheduled Castes 47
Schimmel, Annemarie 195
Scotland 71
secularisation 136
secularism xix, 7, 75, 198–199, 216, 239, 246
separation of church and state 45
Serbia 22
Shah, Amit 59
Shah, Aqil 129
Shah Jahan 46, 194, 219, 221
Sharda, Ratan 210
Sharia 6, 57, 93, 244
Shastri, Lal Bahadur 118
Shiva (Lord Shiva) 212, 214, 243
Shivshankar, Rahul 209
Shourie, Arun 198, 210
Shri Ram Janmabhoomi Mandir 75
Sikhism 136
Simon Commission 86
Sind 88
Singapore xiv, 102
Singh, Manmohan 242
Singh, Tavleen 28
Smith, Vincent Arthur 196
Snakes in the Ganga: Breaking India 2.0 211
social exclusion 167, 169–171, 182, 214, 225
Social Hostilities Index (SHI) 153
social inclusion 171, 180–182, 226, 235
social reproduction 174
Society of Righteous and Harmonious Fists 133
Solomon Islands 6, 7

Somalia 15
South Africa 6, 7, 47, 112
South Asia Scholar Activist Collective 178
South Korea 115
Soviet Union 112, 118, 123, 125, 215, 250
Spain 22, 71
Sri Lanka ix, xiv, 6, 7, 85, 108, 115, 129, 197
Statue of Unity 104
status of Muslims 175–177
St Stephen's College 155
Sudetenland 97
suffrage 11, 13, 15–17, 23, 37, 88, 126, 148
Sufism 195
Suhrawardy, Huseyn Shaheed 79
Supreme Court 41, 75, 121, 124, 173
Switzerland 147–148

T

Taj Mahal 46, 219, 221
Tamil Nadu 36, 106, 127, 138
Thackeray, Bal 144
Thailand 15, 30
Thakur caste 54
Tharoor, Shashi 184, 211, 232, 237, 246–247
The Arctic Home in the Vedas 251
The Discovery of India 90, 196, 249
the Emergency 2–3, 5–6, 19, 29, 121–122, 127–128, 137–138, 140, 143–144, 150
The Hindutva Paradigm 211
The Indian War of Independence of 1857 220
The Open Society and Its Enemies 186
The Political Future of India 251
The Sangh & Swaraj 211
The Soul of India 252
The Story of My Deportation 251
The Struggle for India's Soul 211
The Times of India 1, 25, 79, 137, 197
The United States of America: A Hindu's Impressions and a Study 251
Tilak, Bal Gangadhar xi, 250, 251

Times Higher Education 32
Tipu Sultan 212
Tomb of the Unknown Soldier 206
Treaty of Versailles 97
Truschke, Audrey 197
Tryst with Destiny 105
Tudor, Maya viii
Tulsidas 200
Tunisia 37
Turkmenistan 10, 158
Turnverein 132–133
'two-nation' theory 96

U

unequal representation 36
uniform civil code 57, 171–172
United Arab Emirates (UAE) 15, 18
United Kingdom (UK) ix, xix, 4, 30, 33, 45, 71, 80, 89, 130, 147–148
United Nations Office of the High Commissioner for Human Rights 152, 165
United Nations (UN) xiv, 152, 156, 165, 232
United States Commission on International Religious Freedom (USCIRF) 156
United States Constitution 43, 148
United States Holocaust Memorial Museum 8
United States (US) v, x, xvii, xviii, xix, 4, 8, 27, 29–30, 40–41, 43–45, 110, 130, 132, 145, 147–148, 152, 155–156, 159, 161, 168, 179, 184, 202, 206, 222, 251
University of Würzburg 8
Upadhyaya, Deendayal 211, 223
Uttar Pradesh v, 2, 36, 40, 46–48, 57, 63, 68, 122, 197, 208, 219, 221, 230–231, 243

V

Vadra, Priyanka Gandhi 232
Varanasi 46, 197, 208, 209, 212
Varieties of Democracy Institute v, vii, 4, 7
Varma, Pavan K 193, 198
Varshney, Ashutosh 233
Vedanta 184, 195
Verma, Rahul viii, 18, 235

Vietnam 16, 18
Vijayan, Pinarayi 239
village councils 117
Vishva Hindu Parishad (VHP) 135
vishwa guru 245, 248
Vivekananda, Swami 183–187, 190, 200, 217, 247
vote buying 17–18

W

Waiting for Shiva 212
Washington, Booker T 251
Washington Post 25, 224
Weber, Max 231
WEIRD rule 116
Welles Hangen, Putnam 119
West Bengal 138
When China Rules the World 203
White, Gordon 143
Why I Am a Hindu 237
Wikipedia 9, 134
Wilson, Woodrow 98, 100, 113
World Justice Project 8
World Values Survey 126
World War One xiii, xiv, 81, 97–98, 106, 111–112, 132–133, 147
World War Two xiii, 81–82, 89–90, 215
Worshipping False Gods 210

Y

Yadav, Akhilesh 59, 65, 243
Yadav caste 59, 243
Yadav, Mulayam Singh 59
Yemen xiv
Young India 251
Young Italy 133
Yugoslavia 112

Z

Zimbabwe 22